Kilmichael: A Battlefield Study

KILMICHAEL
A BATTLEFIELD STUDY

SEÁN A. MURPHY

FOUR ROADS
PUBLICATIONS

ISBN: 978-0-9931164-0-7

Published by Four Roads Publications 2014
Reprinted 2015

www.kilmichaelbattlefield.com

INSPIRE DESIGN AND PRINT
Cork Road, Skibbereen, Co. Cork, Ireland.
www.inspire.ie

Contents

Preface

THE IDEA TO produce this book has been gestating for twenty years but it wasn't until about seven years ago that I actually decided to do something about it. The first drafts were put together in my last year of service in the Defence Forces in 2007-2008, but with a change of career the project was put on hold until I dusted it off in 2012 and introduced the more current references.

It has been an interesting journey but also one that required considerable patience. A lot of information concerning the Kilmichael ambush is in the public domain, some very accurate and relevant, some wildly misleading. All "facts" have to be treated with caution. As part of the research experience I was struck by the number of people who were willing to provide details or even a view as to what occurred on 28 November 1920 but only on the condition that they were not identified as a source. It wasn't that they were afraid to do so; it was more the concern that they would be seen to have allied themselves with a particular "camp." A notable suspicion is reserved for "revisionists." That attitude might change, and hopefully in the near future, thereby assisting whoever decides to engage further with this fascinating incident.

I can report that in the course of my research I have come to the conclusion that there are still, as yet unseen, details concerning the ambush which are not in the public domain. People are holding onto mementos for a number of reasons, preferring to consider them as private family keepsakes rather than historical items to be shared with the wider community. They are perfectly entitled to do so, and I only make this point in order to counter any argument that all the "facts" of Kilmichael are known and available.

I received support, encouragement, and assistance from so many people over such a long period of time that it would be impossible to name all, simply because I would forget someone. There are, however, those that went beyond the call and devoted evenings (normally after 2100hrs!) and weekends listening to my theories and descriptions. I engaged with these at length because I respected their views, knowledge, and experience of the subject matter:-

Comdt Ian Harrington who competed with and against me in many shooting competitions both at home and abroad; a fine marksman with a shooter's eye for detail. Lt Alan Kearney, who possesses an unmatched knowledge of weapons generally but is particularly strong on those in circulation at the turn of the 20th century. Comdt George O'Connell, in my opinion the most technically proficient Ordnance Mechanical Engineer in the Defence Forces; he has an encyclopaedic knowledge of ammunition and a great ability to identify the questions to be answered. Lt Col Stephen Ryan, a fine academic and military historian in his own right; he didn't hesitate to administer "the red pen" when requested to do so and also put some very relevant texts my way that I would otherwise have missed.

A special word of thanks is reserved for Eithne Scallan and Dr Mark C. Nolan who assisted greatly in negotiating the final hurdles by casting cold, uncompromising eyes over the near final text.

Kaz Balinski, Capt (Retd) Donal Buckley, Comdr (NS) Pat Burke BL, Dara Carberry, Dermot Carberry, Mick Cowan, Comdt (Retd) Peter Daly, Comdt Larry Devaney, Gabriel Doherty, Comdt (Retd) John Guinane, Eoghan Harris, Michael Hurley, Diarmuid Kingston, Eve Morrison, Fr Brian Murphy, Cathal Murphy, David Murphy, Comdt Fintan McCarthy BL, Gordon McMillan, Andrew Nelson, Michael O'Dea (RHA), Comdt (Retd) Páraic O'Gallchóir, Mary O'Leary, Luke Rochford, Caleb Sheehan, Richard Sterritt, the library staff of UCC and UCD, the Defence Forces Military Archive, the Royal Navy Historical Branch, Noel Howard.

To those that did not wish a public acknowledgement: you know who you are and I extend my sincere gratitude for your valuable assistance.

Finally, there are those who are so close to me and have been so supportive that they do not require a public acknowledgement but deserve one nonetheless. I refer to Trish, Ali, Jane, and Sarah who had to put up with the risk of every family car journey ending up in Kilmichael. The "threat level" in that regard has now been reduced to LOW. It's safe to come out!

Seán A. Murphy
Cork, 2014

CHAPTER 1

Growing up with Kilmichael

"In West Cork, and in Ireland as a whole, Kilmichael became the most celebrated victory of rebel arms, the archetypal ambush. Tom Barry, the column commander, became a folk hero and a revolutionary celebrity."[1]

IN WEST CORK it is difficult when discussing the War of Independence to avoid a consideration of what happened on 28 November 1920 at Kilmichael, an event that must be regarded as unusual when seen in the context of the conflict as a whole. Even those with just a passing interest are likely to have strong opinions about what transpired – opinions that have been shaped by any number of factors, including the Irish education system, family backgrounds, political allegiances, and the great volume of words in historical texts and journals detailing the conflict in West Cork. The Kilmichael ambush has remained part of the popular culture, with historical detail passed from generation to generation by word of mouth and by the activities of the commemorative societies established to retain the events in the public consciousness. Recently, however, a different understanding of what might have occurred at Kilmichael has been made available due to the efforts of professional and amateur historians taking it upon themselves to question accepted accounts and thereby form their own view as to the accuracy and veracity of what has been presented to date.

The historical allure of Kilmichael is arguably more concerned with the controversy that surrounds it than with its military significance. The debate continues to reverberate around whether the British combatants, who were considered to be part of an elite auxiliary police force, were killed after they had shot dead two IRA volunteers and injured a third (who would die later of his wounds) while pretending to surrender, or whether they were simply executed and the false surrender story concocted after the event in order to explain why the IRA did not take any prisoners.

To date, the debate has been dominated by two main personalities, Meda Ryan[2] and Peter Hart[3], who have each presented polarised views on Kilmichael. They are now as closely associated with Kilmichael as Tom Barry himself. Torch bearers are available and awaiting in the wings for each of the opposing schools. Their day will also come, but hopefully in the absence of the petulance that has characterised the debate so far.

It is not surprising that personalities have played such a big role, as Kilmichael itself has always been wrapped in a cult of personality: that of Tom

Barry who continues even after ninety years to loom large over the battle site. There were probably fifty-four other combatants (thirty-six IRA and eighteen members of the Crown forces[4]) involved in the engagement, yet most casual observers would be hard-pressed to name another participant besides Barry. Such a focus on personality has a consequence for "the bigger picture"; perspective becomes lost in the noise, with commentators tending to align themselves with the personality rather than the event, thus losing sight of the fact that twenty other "personalities" were to end their lives on a 200-metre stretch of a rural West Cork road.

Although I have had an on-going interest for nearly thirty-five years in Kilmichael, prior to this publication I have never written anything about the event other than a letter to the editor of the *Irish Examiner* (14 September 2013), which had more to do with the preservation of the ambush site than with the engagement proper. A number of individuals, military and academic, were aware of some of the views I had in relation to the engagement; this was primarily on the basis of casual conversations usually initiated by my "ambushing" of them in the environs of UCC, emailing them directly or conversing with them when opportunities arose.

Professor John A. Murphy (ambushed twice in fleetingly short engagements) and Gabriel Doherty of the School of History, UCC, (brief but more sustained engagements) were particularly "targeted." It must be said that both Gabriel and I were already known to each other, having attended UCG, now NUIG, at the same time and having played an enthusiastic yet poor standard of rugby together for the college. Almost everyone I approached offered encouragement, but a singular piece of insight from Gabriel Doherty has remained with me from the outset. He informed me that the majority of historians he knew had no military experience or background. They may have studied battles, read about battles, watched battles on TV and the Internet, and had even written books about battles, but the military detail sometimes escaped them. Without any experience of a weapon jamming, or appreciation for the measured concentration necessary to successfully fire an accurate shot, their analysis would always be missing that "coalface" experience. There was a gap, as such, in the narrative that could and should be addressed by someone with that relevant knowledge.

Armed with such awareness, the mission became one of considering the Kilmichael ambush from such a "coalface" perspective. As will be shown, the existing narratives and the engagement area itself are a treasure trove of hidden inklings and whispers which individually are open to interpretation but cumulatively offer some compelling ideas that challenge the prevailing views. I have been informed by those whose opinions I have sought before publication that the analysis that this study contains and the questions it raises will cause certain attitudes to be reviewed.

My interest in Kilmichael started when I first became aware of it in my national school days in Skibbereen. Kilmichael doesn't creep up on you; almost like any ambush, you find yourself engaged with it before you even realise where you are. Although I spent much of my formative years in Skibbereen, I am not a native of the town and therefore don't consider myself a "West Corkonian." I was born in Cork city and moved with my family to Skibbereen in the early 1970s. My father, a civil engineer, took up a position with the local county council and we settled quickly in the town. Skibbereen is a welcoming place. It is an inclusive town that facilitates the coming and going of different nationalities and religious persuasions. It is also an open town in the sense of allowing artists and "alternatives" opportunities to be, as *The Southern Star* declares, "Seen and Heard." I have maintained my associations with the town ever since.

To a young boy in Skibbereen during the 1970s the ambush at Kilmichael conjured up many images. Much like Sean Keating's magnificent painting, "The Men of the South", the West Cork Flying Column led by Tom Barry was steeped in romantic imagery. The War of Independence was not about the grim realities of combat with is pain and suffering but about patriotism and a steely determination to be free. It was about idealism. A distinct mythology was fuelled by classroom discussions suggesting comparisons between the actions of Tom Barry's column and those of Cúchulainn and Na Fianna. I recall recounting to my father the stories we had heard during our history lessons about Tom Barry, the destruction of Rosscarbery RIC Barracks, the escape from encirclement at Crossbarry, and, of course, the resounding victory at Kilmichael. I also recall, shortly after recounting those stories, my father giving me my first copy of *Guerilla Days in Ireland*, Barry's own account of all those historic events.[5] I was 12 years old at the time. Why *Guerilla Days*? I'll never know other than he simply thrust the book into my hands and thereby catapulted me into a relationship with the Kilmichael ambush that has remained ever since. I was enthralled by the notion of this band of freedom fighters roaming the countryside at will, outwitting enemy forces in a Robin Hood-v-Sheriff of Nottingham style of engagement. The bloody aspects of the encounters bypassed me in the same way that a young boy watching a cowboy film doesn't keep a casualty count. Tales of the West Cork Flying Column were tales of pure, unbridled excitement.

It was only in later years that my father told me about meeting Tom Barry on a number of occasions when he was staying in lodgings as an engineering student at UCC. Barry and some of his old IRA veterans would meet in the house on College Road of Jim Hurley , a former column member who subsequently became the bursar of UCC, and recount tales of the struggle into the small hours.[6] My father remembered the tally of casualties as being considerable yet never contested. Unfortunately for my purposes, he never remembered Kilmichael being discussed.

I never encountered anything in Skibbereen other than admiration for Barry, even though he appeared to have an awkward relationship with the townspeople. Barry described them as,

> . . . a race apart from the sturdy people of West Cork. They were different and with a few exceptions were spineless, slouching through life meek and tame, prepared to accept ruling and domination from any clique or country, provided they were left to vegetate in peace.[7]

I have taken steps to ensure that Barry's depiction of Skibbereen's involvement in, or attitude to, the conflict has not influenced my objectivity. This book, therefore, should not be considered as a "revenge for Skibbereen"! There is little doubt but that Barry was unfair by presenting such a generalised assessment of the people of the town. If Skibbereen did not provide volunteers to the required number as expected by Barry, then maybe there were practical reasons for this. Michael Hopkinson describes Skibbereen and the area west of it as not being ideal for sourcing volunteers due to the predominance of poor farmers and fishermen.[8]

If the town's engagement with the IRA got off to a slow start then certain elements ensured that it finished on a republican high. It remains a fact that one of the last RIC men to be shot in the course of the War of Independence was shot in Skibbereen on the morning of the truce. Diarmuid Kingston describes the incident as follows:

> The truce came into effect at noon on 11 July 1921. At 11 o'clock on that morning, Constable Alexander Clarke (No.52442) was walking on his own to his lodgings in Townshend Street, Skibbereen. For security reasons, he had been sleeping in the barracks and that morning, knowing the truce was imminent, was unarmed as he made his way home. He was ambushed by four men and shot dead. He was a fifty-two year old married man and had completed thirty-four years of police service.[9]

Skibbereen's hinterland certainly had very firm British military connections. Castletownshend, described as "a sheltered little corner of the empire"[10], had a long and strong association with the Royal Navy, supplying many recruits, both Catholic and Protestant, from the local population. Vice-Admiral Henry Boyle Sommerville paid the ultimate price for assisting young local men gain entry to the Royal Navy when he was assassinated by the IRA on 24 March 1936. Jane O'Hea O'Keefe, quoting from the book *Blood-Dark Track* by Joseph O'Neill, suggests that the admiral was shot for two reasons:

> *Firstly, the IRA wanted to generate some kind of momentum behind what was, by then, a flagging campaign. Secondly, they chose him because he was a Protestant and also because he was an admiral, and they knew his shooting would make the headlines. He was given no warning. He was somebody who was simply trying to do a good turn in helping to get employment for local boys, rather than to recruit for the Royal Navy.[11]*

His murder is seen as one of the significant events that provided an impetus to the Fianna Fáil government's decision on 18 June 1936 to declare the IRA an unlawful organisation.

My parents were apolitical. My father often said that "those who declare their political allegiances make no new friends." Both he and my mother were part of that "silent generation" that Gerard Murphy refers to as, ". . . half-afraid of the generation that came before them, the sometimes brave and sometimes savage men who had fought the British Empire."[12] They were the children of the generation who had fought for the nation's independence and who, having gained that independence, refused to yield power or leave the stage until they couldn't physically remain any longer.

On my father's side in west Kerry there is some evidence of republican activity. Both his parents were national school teachers in the village of Camp, outside Tralee. They were certainly Irish language enthusiasts, but more so because of their west Kerry roots and their everyday use of the language rather than the pursuit of a nationalistic ideal. They were not political, but my father's uncle, John Deen, was certainly involved and is listed in the Military Pensions archive as having held the rank of Second Lieutenant in E Company, 4th Battalion, Kerry No.1 Brigade.

The story is somewhat different on my mother's side. Her family is from south Roscommon near the village of Four Roads in a townland called Carncleva. My maternal grandfather, Tom Lane, had little interest in or time for republicanism. He would recount with pride that "his people" were the "chief cattle herdsmen" for the McGann family. The McGanns were strong farmers and large landowners in the area, and their big house was a

An early edition of Tom Barry's best-selling account of the West Cork Flying Column, which established the conventional republican narrative of what happened at Kilmichael.

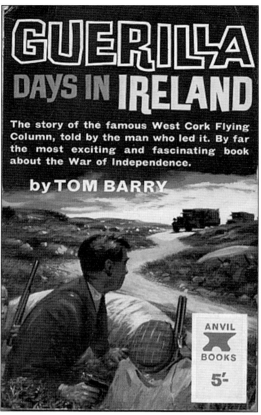

dominant feature on what was referred to as "the high road" overlooking the village of Four Roads. Although my grandfather played no part in the War of Independence, nor wanted to, his sister Bridget was a republican through and through and was married to Paddy Gallagher, who had a similar outlook; to quote my grandfather, "they were both up to terrible devilment!"

As an impressionable young boy, the Gallaghers intrigued me. They lived in Curraghboy, a small village outside Athlone. Paddy had been an active IRA volunteer and had spent time in Pentonville Prison in England for his republican activities. I loved visiting them. I was besotted by the tales of "IRA men on the run, Tans and Auxies." I was fascinated by the fact that Paddy had a shotgun on clear display in the corner of the room and cartridges scattered liberally in close proximity to it. "For the Tans or Freestaters!" he would declare. "You're not a Freestater, are you?" he'd whisper with mock seriousness. I knew that to answer in the negative meant Paddy, the gun, and I going out the back "for a few shots." Bridgie, as she was known, would shout out after us, "Mind that gossoon!" which was in itself a futile exercise as Paddy was as deaf as the proverbial stone.

Bridgie was interviewed in the 1970s for a documentary that RTE were preparing on the Troubles and both my grandfather and I were glued to the radio as she recalled raids by the Black and Tans on her house, as Paddy, who was "on the run" at the time, was well known to them. She described storing ammunition in the kettle beside the fire and the fear that the Tans would find it. "Oh the Lord Jasus!" my grandfather would mutter after each of the anecdotes, "She's bringing a total disgrace on the family! We won't be able to walk outside the door!"

Paddy fought on the anti-Treaty side during the Civil War, and I was told that he had been involved in the shooting of a Free State soldier in Athlone. The shooting was widely condemned in the area, and the parish priest at the time is reported to have put a curse on those involved, "that their hair may turn white." Paddy had what would be described as a "shock" of white hair. My fascination was secured!

Although my maternal grandfather was anti-republican, his wife, my grandmother, Jane Hynes, was a different proposition. She had been associated with, but not a member of, Cumann na mBan, and her family were as active as any others in south Roscommon. Her contribution to the War of Independence was to paint a slogan on the wall of the RIC barracks, "RIC soon RIP." "A well paid piece of work," she would chuckle. It is fortunate that my grandfather predeceased her, as I'm not sure what his reaction would have been to the volley of shots the Irish Defence Forces fired over her grave in 1991. The war was mentioned by my grandparents in my presence on only the rarest of occasions, but they are memorable for the short-lived hostility and the long silences that followed. I felt both sides hurt for their own reasons. There were no winners in those rare arguments.

With that lineage it is not surprising that in our family there was always an interest in Irish history, and *Guerilla Days* was always within arm's reach to fuel some of the debates among the elder siblings. It remains a great read. It is well written and it is one of those texts that embrace the reader from cover to cover. It draws the reader into life with the column, and shares all aspects of its activities. The tales of martial life, of service with the column, imbued me with a fascination for all things military. In its own way I'm sure it had some influence on my own decision to enter the military. I never envisaged that I would do anything else in the course of a professional career other than to pursue an occupation in the profession of arms. I was most fortunate after my leaving certificate to be offered a cadetship in the Irish Permanent Defence Forces. No reflection time was required or availed of, and in 1985 I entered the Cadet School of the Military College with a suitcase in one hand and *Guerilla Days* in the other.

The first seeds of doubt

Part of my initial training as an officer cadet involved developing my presentation and public speaking skills and so, along with every other cadet, I was required to give a twenty-minute presentation on a military topic that was of interest to me. Without hesitation I sought and was granted permission to base my presentation on the events at Kilmichael. Preparing the presentation wasn't difficult; it was a welcome break from the intensity of the training that I and fellow members of the 62nd Cadet Class (a "flying column" in its own right under the command of a Kilkenny man and renowned hurler, Captain Kieran Brennan) were enduring at that formative time. At night, in the confines of my room, I prepared plastic overheads setting out the area in which the action occurred. I prepared index cards, quoting freely from *Guerilla Days* in order to support my theory that this was a military action in which the IRA had demonstrated their superior military effectiveness and prowess. I was going to inform the Cadet School about this elite unit of freedom fighters which had taken on the best the British could offer and scored such a remarkable victory. I had access to a small military library, but none of the texts appeared to be of much use as they were primarily concerned with military encounters where both combatant parties were more akin to conventional military forces such as in Indochina and Algeria. There were some counter-insurgency texts available, but these generally prescribed that victory was more often than not in the hands of the conventional forces. Faced with few other sources of research, I decided to analyse the events on the basis of the basic military knowledge I had picked up in my first six months of training. This was the first time I had to critically consider the events through a military lens, albeit the crude and rudimentary lens of a cadet. As I tried, however, to reconcile my training with the actions of the column I began for the first time to have concerns that the events may not have transpired exactly as Barry and others had described. At that stage of my cadetship I was learning the basics of military tactics, field craft, unit cohesion in addition to command and control in small military units. It was, however, our weapons handling and marksmanship training that really cast the first doubt as to what an untrained civilian could achieve with a military rifle and military grade ammunition.

Our first encounters with weapons were intimate ones. Within days of entering the Cadet School, each cadet was issued with a 7.62mm FN automatic assault rifle. We lived with that weapon, literally, twenty-four hours a day. It was chained to the radiator in each cadet's room. If it wasn't chained to the "rad" it was in your hands. Stripping and assembling this rifle became second nature. Each rifle was spotless and rigorously inspected by the instructors on an on-going basis. It was never unattended, as to leave it as such would result in the strictest of sanctions. I knew my rifle so well that I thought I could do almost anything with it. That was true, I could do almost anything with it, except the first time I fired it I struggled to hit

8

the standard target! After intense classroom instruction in marksmanship and weapons-handling and having passed our TOETs (Test of Elementary Training) we were brought to the No. 3 Range in the Curragh for our first introductory shoot. This initial sortie was very instructive and provided an insight into what an untrained civilian might accomplish with a military weapon. Even though this first introductory shoot was in the presence of instructors in a very controlled environment, the results were illuminating. In summary, some cadets were good shots, some cadets were poor shots, and some were very poor shots indeed! I was a card-carrying member of the final group. I remember an instructor approaching me and asking me if I had been in the FCA[13], to which I replied that I had, the 11th Infantry Battalion, West Cork. "Did ye not fire the .303?" he asked. I replied that we had. "How did you get on?" I informed him that whilst we had fired the Lee-Enfield Mk IV .303 nobody had been allowed to inspect their target, so in fact we didn't know how we had fared. "I'm not surprised," was his simple retort. Our weapons training continued and through good instruction, more days on the ranges, and perseverance we were all brought to a proficient level of marksmanship, but I had witnessed at first-hand what it took to achieve that proficiency.

The objective of cadet training is to produce an officer who is capable of leading and commanding a platoon-sized formation of thirty trained soldiers. The Defence Forces consider a training programme of between eighteen months and two years necessary to achieve this objective. Within that time frame the first eighteen weeks are dedicated to transforming the civilian into a trained soldier equivalent to the rank of private. The second phase of training was devoted to troop leading while the third phase was focussed on junior leadership. All phases of training were relentless and intensive. Having in the first six months seen and experienced the effort required to achieve this level of military skill and proficiency, I again began to wonder how Barry could have led a platoon of untrained civilians to engage a considerably sized military party and defeat them with such devastating effect.

On graduating from the Cadet School of the Military College as a commissioned officer with the lofty rank of second lieutenant, I was posted to a cavalry unit and soon afterwards found myself stationed on the Border as a young troop commander. In my time with the 4th Cavalry Squadron I was fortunate to be involved with the training of young recruits and had the opportunity to witness at first hand the challenges in progressing from civilian to trained soldier.

In 1988 I was sent to Galway to study science where I took chemistry and mathematics as my primary subjects. With a Bachelor of Science degree, a career in the technical units of the Defence Forces was open to me. After finishing my studies in NUI Galway I became an ordnance mechanical engineer (OME) with the Army Ordnance Corps and spent the majority of my military service as a weapons and ammunition engineer. Incidentally, in the course of my ordnance training, the first weapon we examined in detail was the Lee-Enfield Mk IV, a successor to the Lee-Enfield Mk III which some members of the flying column may have used at Kilmichael. The Ordnance Corps gave me an appreciation of weapon and ammunition capabilities in terms of effect and complexity, and once I qualified as an OME I was very fortunate not alone to serve in an exceptional corps but to be posted to an exceptional unit, the 3rd Garrison Ordnance Company based in Collins Barracks, Cork.

A significant part of a young ordnance officer's duties is to attend shooting practices in a supervisory capacity. In my fifteen years' service with the Ordnance Corps I attended many such events where the shooters were either novices or reservists (FCA). The rifles being fired were the .303 Lee-Enfield, the 7.62mm FN, and the 5.56mm Steyr assault rifle. There were always some naturally good shots present, but equally there were also those who, despite their best efforts, couldn't hit the proverbial barn door. In support of the adage that "a little knowledge can be a very dangerous thing", I once came across an enthusiastic reservist who was visibly firing over the top of the target. I asked him to explain why he wasn't aiming at the target. "Simple," he replied, "a lot of people aren't aware that bullets don't travel in straight lines. They have a trajectory." He further explained that he was hoping to "lob" the rounds onto the target. Such were the challenges faced by the instructing staff!

The 3rd Garrison had a long and proud tradition of competitive shooting and always encouraged new arrivals to get involved in unit shooting activities. As the only lieutenant in the unit at that time, I didn't have any option other than to involve myself, as the unit teams required an officer member to participate in the competitions. My less than auspicious introduction to rifle-shooting apart, I became very involved in competitive shooting. With solid instruction and assistance from the NCOs and men of the unit, my shooting improved to the extent that in 1997 I won the All-Army senior rifle-shooting competition,[14] a victory I attribute to being very lucky on the day but a victory that was very welcome nonetheless. An officer had not won the competition in years, and I was consequently appointed as team manager/coach to the Defence Forces combat shooting team. We competed in the British Army's Central Skill at Arms Meeting (CENTSAM) competition in Bisley, Surrey, on four occasions before I ended my involvement with

The Defence Forces' top marksmen: the author (seated, second from left) with other members of the the Irish Defence Forces' Combat Shooting Team which competed successfully in the British Army's CENTSAM (Central Skill at Arms) competition at Bisley in the UK.

shooting on joining the Defence Forces Legal Service (DLS), where officer engagement with weapons was not pursued to any great extent other than firing an annual range practice as required by Defence Forces' Regulations. The DLS had some fine staff, professional, capable and competent lawyers whose lack of prowess with the rifle was more than compensated by their ability with the pen, an infinitely more dangerous weapon!

It was while participating in the CENTSAM competitions that I encountered a number of civilians who had their own personal military standard weapons, including Lee-Enfield rifles, and I spent a number of evenings listening to their personal experiences with the weapons and about the time and effort that each had expended in attaining their levels of marksmanship. Their levels of knowledge were amazing, as too was their commitment to what was in effect their hobby. Even though they were recreational shooters, their dedication to the weapon was total. Being aware of political sensitivities, I gently pressed for their views on what could be expected of a civilian with a modicum of training in an operational environment armed with a weapon such as the Lee-Enfield. The responses were varying but informative. More than once a view was expressed that the firing of the weapon was the easy part; what had also to be considered was what an inexperienced shooter would do if the weapon failed to fire or developed a stoppage. With no exposure to, or training in, immediate action drills, it would not be beyond the bounds of possibility that a shooter could be out of action for more than a few minutes while he tried to rectify the difficulty. There were even more fundamental aspects to consider, such as how fast and effectively could an accurate rate of fire be maintained? What were the firing positions like? How would the shooter react to firing his weapon in the knowledge that there were .303 rounds heading in his direction also? What types of targets would such untrained civilians be engaging: static or moving, active or passive? I was asked had I considered the difficulties with maintaining an aim (sight picture) in the aftermath of a considerable physical exertion? The questions were reasonable and stemmed from practical considerations. They were a departure from the simple view of volunteers "pouring lead" into the enemy from perfect firing positions with perfectly functioning weapons in perfect conditions.

The more I reflected upon the engagement at Kilmichael, the more the clarity of the earlier years blurred. I became less convinced that events could have transpired as detailed in Barry's account. This change was occasioned by a combination of my own military experiences and weapons knowledge, which allowed the action at Kilmichael to be considered from a better informed basis. This book, therefore, is an opportunity to share with others the knowledge and experience gathered in my service in the Irish Defence Forces with the objective of sparking an interest in considering the events at Kilmichael from a newer perspective.

It is against this background of having once accepted, word-for-word, the narrative in *Guerilla Days* to subsequently revising it in line with my continuing military education and experience that this analysis begins.

CHAPTER 2

Conflicting narratives

THIS CHAPTER IS concerned only with the military aspects of the engagement at Kilmichael. I am aware of the broader debates and conflicting views as to a sectarian and/or ethnic cleansing aspect of the IRA's operations in West Cork, but such considerations are beyond the scope of this study.

The debate over what militarily occurred at Kilmichael has been a polarising one. It has amounted to an academic "shouting match", where a view is offered, then countered and returned, but rather than arriving at a synthesis, this dialectic joust never matures to a consensus. Passionate disagreement abounds, and departures from the accepted narrative are assured of a harsh response. Such reactions, particularly when they become personalised, are unfair as they only serve to stifle further investigation and act as a deterrent to new theories. My own view as to what may have transpired has been revised on an ongoing basis, such revisions being commensurate with my own military service, knowledge, experience, and life-learning.

In order to take a more enlightened approach to this study, it is important to understand the significant areas of disagreement: firstly by considering the more established traditionalist views and then the more recently revised version of events. It will then be possible to identify the main areas of contention in advance of any detailed examination.

The traditionalist view

The prevailing view, and the one that I subscribed to in my formative years and early professional career, is that as narrated by Tom Barry in *Guerilla Days*: that a patrol of eighteen members of the Auxiliary Division of the Royal Irish Constabulary (ADRIC), more commonly referred to as "The Auxiliaries" or simply the "Auxies", were ambushed by a party of the IRA consisting of thirty-six members of the West Cork Flying Column. The patrol members were defeated by conventional means in a relatively short but nonetheless intense engagement; and that at some point during the engagement the ADRIC dropped their rifles while pretending to surrender but then drew their revolvers, opened fire, and killed three volunteers. In doing so they sealed their fate, and Barry gave the order not to accept any further offer of surrender and to kill them all.[1]

Barry's version of events has many supporters, among them John Mc-Cann who provided an account in 1946, three years before publication of

Guerilla Days. McCann's sources are not disclosed, but it would appear he sourced his information by speaking to IRA men who were known to have been involved. He describes the action from an IRA perspective in the following terms:

> *For a time the "Auxies" made a fight of it; but being called upon to surrender they signalled their intention of doing so. Barry gave the cease fire order. As he did his men rose to take their prisoners. As they advanced the Auxiliaries again opened fire. They killed Michael McCarthy of Dunmanway, and Jim O'Sullivan, Kilmeeen, Clonakilty while a heroic youth, Pat Deasy, of Kilmacsimon, Bandon, subsequently died of his wounds. The volunteers resumed the attack and when they left Kilmichael, 17 Auxiliaries lay dead on the roadside, and a drenching rain was fighting a losing battle with the fiercely burning lorries.[2]*

An even earlier version was published in 1941 under the pen-name "Eyewitness" in *An Cosantóir*, the Irish Defence Force's magazine, describing the false surrender as follows:

> *. . . they were surprised to hear the Auxiliaries chant "We surrender" as they grounded their rifles. Quickly four Volunteers of No.2 Section stood up to take the surrender but quicker still the Auxiliaries opened fire on them with revolvers, mortally wounding Lieutenant Pat Deasy, Kilmacsimon Quay and killing outright Lieutenant Jim O'Sullivan of Rossmore.[3]*

"Eyewitness" continues a description of the engagement, with the ADRIC caught in a cross-fire between different IRA parties until all were killed in action.

Ewan Butler provides an account of the event that varies little from Barry's, but he gives some revealing detail about Barry's briefing to the column before the commencement of the action:

> *There would, he said, be no withdrawal. The Column would stand and fight until either it or the enemy were destroyed. The action which they were about to fight, he explained was vital to West Cork and to all Ireland. The Auxies would not take prisoners, and neither would the IRA. "See to it," Barry concluded, "that these terrorists die and are broken!"[4]*

Barry took exception to an account which failed to mention a false surrender. Paddy O'Brien, quoted in Liam Deasy's *Towards Ireland Free*, offers a simple view of what, to his eye, had transpired:

> *Meanwhile, the second tender was about one hundred and fifty yards behind, and had become stuck at the side of the road where the driver had tried unsuccessfully to turn it. The Auxiliaries had jumped out, threw themselves on the road and were firing from the cover of the tender. We then opened fire from their rear and when they realised that they were caught between two fires, they knew they were doomed…it had been a short but grim fight.*[5]

Barry unleashed a broadside the following year criticising Deasy in no uncertain terms:

> *I have no alternative but to tear asunder Deasy's published account…of the fight itself…and the fight[depicted] where no false surrender by the Auxiliaries occurred – after which two IRA men were killed – this depicting me as a bloody minded commander who exterminated the Auxiliaries without reason.*[6] *[author's insert]*

The accounts from McCann, Butler, and "Eyewitness" are presented as examples of the type of narrative that support the view that the ADRIC, having feigned a false surrender, were defeated in a fight to the finish. This view was afforded more recent additional support by Meda Ryan, author of *Tom Barry: IRA Freedom Fighter,* whose uncle, Pat O'Donovan, had participated in the ambush. This version of events, where the ADRIC had sealed their fate by offering a false surrender, had entered the popular culture and has remained there for many years by and large without criticism.

The revisionist view

The more commonly held views, as provided above, have more recently been challenged, most prominently by the late Peter Hart in his 1998 study published as *The IRA & Its Enemies: Violence and Community in Cork 1916-1923.*[7] Hart suggests that Barry's account over the years changed in the telling and that what actually transpired was possibly less dramatic, less glorified but more controversial. Hart has questioned in no uncertain terms the credibility of what Barry described. In Hart's opinion:

> *Helpless wounded men and prisoners were killed after the battle was over . . . Barry's "history" of Kilmichael, on the other hand, is riddled with lies and evasions. There was no false surrender as he described it. The surviving Auxiliaries were simply "exterminated."*[8]

15

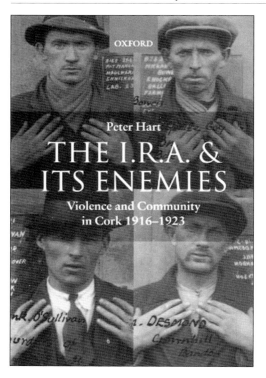

Peter Hart's 1998 study of the War of Independence in West Cork provided a major challenge to Tom Barry's account of events at Kilmichael.

Hart's view has attracted support from some notable quarters, including Professor Diarmaid Ferriter who, when describing the Kilmichael ambush, refers to a "cowardly massacre which involved the deliberate killing of already surrendered soldiers."[9]

One of the central pillars of Hart's challenge to the accuracy of events portrayed in *Guerilla Days* is his contention that the report reputedly sent by Barry to his superiors in the immediate aftermath of the ambush undermines his subsequent depiction of events. The report, which Hart alleges was intercepted by the British Army, formed part of the 6th Division's history of the conflict between 1916 and 1921. The 6th Division was the British military formation responsible for the southern part of Ireland, in whose area the Kilmichael ambush took place. Barry's captured report does not refer to a "false surrender" and gives a version of events quite at variance with that given in *Guerilla Days*. In the captured report, Barry attributes the deaths of the IRA men to,

> . . . *the fact that those three men were too anxious to get into close quarters with the enemy. They were our best men and did not know danger in this or any previous actions. They discarded their cover, and it was not until the finish of the action that P. Deasy was killed by a revolver bullet from one of the enemy whom he thought dead.*[10]

In the interests of balance it should be recognised that a number of authoritative historians, in particular Meda Ryan and Brian Murphy, have taken issue with the authenticity of this report, questioning the accuracy of some of the detail and in particular its origin. Ryan does not believe that Barry was its author and suggests that "basic elements point to a forgery."[11]

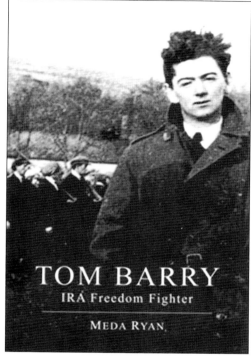

Meda Ryan's 2003 biography of Tom Barry: supporting the traditional view of events at Kilmichael.

TOM BARRY
IRA Freedom Fighter

MEDA RYAN

That Barry would write such a report shouldn't be surprising, however. It is a standard operating procedure to write such an "after action" report to inform higher headquarters. The IRA, according to Tim Pat Coogan, had a propensity to "churn out . . . documents in vast and incriminating quantities, inevitably to be found and seized by the authorities."[12]

Accepting the different views, perspectives, and ideological positions that the historians occupy, it still remains the case that Barry's report was included in a history of the rebellion in the 6th Division area. The report was made available for an internal military audience with an objective that the British might learn something about the IRA's conduct of operations. It would not make sense to forge a captured report when the purpose of compiling it in the unit's history was to contribute to a better understanding of IRA operations.

Hart's public challenge to Barry's depiction of the ambush is not isolated or unique. Questions were already emerging even as *Guerilla Days* was published. Its first appearance was concurrent with the activities of the Bureau of Military History which was gathering statements from War of Independence veterans in an attempt to catalogue events while those veterans could still remember their own roles. What is apparent from the statements, which will be dealt with in detail and relied upon in the course of the analysis, is that there are conflicting recollections of how the events at Kilmichael unfolded. The Bureau statements, for example, outline differences in how the action was commenced, where combatants were located, and the roles they played. There are other variances about what arms were used and the quantities of ammunition available. Inconsistencies are also evident about the quantities of arms and ammunition that the IRA secured from the defeated ADRIC. Of paramount significance, however, and especially for the

"All that remains to mark the tragic scene. The second patrol tender, crippled and forlorn, lies desolate at the edge of the bog." – a picture published in the *Daily Sketch* with its report on the ambush.

purposes of this analysis, are the differing recollections as to how the members of the ADRIC patrol were killed. This study will outline and present an informed comment on some of those conflicting narratives as it examines the specific detail of the combat action.

Summary

Clearly differences of opinion are understandable, but it is the intensity of the academic engagements that catches the eye. The arguments and exchanges might draw comparisons with the manoeuvres in a military operation where the conflicting forces engage in a strategy of continually trying to outflank each other until, finally running out of terrain, they arrive at a stalemate. The stalemate in the case of Kilmichael will only be broken by a new development either through new information becoming available or through a new way of thinking: a new analytical framework.

In a review of John Regan's 2014 book *Myth and the Irish State,* Diarmaid Ferriter makes the following observation on the difficulty of arriving at a determination as to what happened:

> *None of the arguments about the Kilmichael ambush in 1920, when 16 Auxiliaries were killed by Tom Barry's IRA flying column, and in relation to which there were accusations that there was a false surrender by the British troops that resulted in the brutality of some of the deaths have been proved conclusively. The contradictory evidence about what happened does not merit emphatic conclusions from anyone involved in the debate.[13]*

Ferriter's view is understandable when considered in the light of the academic jousting that has characterised the debate thus far. All relevant historical material appears to be either in the public domain or at least known about, thus fresh lines of inquiry have all but disappeared. All the participants are now deceased and it is no longer possible to acquire original first-hand insights. Reliance must be placed on the existing accounts, be they records, reports or published reflections from the pens of those who were directly involved or those who spoke with the participants and dependably reproduced the content of those interviews.

In 2013, Ernest McCall, writing in what is probably the only text dedicated purely to the history of the Auxiliary Division of the Royal Irish Constabulary between 1920 and 1922, outlines a perspective that many will be in general agreement with:

> *The Kilmichael Ambush is celebrated by Republicans and remembered by the Crown Forces as a disaster. It has been surrounded in controversy ever since it happened. A number of academics and writers have explored this ambush in great depth and have written books and papers on the ambush and cannot come to an agreement as to what really happened.*[14]

Although the situation may appear on the surface to be one of stalemate, I believe that a new line of inquiry can be opened by examining the finer military details which, in the prevailing focus on the historical narratives, have not been explored by historians. This lack of exploration is understandable, as without a military background one could not be expected to appreciate the potential impact or significance of some detailed military aspects. It is worth keeping in mind the observation made in 1911 by one of Germany's foremost military writers, Major General Hugo von Loringhoven:

> *In time we learn that war training requirements just cannot be comprehended by those outside the military, or even by those who have only casual contact with it. For this reason, works on military history, written by civilians, may be misleading and dangerous unless written with exceptional care and judgement.*[15]

Some of the relevant texts about Kilmichael have been written with the "exceptional care and judgement" referred to, but others are wildly inaccurate. More importantly though, in this author's view, is the lack of appreciation for the purely military aspects. I would agree with Ruan O'Donnell's view that "the War of Independence is remarkably under researched in terms of in-depth studies for such a seminal transition in the history of Ireland."[16] To support such a view I suggest that the Kilmichael battle site is replete with details relating to the ambush, which have yet to be uncovered. It is arguably the case that the military dimension to the ambush has been neglected as no in-depth study of the site has been carried out to date. There are military nuggets available which, if properly assessed, have the potential to seriously call into question some of the accepted accounts.

A close examination of the Kilmichael ambush through a military lens might provide a new perspective, a new breakthrough. How would this work? Instead of just accepting that a volunteer was armed with a rifle, we will question what kind of rifle was available to him. We will consider what could be achieved with it. We will question the quantities of ammunition available to the combatants and estimate how prolonged the engagement could have been. We will assess the combat capabilities of both trained and untrained troops and how they would be likely to react to the "friction" that will always characterize warfare. Ultimately, such an analysis will provide an additional interpretative architecture whereby the existing historical narratives can be assessed using a methodology that would provide an insight into the combatants' potential actions and reactions due to a number of variables, prior to, during, and after the engagement, and thereby provide an additional understanding of the critical aspects of the action. In this regard, any analysis will be theoretical, as we are seeking to reconcile an outcome with an understanding of what would have been militarily accomplishable. I agree with Meda Ryan's view that "historical discussion progresses by means of interpretation of new evidence and reinterpretation while incorporating previous research."[17] The evidence that this study will reveal is neither new nor sensational. It has always been there, but in this author's opinion its significance has been missed.

It is therefore timely to adopt a new approach and to consider the action through a different analytical process – one that is used by military students to assess what courses of actions were militarily feasible when set against the particular circumstances of an event. Students with a military background, as distinct from military historians with no military background, are ideally placed to conduct such an analysis. Their suitability is grounded on either previous experience of operating in combat situations or by their professional development allowing them an understanding and appreciation of what is and is not possible when presented with a certain set of information. Military analysts will have a view as to how particular combat situations may be conducted. They will also appreciate the potential hazards that accompany high-intensity combat scenarios and how decisions are made under those pressures. The danger, however, is that the military student may often have a preconceived notion about what is being examined, so that there could be a tendency to adopt a generalised approach to the matter or even to fit the facts to a desired outcome. As a counter to that possibility, the military analytical process, if followed correctly, will address that risk. That process, known as a "battlefield analysis", ensures that the matter being assessed is subject to a systematic and rigorous examination. Before we attempt to dissect and examine the action at Kilmichael, I would first like to outline some of the logic behind how we will approach the analysis and consider if such a process can be applied to the circumstances of this investigation.

CHAPTER 3

How to analyse a battle

"One could speculate that five honest men could study any aspect of the war and prove to their satisfaction that five different things were true."[1]

EVERY BATTLE, no matter how small, has its own lessons to provide. Due to the nature of battle, many of these lessons are often hidden and difficult to access. Military historians and professionals therefore utilise various analytical tools to cut through the confusion that inevitably arises from a complex and intense series of events – the "fog of war" that Von Clausewitz refers to. Such tools can uncover and explain the underlying causes for a particular outcome as well as revealing what the potential results might have been, dependent upon certain conditions. Battlefield analysis, which is universally taught on command and staff courses in military colleges throughout the world, consists of critically evaluating the outcome of an engagement against the capabilities and capacities of the conflicting forces and the physical environment within which the engagement occurred. In order to do so, and in advance of analysing the actual combat, a significant effort is devoted to considering the factors that will most likely determine the outcome. These factors are best described by the acronym METTS —Mission, Enemy, Troops (own), Terrain, Space (and time).

The METTS model

The necessary requirements to accomplish an objective are determined by the mission (M). The mission can be of a general nature or specific to a task but it should be a clear, concise statement of the task and its purpose. Both combatant parties may have different missions which would influence their frame of mind and their subsequent conduct in the course of the operation.

Having considered the mission, the METTS model next considers the opposing forces. The enemy (E) and troops (T) are assessed against their potential to accomplish their missions. Such potential is determined by the capability and capacity of the respective forces, starting with the size and composition of the forces and the military effectiveness of the individuals involved. Unless an individual possesses the necessary skills to use the weapons at his disposal and to avail of the opportunities that the physical environment presents, he will not be in a position to contribute to the overall effort of his unit.

Members of the Irish Army receiving a battlefield briefing on the high ground overlooking the Kilmichael ambush site on 18 December 1966 (*Irish Examiner Archive*).

An examination of the use of space (S) and time involves critically considering where the troops were located and whether such deployments were adequate to achieve the task at hand. The time at which the operation commences and the time required to accomplish the mission will have an impact on any decision about the quantities of ammunition required and the likely duration of the action.

Application

Once the METTS aspects have been assessed, the inquiry moves to the next stage of applying the results to the existing accounts of what allegedly transpired – dissecting the historical "facts" of what is said to have occurred against the possibilities of what could have occurred. In order to do so it is necessary to establish the central point of reference from which the analysis will extract such detail. In the case of Kilmichael, the analysis will follow the trail of events as detailed by the combatant closest to the action: the account given by Tom Barry in *Guerilla Days*.

In the study of military events this is a well-established approach, whereby the terrain and known weapons capabilities are used to reconstruct the engagement, and the reconstruction is then compared with the existing written accounts. This approach was pioneered by a German military historian, Hans Delbruck (1848-1929), whose system of research,

> . . . essentially involved a severely critical evaluation of the written sources in the light gained through an examination of the actual terrain; a consideration of the actual capabilities of weapons, equipment, and logistical means; and a comparison of suspicious accounts with more reliable records from similar battles.[2]

The critical examination referred to above is more commonly referred to as "factual criticism" which complements the more commonly used "source criticism." Source criticism has dominated the Kilmichael inquiries so far, and it would seem that once the source of a piece of information has been established and verified then it is accepted as fact. An examination of the Kilmichael ambush has to move beyond simple source criticism. Delbruck's methodology takes this a stage further by testing these facts against what realistically could have occurred; in other words these facts are given a "reality check."

Using this methodology, a detailed examination of the smaller aspects of the battle can allow a fuller consideration of what the real capabilities and capacity of the IRA and ADRIC forces were at that time. Such an examination will then allow us to consider if events as reported really could have occurred when compared with the realities of warfare. Gunnar Artéus describes three features (which he calls "correctives") by which this process can be conducted. In his opinion, the operation should be examined in light of:

- the "laws" (condensed historical experience) of the theory of war;
- historically unchanged topo-geographic conditions;
- what we know is physiologically or technically possible.[3]

Rather than treating the three "correctives" individually, we will consider them as a collective, a collective that will accompany the analysis throughout. Using these correctives will allow us to reflect in an ordered manner on alternatives to the prevailing consensus as to what transpired.

The correctives allow the engagement to be assessed in a coherent way and introduce a disciplined approach to the study. They require the ambush to be assessed in the light of what previous, similar engagements between regular and irregular forces had resulted in. It then requires us to consider the physical environment and the advantages, disadvantages, and challenges that the "lay of the land" presented to both sides. Finally, an assessment of the capacity of both sides, given their physical and weapon capabilities, is conducted to determine what result was realistically possible.

In light of this approach, an assessment of an engagement such as Kilmichael would not restrict itself to considering the weaponry and terrain alone. The responses of the combatants on both sides, as individuals and also as a group, will also form a productive line of inquiry, employing a method known as "inherent military probability" (IMP). It describes a simple methodology used to assess and compare the documented response of the combatants to a particular action against how one would expect a trained soldier to respond when confronted with a similar set of events. A consideration of the actions by the application of the IMP may not be appropriate for all the combatants, when one considers that the members of the attacking party at Kilmichael were more akin to armed civilians than professional soldiers, but its benefit is in introducing a common standard against which all can be measured.

This battlefield study will focus particular attention on the level of unit cohesiveness that would be necessary for the IRA to successfully accomplish the mission and for the ADRIC members to extract themselves from the danger. In assessing this, the study will allow for consideration of a number of possibilities such as whether the IRA had more than their fair share of good fortune in how the engagement played out, or was it the case that the ADRIC patrol failed to react and respond as would be expected of professional soldiers when faced with similar threats, or were they simply dogged with misfortune?

The sources used to aid the interpretation will vary from historical records and commentaries to the most current understandings of weapons and ammunition technology and, of course, the psychological understanding of how troops react in battle.

An engagement amenable to analysis?

Although it is clear that a process is needed which would allow the events at Kilmichael to be examined in a dispassionate way, it should be asked if such a process is appropriate in this instance and if the engagement can be analysed in a meaningful way by using established military analytical methods. The answer will depend on the following questions: Can what occurred at Kilmichael be considered a "battle"? Can the area in which the engagement occurred be considered a "battlefield", and does an examination of the events at Kilmichael deserve to be referred to as a "battlefield study"? Even if the engagement can satisfy these prerequisites, some may also naturally question whether there is a benefit to be gained from such a study.

The Battle of Kilmichael?

The noun "battle" is defined in the *Oxford English Dictionary* as "a sustained fight between large organised armed forces." It may be difficult to describe the action at Kilmichael as a battle when measured against this description, but such categorisations have not prevented similarly scaled actions in the past being afforded this status. Throughout Irish history there have been numerous instances in which confrontations with the Crown forces have been afforded the status of a "battle." The progression from skirmish to battle is often a short journey, and in Ireland the final classification is often more dependent on how the local population or remembrance committee decides to categorise the engagement rather than the scale of the action itself. In the case of Kilmichael, there is little doubt about its status locally; the headstone in Castletown-Kinneigh over the graves of the IRA volunteers killed in the course of the ambush refers to them as having been killed in "the battle of Kilmichael."

To describe the ambush as a "battle" requires a liberal interpretation or, at the very least, an extension of the current understanding of what constitutes a battle. The engagement was certainly not one which could be considered as, in the words of one definition, "a general action involving most of the frontage of rival armies."[4] It should, however, be borne in mind that if Kilmichael was undertaken with the sole purpose of obtaining a decisive victory, then it sits easier with Von Clausewitz's definition of a battle as "a conflict waged with all our forces for the attainment of a decisive victory."[5]

Kilmichael, in tactical terms, was an ambush, and in modern military terminology such an ambush would be more likely categorised as a small-scale contingency operation (SSCO) as opposed to a battle. The SSCO at Kilmichael was a small-unit action, the outcome of which was arguably more influenced by individual actions and personal motivations than through an integrated, collective effort. That said, the Kilmichael action does have elements which one would associate with larger engagements. In order to be successful, for instance, the unit would have to be able to co-ordinate its actions to maximum effect. This is evident in Barry's initial concept as to how the ambush would unfold. For example, troops had to be deployed with the dual purpose of driving home an offensive action and at the same time mutually supporting each other should events not go to plan. The uncertainties would necessitate providing a reserve element to be deployed as required.

The communications, command, and control measures required during the exchange would thus echo those of a larger confrontation.

Kilmichael may have displayed certain commonalties with what is generally understood as a battle and may be described in the popular culture as such. There exists, however, a more compelling argument to suggest that it was a small-scale contingency operation. As a consequence of this categorisation, another crucial question arises: can the ambush area then be described as a "battlefield"?

Battlefields are more generally associated with symmetric warfare, not the asymmetric actions that were so characteristic of the on-going engagements between the IRA and Crown forces. The word "battlefield" conjures up images of the Somme, Normandy, Kursk, and Balaclava, expansive areas with significant terrain features within which large military forces engaged in offensive and defensive actions, attacking and counter-attacking until finally arriving at an outcome.

Studies of such battlefields and of the events that unfolded on them are regarded as strategic studies. Strategic military studies entail the study of warfare at the highest level, where students and analysts consider the build-up and preparation of forces prior to the engagement as well as the planning of the conflict and its conduct.[6] These considerations are accompanied by an awareness of the broader contexts such as the political, economic, and cultural backgrounds that prevail at that time.

Given this broader background, the word "battlefield" suggests an event more comfortably positioned on the macro as opposed to micro spectrum, another reason why it is difficult to categorise a study of the Kilmichael ambush as a strategic study.

On the other hand, battlefields may also be defined in terms of space and duration, and to this end Kilmichael satisfies these considerations, albeit on a smaller scale. Even though the area within which the engagement was conducted was confined by the tight deployment of the attacking force, the terrain, similar to any large battlefield, would act as a decisive feature of the conflict area. The effect of the narrow boundaries of the engagement area, or "killing zone" as it is more commonly referred to, is worth noting. Instead of the square miles or kilometres that one associates with large battlefields, at Kilmichael we are more concerned with square metres, the area of engagement being no more than 400m x 200m at its extremes. Within such a tight battlefield it is still possible to divide the action into a number of constituent parts. These parts had a conjunctive relationship with the success or failure of every other part, each part thus influencing the eventual outcome. Most battlefields, regardless of the territorial dimensions or size of the combatant units involved, still have areas within which small independent engagements or clashes are played out, and in that respect the Kilmichael site has much in common with the larger, more easily recognisable theatres.

If the space over which the engagement takes place distinguishes a strategic from a tactical categorisation, then of equal importance is the time factor. By "time" we are referring to the time-frame within which the operation is conducted. Although strategic battles are more likely to last days, weeks and, in some cases such as Stalingrad, months, the action at Kilmichael, if we are to accept Barry's account, would appear to have lasted no longer than thirty to forty-five minutes. Kilmichael can be said to have been many things, but never a protracted engagement.

Accepting such a time difficulty and even that the action didn't proceed along predictable lines (an issue to be dealt with later), Kilmichael still demonstrates many characteristics of what is encountered in the larger battlefields. Within a large battle, there are often smaller contained actions independent of the main effort, where smaller engagements take place. The actions in the course of the contact replicate those activities that one would expect to unfold at a time and place within the larger battle piece.

Can the action at Kilmichael be subjected to an in-depth battlefield analysis?

In considering the question posed there are two fundamentals to be addressed. The first is whether the battlefield can accommodate the more common methodologies that will be employed, i.e., is there enough to work with? Secondly, if that can be satisfied, then the more philosophical question remains as to whether there is an actual benefit in conducting such an examination.

If the difficulties associated with defining the ambush at Kilmichael as a battle are balanced with allowing the area in which the engagement occurred to be considered a battlefield, the logical conclusion would be that it is so suited, but such an examination would need tailoring to adjust for the unique aspects of the engagement.

An additional objection to analysing the events at Kilmichael could be made along the following lines: that any examination is of little consequence when all that mattered was the outcome of the engagement. Such an objection would relegate the events and personalities to the status of a sideshow to the main event. Details on how the ADRIC members were killed would matter little or be of minor relevance. Proponents of such an objection would declare that what mattered was that the IRA had laid down a marker and that any quest to develop an accurate understanding of how the engagement played out had little relevance. But is that really the case? The answer must surely be in the negative. The benefits, in this writer's opinion, are obvious. Understanding the finer detail of what transpired can assist in looking at other operations with a different perspective. It provides a much greater appreciation of the combat proficiency of the units involved. It can also provide an insight into how the IRA and ADRIC would deal with each other should they have come into further contact as the conflict progressed. Did the outcome, in the absence of a detailed understanding of what actually transpired, cause the British to overestimate the combat capability and capacity of the IRA in West Cork? Until this particular engagement unfolded it is unlikely that the British considered the IRA capable of organising and executing such an operation. Was it now realistically within the military reach of the IRA to defeat the ADRIC patrols by conventional tactical means?

A weaker objection would suggest that enough time and academic resources have been devoted to this issue, and that any further examination would only add to the existing confusion. Such a weaker objection would be countered by highlighting the usefulness of something new being added to the existing deliberations and thereby opening a new channel of exploration. This analysis should not be seen as a challenge to the existing historical examinations but as something that would complement the efforts to date, thereby serving a useful intellectual purpose. Stephen Morillo offers a view that historical studies undertaken by different historians with different perspectives and philosophies are in practice,

> ...*much more a cooperative venture in which separate interpretations complement each other, creating a more rounded and complete picture of the past, than it is a competitive one.*[7]

The focus of this battlefield study is to consider what was militarily possible and then inherently probable as an outcome, having assessed the military capacities of the opposing units. I am not aware of such an approach previously being applied to the Kilmichael ambush and therefore this study will hopefully provide readers with a new "separate interpretation."

Summary

The confrontation at Kilmichael is not easily defined as a battle. A more realistic definition would be to categorise the engagement as a small-scale contingency operation that occurred in a tight battle space. However, given the tight dimensions of this battle space and the number of combatants involved, the force/space ratio would suggest an unavoidably high combat intensity. Such levels of intensity are more associated with larger encounters.

For the purposes of this examination the terrain can be considered as a battlefield in its own right. It is therefore amenable to a battlefield analysis, and there is a benefit to such an examination which will allow a newer perspective and a fresher examination of the existing historical narratives.

Applying the METTS model

B EFORE APPLYING THE METTS model to the engagement at Kilmichael, we should be aware of the prevailing political and military
climate, in particular what led to the deployment of the ADRIC
by the British government, particularly in West Cork.
The situation in certain parts of Ireland between 1919 and 1921 has
been categorised as being in a state of undeclared war.[1] By November 1920,
however, the IRA was particularly active in West Cork where, more than
in any other area in the country, engagements were becoming increasingly
destructive and vicious. Gerard Murphy, recognising the increasingly violent
nature of the conflict, does not disagree with Peter Hart's assertion that West
Cork was the "Gaza Strip of the Anglo–Irish war."[2] The conflict was moving from sporadic clandestine attacks on people and property to a situation
where IRA operations were becoming more organised and on a larger scale,
thus presenting a greater challenge to the Crown's authority. Its character
has been described as a "prototype of modern irregular war."[3] In parallel,
the Crown's civil administration was being usurped by republican efforts to
replace key institutions. The IRA now represented a direct threat to the rule
of law. The threat could not be contained or challenged by a normal police
response. For political reasons there was no desire to acknowledge the scale
of the rebellion by handing over control to the military authorities. However, this decision may have been based on the intelligence assessment at that
time, as Peter Hart offers a view that "guerilla warfare was the only military
action to be expected of the IRA and that a general rebellion was unlikely."[4]
In 1999, Jeremy Black, commenting generally on the increasingly violent
nature of internal conflicts, describes the authorities' response, arguably applicable in this instance, in the following terms:

> *Although the governmental response is presented as policing, it can entail a
> level of military commitment that deserves the description, War.*[5]

The nearest the British authorities came to declaring war was in imposing martial law in eight counties in the south of the country. In order to
maintain the semblance of a "police primacy" policy, a decision was made
to augment the existing police service with additional constabulary forces
– temporary constables (Black and Tans) and temporary cadets (Auxiliaries).
By recruiting ex-members of the British army, the police had effectively

been issued with a military capability. The RIC, in the absence of a declaration of war, was now on a war footing. Rather than policing, the efforts of the ADRIC can be firmly considered as within the realm of a counter-insurgency role.

In summary, the situation existing in West Cork from mid-1920 could be best described as that of a state of emergency. All sectors of society were impacted. Patrick Bishop and Eamonn Mallie make the general point about the popular attitude to the conflict, stating that:

> *Despite later myth-making this was not a heroic war. There was considerable popular acquiescence among the population to the IRA; but when it was not forthcoming there was intimidation.* [6]

Militarily, the momentum was with the republican side as the Crown struggled to maintain law and order. Morale in the RIC was plummeting as a consequence of being directly in the firing line both socially and militarily. As a force the RIC was becoming more and more isolated and vulnerable. The IRA's ambition, buoyed by the success of its operations, was only limited by the personnel and equipment it had at its disposal. Against this backdrop the METTS analysis begins.

(M) Mission

A discussion about the overall mission of the IRA during the War of Independence is beyond the scope of this study, yet it is important to realise that "the objective of the military act is to support the achievement of the confrontational objective of getting the opponent to change his mind."[7] Kilmichael, when considered in this context, was a supporting confrontation in what can be defined as a *small* war (and it is interesting to note here that *guerilla*, a Spanish word, translates as "small war"). Small wars have been defined as "messier, lesser conflicts: the adversary skirmishes, snipes, ambushes, and sets off booby traps; often there is no clear distinction between combatants and non-combatants."[8] Up until the Kilmichael incident the intensity of this small war in West Cork was sporadic and low-level. The conflict was an asymmetrical confrontation between two forces whose differences in terms of weapons, tactics, and field organisation were stark. However, with the formation of the West Cork Flying Column, the IRA created a decentralised combat unit that was capable, intermittently, of bridging the disparities between the forces.

It is difficult to view the specific mission of the IRA column on that morning other than seeking an engagement with British forces as part of the overall campaign and "...to inflict more casualties on an enemy force than those it would itself suffer."[9] *An t-Óglach* , the official organ of the Irish Volunteers, was already urging its members to increase the tempo of the conflict and "to see that it continues, grows more intense and more menacing to the invader."[10]

This general direction is typical of what is more commonly referred to as "mission command", where a broad objective is given to unit commanders but the ways and means as to how this objective is attained is left to the commander's own decisions and resources. Tom Barry tells us he was looking for a confrontation with the ADRIC. He was thus ready to exploit whatever opportunity presented itself and was prepared to challenge a motorised patrol of approximately two sections in strength (eighteen men) with a column that was little more than platoon strength (thirty-six men). Before arriving at the ambush site, Barry had provided little by way of detail to the column as to what the mission was. Immediately before deployment, however, he left the column members in no doubt that the mission was to ambush and to destroy the patrol in order to lay down a statement of intent.

How exactly the operation was to be conducted in order to achieve the mission is still unclear, and I would suggest that it was unclear to Barry also. His intent, however, was abundantly clear. Barry saw no other outcome to the engagement than kill or be killed. IRA prisoners would be either summarily executed on the spot or tried by courts martial and probably face the same outcome. The stakes were therefore high and retribution from the Crown forces guaranteed. This, for the volunteers, was an objective reality and a prime motivator in the desire for a successful outcome. Barry believed this to be the case and intended the engagement to be a fight to the death, with either the column or the ADRIC being annihilated. How Barry intended arriving at this end-state is not clear, and this lack of clarity has been a significant factocr in fuelling the controversy surrounding the engagement.

It must be recognised, of course, that even where a commander has a clear concept of how operations should be conducted, he must accept that uncertainties will arise. Von Moltke was quite categorical on the uncertainties that accompany warfare:

> *Certainly the commander in chief will keep his great objective continuously in mind . . . but the path on which he hopes to reach it can never be firmly established in advance.*[11]

£1 a day and extras – the recruitement advertisement aimed at former officers.

(E) Enemy

In order to help the RIC maintain public order, a decision was made to recruit former army officers as "temporary cadets" and assign them to a paramilitary division that would have quasi–police functions. This division was named the Auxiliary Division of the Royal Irish Constabulary (ADRIC) and its members become more commonly known as "Auxies." They were deployed to those areas where the IRA was most active.

The ADRIC consisted of World War One veterans drawn exclusively from commissioned ranks. They were considered to be well equipped, well resourced, well paid and well trained. They presented a formidable adversary for the numerically superior but otherwise militarily inferior IRA. Barry recounts that they were drawn,

> . . . from ex-British officers who held commissioned ranks and had had active service on one or more fronts during the 1914-1918 war . . . Each carried a rifle, two revolvers, one strapped to each thigh, and two Mills bombs hung at the waist from their Sam Browne belts.[12]

Sean Edmonds describes them as "ex–officers of the British Army, battle hardened and tough, whose records showed them to be fearless and first class fighters . . . they were to be the crack storm troops who would break the back of the IRA."[13] The ADRIC have also been described as "special shock troops", supporting a view of a force capable of performing above normal military standards.[14]

The ADRIC patrol attacked at Kilmichael consisted of eighteen members drawn from "C" Company which was part of an overall strength of 160 members based at Macroom Castle. They had arrived in the area during the summer of 1920 to augment the RIC force in the town and to engage in

Members of the Auxiliary Division of the Royal Irish Constabulary, more commonly known as "Auxies". They were regarded as an elite force, but were the members of "C" Company ambushed at Kilmichael really up to that standard? (*From a painting by Michael O'Dea RHA.*)

counter-insurgency operations. Views about the calibre of these personnel included "invariably overbearing and arrogant"[15], "classic members of sibilant and sinister raiders"[16], and "many appeared to be amiable, but time was to prove that most of them were ruthless killers."[17] John Ainsworth describes the attitude of the IRA towards the Auxiliaries in the following terms: "The Auxiliaries were considered by Irish adversaries who knew them well to be more ruthless, more dangerous 'and far more intelligent than the Tans.'"[18] They have also been described as "anti-IRA irregulars, unlike the army, [who] responded with a campaign of counter terror, militarily quite effective but politically counterproductive."[19]

As former commissioned officers, there was a certain standard of conduct expected of them, and initially they were deemed to be a cut above those former soldiers who made up the force of Temporary Constables known more commonly as the "Black and Tans." However, it wasn't long before their indiscriminate violent behaviour cast them in a poor light, as the following quote from Sylvain Briollay, a journalist covering the situation in Ireland at the time for the *Revue de Paris* and *Le Correspondant* during the winter of 1920-1921, testifies: "And stranger still, the cadets of the ADRIC Force, though all officers, seemingly go as far as the Black-and-Tans."[20]

A.J.S. Brady writing in his memoir, *The Briar of Life,* and having lived in Macroom when the ADRIC were deployed there, gives a further insight into the capability of the force with the following observation:

> *The section of the force that was known as "C" Company, was well equipped, and comprised many hardened warriors of the First World War. It did not seem possible that the Flying Columns of the IRA could defeat the Auxiliary Police . . .[21]*

The fact that they were well-equipped is supported by recent research conducted by Ernest McCall, who states:

> *Each ADRIC Cadet had a selection of weapons to choose from before going on patrol and could select from the following:-*
> 1. *Webley/Smith & Wesson/Colt, revolver/semi-automatic pistol and 50 rounds of ammunition*
> 2. *Lee-Enfield rifle, bayonet and forty rounds of ammunition*
> 3. *Winchester repeating rifle and forty rounds of ammunition*
> 4. *Winchester shotgun and forty rounds of ammunition*
> 5. *Lewis machinegun and five drums of ammunition*
> 6. *Vickers heavy machinegun and 1000 rounds of ammunition for armoured cars*
> 7. *Verey flare pistol and twenty five rounds*
> 8. *Mills hand grenades*

McCall further asserts:

> *The ADRIC performed their own firearms training and obviously had a military mindset in relation to the use of firearms compared to that of a police officer.[22]*

Gleeson informs us that the ADRIC had received no training except in revolver firing and bomb throwing and that the ADRIC personnel in

Macroom were allowed as much ammunition as they wanted and would hunt rabbits and game in the Macroom Castle domain and also "did a lot of revolver shooting at bottles thrown in the river"[23] ,thus possibly hinting at the relative boredom when not engaged in patrolling.

The perception, therefore, from the start was that the Auxiliaries were a "super force" or elite unit that the IRA could not match in combat on a like-for-like basis. But how correct is this? The fact remains that its perception as an "elite" is one based wholly on the requirement that qualification to be a member was determined by an applicant's previous status as a commissioned officer.

The terms "elite" or "special" have been attributed to the ADRIC without, in this author's view, any real consideration as to what it takes to attain such a status in the military hierarchy. In order to fully understand what is in effect a "special forces" status, it is necessary to consider a working definition. Eliot Cohen, writing about special forces, presents three criteria to be satisfied in order for a force to be considered elite:

- *The force is usually assigned extremely hazardous missions,*
- *The force is normally small in size and membership is restricted to those who meet a high threshold in terms of training and physical fitness,*
- *The force must by its actions attain a reputation for bravery and success.*[24]

It is clear from the historical accounts that the ADRIC didn't perform any missions above and beyond what the ordinary military or RIC performed. As we will see when we consider the training and physical fitness possessed of the patrol members, it is far from certain that the general membership of the ADRIC were so gifted or capable. In terms of a reputation for bravery and success, it was more the case of a reputation for excess and violence. The impact of the ADRIC's heavy handedness and ruthlessness is probably best surmised by Roger Beaumont:

> *The spectacle of these counter-terrorist forces acting much like the lately de-rided "Hun" brought down the seemingly invulnerable Lloyd George, not the last liberal-minded politician to learn about the limits of military force the hard way.*[25]

The ADRIC as a force did not satisfy any of Cohen's criteria. Ex-officers who had been demobilised following the armistice in 1918 had merely responded to newspaper advertisements, and there is little evidence to suggest that there was anything that resembled a selection course or even selection criteria to choose who would become a member. Also, what is often over-looked is that the ADRIC was a relatively new force and, unlike a traditional military unit, its members came from quite disparate backgrounds. In the case of the members of "C" Company who would fight at Kilmichael we find a mix of infantry, artillery, and even Royal Air Force (previously known as the Royal Flying Corps) officers present. Because of the method by which they were recruited and the speed that they were allocated to their respective units, they would not have had the opportunity to foster an *esprit de corps* characteristic of more established military units. The training and combat experience that each had would have differed considerably. Being described as a veteran did not automatically mean having direct combat experience. An RAF officer, for example, would not have been exposed to close infantry combat, and officers with an artillery background, as an indirect combat support element often miles to the rear of the front lines, were also unlikely to have had such exposure.

Since they had all been officers, it may well have been the case of too many chiefs. So many authority figures within a small grouping would not have helped their effectiveness. In military units, issues such as how individuals are recruited and what constitutes "officership" are important for cohesion and morale and thus for effectiveness in battle conditions.[26]

Fortunately for the purposes of this study, it is possible to make a realistic assessment of the combat capabilities of the patrol members.[27] Existing military records paint a clear picture of the members of "C" Company, all of whom had diverse wartime service and experience. They would be best described as a motley assortment with various military skill levels, and in the case of some patrol members there is evidence that they were either deficient physically or impaired psychologically. Although all had served in the armed forces, the length of that service and the rank attained differed from member to member. S.P. MacKenzie, when describing the nature of the British Army that fought from 1914 to 1918, declares that the volunteers and conscripts were a far less homogeneous body of men than the pre-war regulars, "regarding themselves first and foremost as citizens and only secondarily as soldiers."[28] This is evidenced by the assortment of backgrounds which the patrol members had engaged in prior to the outbreak of war in 1914. If their military service was diverse, then so too were the civilian occupations they held before enlisting.

Previous occupations and enlistment

Cadet Frederick Forde was the only member of the patrol who had been a commissioned officer at the outbreak of the war in 1914 – he was also, incidentally, the only ADRIC member to survive the ambush. Cadets Christopher Wainwright and William Barnes had both enlisted before the outbreak of hostilities and were commissioned as officers in April and May 1917 respectively.

Cadets Francis Crake (an insurance clerk), Philip Graham(a fruit farmer), Frederick Hugo (a language teacher), and Albert Jones (a grocer's assistant and former gamekeeper) had all joined on the outbreak of the war and received their commissions at various intervals in the course of the conflict. The remaining members of the patrol, Cadet Cyril Bayley (an insurance clerk), Cadet Leonard Bradshaw (a printer), Cadet James Gleave (a machinist), Cadet Cecil Gutherie (a law student), Cadet Ernest Lucas (a used car buyer), Cadet William Pallister (occupation unknown), Cadet Horace Pearson (a railway clerk), Cadet Frank Taylor (a medical student), and Cadet Benjamin Webster (occupation unknown) joined the army at various dates between 1914 and 1917. There is no detail available for Cadet Stanley Hooper-Jones.

Rather than being career soldiers, it is safe to assume that but for the outbreak of hostilities in 1914 the majority of the ADRIC involved in the ambush would have had different careers. They were therefore "accidental" combatants. Their presence in West Cork, with the privations and hardships of active service, were more to do with well-paid employment than with any idealised purpose.

Wartime service and decorations

Eight members of the patrol (Barnes, Bradshaw, Crake, Forde, Jones, Pearson, Wainwright, and Webster) had previous combat experience. Three members of the patrol (Graham, Lucas, and Pallister) had lesser experience. Hugo acted as an interpreter and would appear to have spent the majority of his time in the rear echelon as a railway transport officer. Four members of the patrol (Bayley, Gleave, Gutherie, and Taylor) served with the Royal Flying Corps and would not have had any land-fighting experience.

A number of the patrol members had received wartime decorations. Crake, Ford, and Hugo had been awarded the Military Cross. Barnes had been awarded the Distinguished Flying Cross, and Gutherie had been mentioned in dispatches.

Physical and mental fitness

It would appear that Crake, Hugo, Pallister, and Taylor didn't suffer any injuries in the course of their military service, so there is nothing to suggest that their fighting ability was in any way impaired. Similarly, Gutherie's record indicates a period of four weeks in hospital in 1918 (September–October) but nothing to suggest a lack in his fighting ability.

Lucas, while appearing to be physically sound, was described by his commanding officer as being very nervous and suffering from a lack of self-assurance. Jones had been shot in the head in 1915 and had contracted syphilis in 1917. Bayley is reported in October 1917 to have been suffering from "nervous debility" as a result of a crash and had been hospitalised twice in 1918. Bradshaw had been shot in the chest in August 1916 and had been gassed in March 1918. Pearson had been gassed in October 1918. Webster had been shot in the abdomen in 1916 and returned to Britain in April 1917 suffering from "trench fever" and lumbago. He sustained a gunshot wound to the shoulder in October 1918.

Graham had been diagnosed in March 1916 with neurasthenia (shell shock) due to the stress associated with his service in the trenches. He was again repatriated in June 1916 with neurasthenia and didn't return to action thereafter. Gleave had been wounded in July 1918 and invalided back to the UK at the end of August 1918 where a medical board recommended him as suitable for sedentary employment only.

Forde had been invalided back to the UK with a combination of kidney and malarial problems; in August 1920 he was categorised as permanently unfit for duty. Barnes had been wounded in March 1915 and again in August 1916. He was also categorised as suitable for sedentary employment only. In January 1920 he relinquished his commission on account of ill health. Wainwright had suffered extensive damage to his hearing as a result of a heavy bombardment at the Somme in May 1917. In July 1917 a medical board found him permanently unfit for duty in the front line, and he was then posted to a convalescent depot.

Instead of the popular notion of an elite cadre entirely composed of battle-hardened, capable veterans, the reality therefore was quite different. The ADRIC patrol consisted of members who were militarily experienced but only half of them could be said to have had any prior combat experience. It is obvious from the medical categorisations that a third of the patrol did not meet the required combat physical standards and even in the case of those that did, such as Lucas, questions remain as to their capacity to perform in a pressurised environment.

The ADRIC was a short-term measure, a response to the real risk of losing control to the insurgents. It had a poor organisational structure and operated as a parallel force without any clear ties to the police or army. The British Army's *Record of the Rebellion in Ireland* describes the ADRIC role succinctly: "Nominally they acted under the orders of the County Inspector, RIC; but in practice they worked very much on their own or in co-operation with the nearest troops."[29] The ADRIC as a force was created as a reactive measure and had been generated quickly – too quickly. It was therefore lacking in the unit training, experience, and traditions that are so important in the creation of effective units. The motivation behind an individual's decision to join such a force is plainly obvious from the press advertisement, which gave central prominence to the fact that each member would receive an eye-watering £1 a day for each day of service. Its members were contracted for a specified duration, their service being seen as a temporary measure. Given the quasi-independent nature of the ADRIC's role and its paramilitary character (neither police nor military), the external command and control of the force and its position within the British security architecture was ambiguous.

In summary, due to the pressing security situation, by mid-1920 there existed a "market for force" in Ireland. The authorities had an immediate need for trained personnel to augment a deteriorating RIC. Fortunately for the government, due to the abundance of demobilised officers and the straitened economic climate, it would have no real difficulty in attracting the necessary numbers. The ADRIC's modern equivalent would be more likely that of a private military contractor. In the words of one of the ADRIC who had served with "C" Company, "The Corps was advertised as a '*Corps d'Elite*', which of course made it more attractive… it may appear that we were little more than mercenaries."[30]

Overall enemy assessment

Given the improvised nature of the unit, the motivation of its membership and its relatively short operational existence, "C" Company is unlikely to have been a cohesive, properly integrated and effective fighting force. Its efficiency, therefore, would be determined by the actions and initiatives of individual members rather than depending on a collective, co-ordinated response. However, General William H. McRaven, a leading US special forces commander and commentator, makes the point that "brave men without good planning and preparation and leadership are cannon fodder in the face of defensive warfare."[31] Once the patrol entered the ambush killing area they would be faced with fire of a defensive nature from prepared positions.

ADRIC mission

In the case of "C" Company, Richard Bennett states:

For three months the Auxiliaries had been raiding, searching and patrolling the district without being attacked; they had rounded up suspects and had frequently added physical injury to insults.[32]

There is a possibility that the ADRIC had an overall mission objective of countering or disrupting attempts by the IRA to conduct ambushes. An ADRIC member, Bill Munro, who had served with "C" Company alongside those who were to die at Kilmichael, reveals the following:

Reverting to ambush hunting in general, it became obvious that false information was being spread purposely by the other side so that in finding so many mares' nests we would become careless, which in spite of so many warnings by our C.O. turned out to be the case and later cost us twenty lives.[33]

One of the foremost British counter-insurgency experts, General Frank Kitson, has succinctly declared that in counter-insurgency operations, "the problem of defeating the enemy consists very largely of finding him."[34] The ADRIC mission on 28 November was, therefore, probably in line with Bennett's view of raiding, searching, and patrolling.[35] The patrol's actions that day could be considered as part of an overall strategy to recover whatever authority had been lost to the IRA over the previous number of months and to re-establish a military dominance in the West Cork area generally. In pursuit of this strategy they were having considerable levels of success, and it was probably inevitable that a significant confrontation with the IRA was unavoidable. The Kilmichael incident followed on closely from the events of "Bloody Sunday" a week earlier on 21 November 1920 during which the IRA conducted a very successful counter-intelligence operation, killing twelve British intelligence operatives. There is a suggestion that these killings provided the impetus to the British government to exercise the extensive powers available to it under the Restoration of Order in Ireland Act 1920, which had only been introduced in August, and that as a consequence orders were given to intern all known officers of the IRA and other suspected men.[36] It may well have been that this was indeed the mission of the "C" Company ADRIC patrol that day. It is unlikely that they were expecting to be attacked.

Given their mission and the nature of the ADRIC, and the complacent attitude that they had adopted, it is clear that their culture and practices, characterised by a sense of superiority and heavy-handedness, may have ultimately contributed to their demise.

*Howe's Strand whereby any ship could train its searchlight upon the Coast-
guard station is treacherously close to that. It is more likely to have been a
smaller patrol vessel based in Queenstown, such as HMS Badminton, a
Hunt-class minesweeper.*

There were seven Coastguard officers employed in the Howe's Strand
station yet they were issued with ten Ross rifles and subsequently a further
twelve. It should also be borne in mind that one of the volunteers who took
part in the raid states that twenty-five rifles were removed.[42] Whatever figures are accepted, it is strange that the number of rifles available exceeded
the number of those available to use them. A volunteer involved in the raid
made a very astute observation by declaring that following the capture of
the rifles there was "surprisingly little military or police activity."[43] Almost
a year later, on 8 June 1921, the Courtmacsherry Coastguard station was
attacked by what the chief officer described as "an armed force of civilians"; the chief officer also reported that in order to defend the station he
procured "a loan of two rifles and ammunition from the military."[44] The
seriousness of the attack is evidenced by the death of a lance corporal and
the wounding of a private who were attacked in the village in the course of
the engagement. The attack was beaten off within thirty minutes with no
damage to the building, thus demonstrating that when the station needed
to be defended it could be, and that two rifles were sufficient for its defence.
Another Coastguard station, at Ballycrovane on the Beara Peninsula,
also within the West Cork Brigade area, which the IRA had presumed was
occupied by unarmed coastguards, was unexpectedly armed by the Royal Navy and the coastguards were augmented by a detachment of Royal
Marines.[45] The Marines charged with protecting the Coastguard stations
along the south-west coast were from 8th Battalion, "D" Company and were
headquartered at Castletownshend and later at Berehaven. The magazine of
the Royal Marines, *The Globe and Laurel* for 1922 reports the return of the
8th Battalion to headquarters in February 1922, having been deployed since
June 1920. The IRA learned of the presence of arms at the station when a
Coastguard officer was conveniently seen outside the station cleaning a rifle.
The IRA duly raided the station and recovered either eleven or nineteen
Ross rifles (depending on which of the two statements given to the Military
Bureau is the more accurate).[46] What is interesting is that the IRA managed
to overwhelm a detachment of Royal Marines after a brief fire-fight and
that the marines would appear to have been armed with Ross rifles, which
is puzzling since the Lee-Enfield was the standard issue rifle for them at
the time. Further evidence to support a view that these Marines would

have ordinarily been issued with Lee-Enfields is found in "The Monthly Records of the Questions and Answers dealt with by the Director of Naval Ordnance 1918-1922." Minute 242 of January 1919 states:

> *It is proposed to outfit the Fleet generally with Charger Loading MLE short rifles [Short Magazine Lee-Enfield rifles] which is the standard Army weapon and which is now being supplied in certain limited quantities to the Fleet. [Author's emphasis]*

This would suggest that the Royal Navy and Royal Marines were being equipped with Lee-Enfields in 1919 if not before.[47]

Stranger still was the request of the "defenders" to increase the damage to the building "so that their authorities would be impressed by the stiff resistance they had put up."[48] The IRA duly obliged by breaking doors and windows and firing a few shots as they left. One of the Coastguard officers later in the day remarked to one of the IRA raiders that they were "very slow in carrying out that job"[49], thus reinforcing a view that the Coastguard were a Crown force in name only and enjoyed good relations with the local population.

Subsequent to this raid, the same company of the IRA intercepted a military detachment supplying the unit stationed at Eyries and once again managed to gain possession of a Ross rifle. The rifle was not on issue to the British Army, which would force one to question how it was part of a British supply detachment in West Cork.

It should also be noted that ten Ross rifles had also been "acquired" late in November 1919 by the Bantry Battalion of the IRA when they raided a naval sloop that had carelessly tied up "alongside" in the harbour, thus facilitating the passage of the rifles from British to republican hands. One might well question why ten practically unguarded Ross rifles were on board and an opportunity was afforded to the IRA to steal them. This point will be further explored.

Following the various "acquisitions", the majority of the rifles that the West Cork Flying Column had at its disposal by the end of summer 1920 must have been Ross rifles and not, as has been commonly thought, Lee-Enfields. This has a major consequence for how we assess the conduct of operations at Kilmichael because the Ross rifle, although it had a well-earned reputation for being a very accurate high-velocity weapon, had a significant downside: it was totally unsuited to combat conditions. The Ross was a precision weapon that required careful handling and a specific type of ammunition. In expert hands it was clinically efficient, in untrained hands it could pose more of a danger to the user than the individual being fired at. It suffered from a number of design defects, primary among these being that when engaged in rapid fire under wet conditions it was notoriously unreliable as the weapon's mechanism was prone to locking. In fact, its performance in the first two years of the First World War was so poor that the Canadian forces ultimately abandoned it, and the controversy surrounding the weapon contributed to the dismissal of the Canadian Minister of Defence, Sam Hughes. The history of the rifle and how its defects were uncovered are outlined in detail in Appendix II.

The defects of the Ross rifle, as we shall see later, play a significant role in our analysis of what was supposed to have happened at Kilmichael.

There is testimony to support a view that bayonets were used by the IRA since ammunition was always in short supply, and by the time volunteers finished their training they would have managed to fire only a small number of rounds. In the case of Kilmichael, the storage and supply of ammunition to the column was unorthodox. A member of Cumann na mBan stated in her application for a military pension that she had supplied one of the IRA men killed in the ambush, Michael McCarthy, with a hundred rounds of ammunition, which had been stored in her house since 1917.[50] McCarthy may have distributed this ammunition even further, as Barry describes each volunteer being issued with only thirty-five rounds for the engagement. It is not clear if this was rifle, shotgun, or revolver ammunition.

The poor supply of ammunition was matched by the column's lack of training. In fact it is possible that some volunteers fired their weapons for the first time in the course of the ambush at Kilmichael.

In the course of preparing this analysis I was fortunate to be given access to a taped interview of a flying column member from Newcestown, County Cork, by the name of Denis O'Callaghan. The recording is a straightforward account of aspects of his engagement with the republican movement and in particular his involvement with the flying column. Denis O' Callaghan did not fight at Kilmichael but he was at Crossbarry. His description of life with the column is illuminating. It is obvious that he considered himself to be a soldier and "reasonably well trained in the use of arms." He does, however, qualify such training by stating that the arms he was referring to were shotguns commandeered from their owners and stored in company dumps. He further states that the movement was always short of rifles, and the only way these could be supplied was to take them from the military. He recounts an incident in which the Newcestown Company ambushed a military cyclist patrol moving between Dunmanway and Ballineen by jumping over a ditch and securing the rifles after overpowering the soldiers. O'Callaghan's interview makes obvious the sacrifices that volunteer members of the flying column had to endure. He recounts sleeping in a makeshift "hide" in the fields around his home, as sleeping in his house, once he was known to be actively involved with the republican movement, was impossible due to the risk of arrest.[51]

Adequate training on an organised basis for a flying column was not possible. The logistical and operational aspects of maintaining a platoon-sized formation on full-time active service would have drained brigade resources. It would also have become a prime target for British efforts. For these practical reasons the column was mobilised for specific operations and disbanded or stood down when not engaged. It would also have allowed volunteers who were not "on the run" to return to their homes and occupations without creating suspicion. Matt Flood, an IRA volunteer with a North Cork flying column states:

> *Those were tough times because you were out half the night, you might be on anything, training or raiding for arms but you had to show up for work bright and early the following morning because if you were missing or late for work they would suspect something.[52]*

For those that couldn't return home, O'Callaghan describes the great lengths the republican movement went to in order to assist in the running of farms, such as organising locals to look after the farm and to ensure tasks such as the planting of crops were carried out.[53]

The column's greatest strength of being able to melt into the background when not required was also potentially its greatest weakness in that it afforded a limited opportunity for the members to hone their individual military skills; even more significantly, members would have very limited exposure to military operations as part of a larger unit.

The significance of this training deficit is obvious when one considers that to create a competent soldier of private rank requires at least sixteen weeks basic training. This transforms the civilian to soldier. Further, more advanced training, generally of eight weeks' duration, is required to transform the basic soldier to a fully competent infantryman. The overwhelming majority of the attacking force at Kilmichael did not have any such training, and the assumption therefore is that their weapons handling was rudimentary and their tactical appreciation limited. Their ability to fight in a combined or co-ordinated fashion was therefore questionable.

For planning purposes, the availability of trained personnel to accomplish the mission through a full engagement with the ADRIC was vital,

exhaustion cannot be relayed through communications technology but important salient features are very apparent. The poor weapons' handling and total absence of fire control measures, the gathering of rebel forces in large groups at vulnerable areas, the absence of command or leader figures, the excessive noise levels, and the haphazard conduct of operations – all point to the limitations expected of irregulars. If one were to remove the modern weaponry, the personal protective clothing, the portable radio communications systems and solely concentrate on how the operations are conducted then we would get a similar appreciation of how the volunteers would have reacted when faced with the same threat to their lives. Confusion abounds, particularly evident in those instances where the cameraman captures those moments when a rebel grouping is caught unaware. Rather than a co-ordinated and immediate response, panic is the prevalent result. The reactions are innate. Survival is key. There is nothing to suggest that the volunteers at Kilmichael would have reacted any differently.

In summary, the IRA column was a minimally trained, lightly armed grouping seeking to engage a much better equipped, resourced and trained adversary in a conventional infantry encounter. The odds were significantly against them succeeding in this regard.

Terrain (T)

Although the battle site at Kilmichael has undergone a great deal of transformation because of the large monument unveiled there in 1966 and the more damaging development work undertaken in 2013 and 2014, the salient features of the terrain as it was in 1920 remain, allowing us to appreciate, to some extent, how these were used by Barry in deploying his forces.

Weather and light conditions are equally important; having visited the site many times over the years, I can testify to what these are like on wet, dark November evenings!

The site is located in the western area of County Cork, between Macroom and Dunmanway. Although described as Kilmichael, the site is actually located on the R587 in an area known as Shanacashel, between Kilmichael Cross and Gleann Cross. The terrain is typical of that encountered in West Cork, with rocky outcrops and saturated bog traversed by an S-shaped road.

Key terrain

In considering the terrain I am limiting the assessment to an area of 400m x 200m, taking the centre of the ambush as the focal point. The site location is dictated and chosen by a number of self-serving aspects: the troops at the commander's disposal and the likely force to be encountered. An ideal ambush site allows the attacking party to dominate the key and critical terrain. It should provide good cover from fire and concealment from view to the attacking force and limited cover for the ambushed party. Once the enemy combatants have entered the ambush site, the terrain features should make it difficult for any combatants to escape from it. The terrain should limit or at least impede the capability of the enemy force conducting a co-ordinated response to the ambush.

The Kilmichael site satisfies many of the elements required of a good ambush location. Its predominant feature is a classic S-bend shape to the road. The "S" is dominated by high ground on its eastern flank and an open area to the south which would allow good fields of fire to those deployed on the southern flank.

The terrain offered good security to the ambush party, as the nature of the terrain would make it difficult to surprise the attacking party from the flanks. Conversely, were the ambush party to lose the momentum, the terrain would not have assisted their escape. For the IRA that in itself must have been a singular motivation to ensure victory.

The key terrain features are the road (ditchless), the bog to the southern side of the road, and the three rocky outcrops that dominate the road. For the purposes of this analysis I have assessed the decisive terrain as the high ground on the northern side of the ambush area. When military planners speak of decisive terrain they are referring to terrain that it is essential to control in order to ensure a successful operation. The IRA needed to control this feature; if the Auxiliaries managed to gain control, it could have threatened not alone the success of the operation but the continued existence of the ambush party itself.

Obstacles

It would appear that there were no man-made obstacles such as trenches cut across the road or vehicles placed on the road to block the ADRIC. *The Irish Times* refers to "a deep trench being cut across the road"[57], though this is not supported by any other testimony from those involved and can be reasonably disregarded. The most conspicuous natural obstacle is the wet ground or bog that surrounds the high ground to the south of the road. The advantages that such wet ground often provides to those occupying ground behind it was recognised by the volunteer magazine *An t-Óglach* when it advised its readers that "a much inferior force is safe behind a bog as far as a frontal attack is concerned."[58]

Cover and concealment

Even a cursory glance at the ambush site, which has a number of elevated rocky outcrops, will reveal immediately that the attacking party would have the best cover from fire and concealment from observation. The column also made use of a low stone wall to conceal one position while O'Brien's testimony provides details of some limited construction of a defensive position using stones that were available nearby. From the defenders' perspective, the lack of a roadside ditch and the open nature of the intended killing zone meant any cover would have to come from the vehicle they were travelling in. In this regard, the ambush site is considerably different now from how it would have appeared in 1920. The roadside vegetation that is currently in place was not there in 1920 as the image on page 53 demonstrates clearly.

Observation and fields of fire

There was good observation afforded to the attacking party as the dominant elevated positions would allow the attackers a full view of the battle space. When we speak of "fields of fire" we are referring to an area that the weapons used could fire upon from any given position. The relatively linear aspect of the northern feature would afford good fields of fire; these, however, would be restricted in the event of a flanking fire requirement as the lack of depth on the position would afford limited opportunities to fire parallel

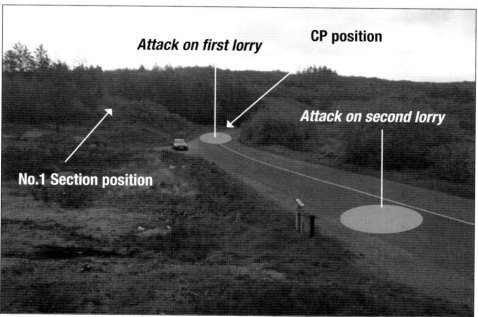

Command Post and No.1 Section positions viewed from No.2 Section position.

No.2 Section position viewed from No.1 Section.

to the feature without engaging other deployed attackers. The volunteers deployed to the south of the ambush position had excellent opportunities to observe the conduct of the ambush but even though they had good fields of fire they would be restricted in engaging in the attack by the presence of volunteers within those areas.

Avenues of approach

There were two unrestricted approaches to the ambush position, from the east and from the west along the road which would be the focus of the ensuing action. There was a restricted approach, cross-country, from north and south of the position, but because the ADRIC patrol was being transported by lorries these approaches can be disregarded for planning purposes.

An assessment of the battlefield area

When objectively assessing the merits associated with the ambush position, one has to not only consider the availability of alternatives but also how the attacking party was deployed to take best advantage of the opportunities that the terrain presented. While I will deal in depth with the deployment in the following chapter, the physical characteristics of the site are worthy of comment

Tactically, the position chosen by Barry was poor. Barry admits as much when he describes the lack of roadside ditches and cover as being "bad for

No.3 Section position taken from No.1 Section.

an ambushing party." Barry, however, justifies its selection on the basis that there were few alternatives available. By focusing on the lack of roadside ditches as a significant weakness we can assume that Barry understood the limitations, particularly in terms of marksmanship, of the troops under his command. This limitation as to the cover available could also work to the IRA's advantage in that the ADRIC would be equally denied firing positions from which they would have to be dislodged.

An objective analysis of the ambush site would point to the lane on the western flank at the entrance to the site as a more significant weakness. In the event that the lead lorry was to become aware of the ambush preparations or that the following lorry was sufficiently to the rear to avoid the first engagement, then this lane offered a last-minute escape from the killing zone. This lane could have offered the ADRIC patrol an escape and access to the only house or hard cover in the vicinity of the site. Had the patrol or elements of it been in a position to avail of such cover, they could have either consolidated a defensive position or organised a flanking manoeuvre and thereby dislodged the volunteers deployed on the southern aspect of the ambush site. Selecting the ambush position so close to such a threat without making any contingency for it was a tactically poor decision. Bizarrely, however, this lane saved the ambush from being compromised by allowing a party of armed volunteers who had arrived late to conceal themselves from the ensuing ADRIC patrol.

Failure to use obstacles that could have assisted in halting the patrol was poor planning on Barry's part. The column could have commandeered digging implements from nearby houses and constructed a trench at the Dunmanway side of the site. Barry was totally reliant on his ruse of appearing in an officer's tunic to slow down or stop the first lorry. He was leaving a lot to chance, something he could have made a contingency for had he constructed an obstacle or cut the road to prevent the patrol driving out of the killing area.

Coincidentally or perhaps by design, *An t-Óglach* in the edition published after the ambush gave instructions to volunteers on the importance of stopping the vehicles being attacked:

> *Barricades, landmines or a combination of the two of these are valuable because if the lorries are brought to a halt they are practically helpless…Trenches can often be dug and camouflaged with straw and earth or road metal. The choice of the best method will depend on local circumstances.*[59]

Space (S) and time

How did Barry use the space provided by the ambush site to deploy his men before the arrival of the Auxiliaries? According to Barry's own account, he split the column into equally sized sections, as detailed below. (It must be noted that a different deployment was described by Volunteer Paddy O'Brien in Liam Deasy's *Towards Ireland Free*[60], where he states that Barry split his men into two sections, one under his own command and the other under the command of Michael McCarthy.)

Command Post and No.1 Section
- Headquarters or command post element of either four or five volunteers, including Barry, deployed to the eastern end of the ambush area.
- A section of ten riflemen was positioned behind the back of a slope on the northern aspect of the ambush site. They would move onto the crest of the slope once the ambush had commenced. This would be the No.1 Section position.

No.2 Section
- A section of ten riflemen was also positioned on what is described as a rocky eminence also on the northern aspect of the ambush position. This also dominated the entrance to the site from the west.

Only seven of these riflemen were allotted to fire at the second lorry whilst the remaining three riflemen were allocated the task of firing on any approaching lorries that could unexpectedly arrive. This would be the No.2 Section position.

• A reserve element of six riflemen was placed to the rear of No.2 Section in order to provide a contingency element should additional unexpected forces arrive.

No.3 Section

• Six riflemen were placed on the southern flank of the site, primarily to deny the enemy use of this feature. This would be known as the No.3 Section position

Time

At the outset it is crucial to establish the timing of the ambush. This will determine the range of visibility and therefore the ability of the combatants to see and engage each other. In Barry's account he refers to the scout signalling the approach of the British patrol a mile from the ambush site at "4.5pm."[61] Did this mean 4.05pm or 4.50pm? This is very significant because sunset for Cork on the 28 November is 4.29pm with twilight at 5.08pm. Deasy refers to the "light beginning to fade" when the signal was received that the patrol were approaching.[62] The police report refers to "dusk falling at about 5pm"[63] while Francis Costelloe describes the action as having commenced as late as 1730hrs[64], which can be discounted as it would have been too dark for the operation. For the purposes of this exercise I am going to suggest a half way measure where the first lorry was engaged at 4.30pm. The day appears to have been particularly overcast, damp, and cold. Therefore, if we are to consider this combined with the impending nightfall, visibility would be deteriorating rapidly.

On a late November evening, ambient light levels would have been low. The potential timing of the engagement is significant in that regard. This was an opportunity ambush, the success of which ultimately depended on the ADRIC patrol arriving at a time when visibility would allow the volunteers to use their weapons to best effect while also maintaining a sufficient level of situational awareness. It was crucial for the attacking force, given its paucity of military experience, that all would be capable of at least seeing what was going on in order to maintain some level of battlefield awareness. From the commander's perspective, in the absence of a communication system, visibility with his deployed sections was of paramount necessity.

CHAPTER 5

How the battle unfolded

WHAT SET THE Kilmichael ambush apart from other IRA operations at the time was the scale, intensity, and result of the engagement. As an armed action it resembled an act that one would associate with partisan warfare, distinguishing it from the IRA's more widely used tactic of assassinating individual members of the security forces. The British Cabinet acknowledged the ambush as a military operation – "it was of a different character from the preceding operations."[1]

The ambush represented a change in focus and an increased ambition about what the IRA felt it could achieve. Such a change, rather than being centrally driven or controlled by headquarters in Dublin, depended on local commanders having the confidence and courage to upscale their efforts and to deliver a maximum return from the personnel and material available. Barry would seem to have been particularly keen to inject an increased momentum or tempo to the existing battle-rhythm of the conflict. As the West Cork Brigade's training officer since August 1920, Barry would have been more aware than most of the potential to depart from the individual actions that had characterised the conflict to date, but it would also appear that he was intent on meeting the ADRIC on conventional tactical terms. Barry was ambitious about developing the IRA's capability, possibly seeking a like-for-like confrontation to reinforce his view that the scale of operations could be increased considerably. A near-frontal collision, even though it constituted the very antithesis of guerrilla warfare, would provide a suitable conduit for this ambition.[2] The IRA were now learning how to keep, "a much larger enemy force in a wearying state of perpetual insecurity by frequent ambush and assassination."[3]

In analysing the pre-combat, combat, and post-combat elements of the engagement, it is best to adopt a process that will focus the analysis on the actions as described in *Guerilla Days* while concurrently considering what would have been the activity unfolding at other positions within the ambush area. There is no fixed approach that is universally suitable for all battlefield scenarios. To try and describe the overall activity as a single narrative would be cumbersome and unwieldy. To assist the reader in gaining a coherent understanding of how the events unfolded, it is necessary to consider the events in sequence, with the conduct of the operation being divided into a number of phases. This will, therefore, involve a consideration of the activities *before* (Preparation, Phase 1), *during* (Engagement, Phases 2,3 and 4) and *after* the action (Phase 5). Considering that Phases 1 and 5 did not involve combat, the outcome of the ambush was determined in Phases 2, 3, and 4.

Using this methodology, the ambush can be considered as a number of localized actions. The first phase will therefore be considered as the movement from the training area to the arrival at the ambush site. Even though the opening engagements on both Crossley Tender lorries occurred virtually simultaneously, the engagements at both sites were evolving at very different rates; consequently, the action is further divided as follows: the second phase, which began the attack, concerns the assault on the lead vehicle, the third phase deals with the attack on the rear lorry, while the fourth phase will be considered as the time Barry's squad assisted in the attack on the rear truck. Finally, the analysis will focus on the fifth stage: the column's activities in the immediate aftermath of the action.

Even after splitting the ambush into distinct phases, difficulties in gaining an overall view are still apparent. Not surprisingly, owing to Barry's direct involvement, *Guerilla Days* gives a detailed description of the combat as engaged in by Barry's group. However, apart from a few descriptions contained in the statements given to the Bureau of Military History, there is little by way of detail available describing the concurrent activity and associated engagements which would have been unfolding at the supporting positions. Reasonable assumptions must therefore be made as to what would or could have been happening there. These assumptions will primarily be based on the testimony supplied by other participants. The deployments of the ambush party and the actions by those deployed at those positions are crucial to gaining an insight into what may have occurred.

In order to appreciate the timings involved and because of the uncertainty as to the exact timing of the commencement of the engagement, H-Hour will be used as the reference time to indicate the opening action of the engagement. The analysis of the conduct of the operation therefore begins by a consideration of events prior to the engagement, moving then through the phases as the engagement begins and runs its course, and then to a consideration of the aftermath of the action.

Phase 1: preparations and movement (H Hour – 7 days)

The column had assembled the previous week on 21 November in an area north-west of Dunmanway known as Clogher. Barry, declaring he "… knew nothing about training a guerilla force"[4], as the training officer was in charge of the camp. He alone would have dictated the activities engaged in. It is assumed that the column members practiced small-unit drills, foot drill, and basic tactics, and there would also most likely have been some level of marksmanship training or weapons handling, but it is not necessarily the case that the volunteers would have fired the weapons.

There is no information to suggest that the column trained specifically for an ambush. The modern approach to preparing a platoon for an ambush is to keep the plan simple and ensure that all participating members understand their roles thoroughly. As a tactical engagement, an ambush is a complex deployment. Adequate preparation is key to its success, with considerable thought and planning being given to dealing not alone with the expected actions but equally with the unexpected. Rehearsals are a prerequisite and are normally conducted by the use of a cloth/model kit or sand table, with "dry runs" being conducted in advance over similar terrain. No training is ever conducted at the actual site for fear of compromising the operation. There is no record, however, to suggest that the column conducted any rehearsals before Kilmichael. Instead, after what was at best rudimentary field training, the column prepared to march to an assembly area known as Ahilina, at O'Sullivan's farm near Castletown-Kinneigh some distance from the ambush site and thereafter commenced their deployment beginning with a route march to Kilmichael.[5]

Captain Donal Buckley in his excellent treatment of an IRA ambush at Tourmakeady, County Mayo, describes the preparatory movements of the local flying column in that engagement:

> *The first principle of an ambush is surprise. It made good sense to move the Column near to where an attack was to take place, obviously the night before a patrol would arrive.*[6]

The route isn't described, but given the relative strength of the column, it is assumed that they used the road when possible and that the road would have been scouted. Since they were moving as a unit, wearing working boots, possibly carrying some rudimentary equipment and bearing arms, it would have taken them an estimated five hours to move from the assembly area to the ambush site – using Naismith's rule of allowing one hour for every three miles travelled. This agrees with Barry's description of having "marched all night."

The descriptions of the weather conditions surrounding the engagement are limited. We are told that the column began its march to the ambush area in "lashing rain" and that they were drenched before reaching the deployment area. We are then given a description of the attacking party having to wait shivering in their respective positions because of the "biting cold." It is not unreasonable to assume that the effect of such exposure on the combat effectiveness of the attacking force would at a minimum diminish their fighting capability.

It is assumed that the column was not exposed to any further rain, as Barry makes reference to the "previous night's rain", but the members were certainly soaked with little opportunity to avail of dry clothing or to dry naturally as they were also deployed in damp areas. If the column began its march at 0300hrs and the engagement was to take place at 1630hrs, then an analysis has to take account of the degrading effect of over 13.5 hours of exposure to wet clothing and equipment on the column's combat capacity.

Having arrived at their rendezvous between 0815hrs and 0830hrs, the column members would have been assigned their respective positions. Barry refers to the column being told of the plan of attack only on arrival at the ambush site, supporting a view that there was little in the way of a rehearsal or drill before deployment at the ambush area:

> We two [Barry and Michael McCarthy] were the only two people who knew up to late Saturday night where we hoped to fight on Sunday.[7] [Author's insert]

If Barry had made a conscious effort not to brief his troops about the location of the ambush, then this is understandable as an internal security or counter-intelligence measure. It might suggest that Barry may not have known his troops well enough to make an objective assessment of their reliability or to discard any suspicion about the presence of an informer. It may also be the case that Barry had not thought the operation through in any great depth. Again, it must be assumed that each volunteer would have been aware of his section, and that each section would have been assigned a section commander as Barry describes each volunteer as having been allocated to a section during the course of the training camp. The ambush's success was predicated on each of these sections being aware of what their role in the engagement was and carrying out those responsibilities efficiently. Command at section level would have to be very effective given the lack of experience among the ordinary volunteers. Section strength is normally ten soldiers, and this is recognised internationally as the limit at which a section commander can exercise effective individual control over the troops under his command.[8] It is probable that the designated section commanders had no experience of small-unit command.

The pre-deployment stage would appear to have been quite casual, and a number of incidents in particular hint at an informal aspect to the column's activities: the late arrival of volunteers and the presence of Lieutenant Pat Deasy at the ambush. In Deasy's case, supported by Barry's testimony, he simply didn't obey an order and followed the column in order to involve himself in the activity. Rather than reprimanding him, Barry allowed him to join the column. The same can be said of John Lordon who arrived late having heard that the column was, "looking for action."[9] Lordon had obviously missed Tom Barry's briefing and was simply posted to No.2 Section's position.

The late unannounced arrival of an additional volunteer party of four volunteers seconds before the engagement began was a far more serious matter. That such armed volunteers would venture to the ambush area in a horse and trap in the knowledge that a large motorised ADRIC patrol was expected in the area tests credulity. They either lacked the necessary level of situational awareness or were unaccustomed to the scale and preparations required for the action being contemplated. They were certainly casual as to their own safety and equally oblivious to the threat they posed to the ambush party. The fact that Barry was obviously unaware of their intended participation and that they could decide of their own volition to participate in the action strongly indicates a lack of cohesion in the operations of the column. It also points to a weakness in internal security procedures that the column's intended operation and location were known beyond the column itself.

With the volunteers in place and the additional late arrivals cleared from the battlefield, the ADRIC patrol in two lorries approached the ambush. The engagement was about to commence.

The engagement and its three phases

Amongst Carl Von Clausewitz's celebrated observations on the nature of war, the following is possibly one of his best known:

> *Everything is very simple in War, but the simplest thing is difficult. These difficulties accumulate and produce a friction which no man can imagine exactly who has not seen war.*[10]

Von Clausewitz's observation about the confusion that military engagements create was as applicable to the events at Kilmichael as to any other battlefield. The "friction" or confusion that Von Clausewitz refers to permeated the engagement with a consequence for how the action must therefore be analysed. This can be somewhat addressed by breaking the combat engagement activity into three distinct phases. We can study the phases separately before reassembling them and taking a holistic view of what occurred.

Each of the phases within the engagement had a destructive element to it. Von Clausewitz recognised the importance of such individual engagements feeding into the attainment of the overall objective and he considered destruction as the ultimate aim of all engagements.[11] The Prussian strategist Von Moltke saw it in similar terms:

> *Only one thing is certain: if one desires to attack, one should do so with decisiveness. Half measures are out of place.*[12]

Barry's actions could never be considered as half-measured, and there was a willingness on his part to expend blood. This can be definitively established by the motivational preparations Barry had embedded in the column before engaging the enemy. The volunteers may not have been adequately briefed about the conduct of the operation, but they would have been well aware that, once it began, disengagement from the ambush would be impossible. Both sides would be locked together, with only one of two options available to both parties: death or victory.

The engagement was to result in the total destruction of the ADRIC patrol, and it was how this destruction was arrived at that has immersed the Kilmichael ambush in controversy. In assessing the course of the ambush over the following three phases, the objective will be to question how this decisive victory was arrived at. Was the ADRIC patrol defeated by conventional military means that accorded with the laws of war? Or was the patrol annihilated as part of a bloody-minded mission, where there was never an intention to take prisoners or allow any of the ADRIC members to escape alive, with the false surrender story being concocted as a way of justifying the annihilation? Or is there an even darker side to Kilmichael, where prisoners may have initially been taken but a decision, for whatever reason, was taken to summarily execute them after they had surrendered? The records are fragmented and inconclusive. It is against these ambiguities that the attack is now considered.

Phase 2 (H-hour): attack on the lead lorry

IRA actions - Command Post and No. 1 Section: It is unclear who or what action initiated the attack. Barry's detailed narrative describes how he stood on the road in a military uniform – an action that he hoped would either slow down or stop the leading truck to enable on attack on it:

> *For fifty yards it maintained its speed and then the driver, apparently observing the uniformed figure, gradually slowed it down until at fifty yards from the command post, it looked as if it were about to stop. But it still came on slowly and, as it reached thirty five yards from the small stone wall, the Mills bomb was thrown, an automatic barked and the whistle blew.*[13]

Barry's description is corroborated, to an extent, by Jim ("Spud") Murphy's recollection. Murphy declares Barry as being with him at the command post on the eastern end of the position. Significantly, Murphy does not mention anything about Barry being in uniform or the lorry slowing down as a result of seeing the uniformed figure:

> *. . . the leading lorry drove into the position. It was allowed to approach to within about 25 yards of No. 1 position. We were ordered to open fire on the driver and occupants of the front of the lorry. The lorry came to a halt within 5 yards of us and Tom Barry threw a bomb into the centre of the lorry himself.*[14]

Barry's description is also at variance with that provided by another participant, Paddy O'Brien:

> *Tom Barry had placed a stone on the road, and had ordered that when the tender reached it fire was to be opened. The opening fusillade killed the driver instantaneously, and the tender came to a halt. Barry appeared on the road and threw a hand grenade into the back of the tender, and all was over so far as that one was concerned.*[15]

The same Paddy O'Brien gave a slightly different account in his earlier statement to the Bureau of Military History:

> *The Auxiliaries in two tenders came along about four o'clock. The driver of the leading one was shot and this tender stopped immediately. Firing had started when Barry threw a Mills bomb and landed it definitely into the tender.*[16]

Edward Young, a member of No.2 Section, describes the commencement of the ambush as follows:

> *. . . the leading lorry in the enemy convoy drove into the position. This lorry was allowed to proceed to the eastern (Dunmanway) end before fire was opened on it by the men of No. 1 Section north of the road.*[17]

Michael O'Driscoll, who was deployed with No.2 Section, describes the attack on the lead truck in the following terms:

> *The first lorry drove past our position. The Auxies were singing. When it got to Tom Barry's position it slowed up. A bomb was thrown into the front of the lorry and No. 1 Section opened fire.*[18]

Jack Hennessy, who was also deployed with No.2 Section, gives a similar but brief account of the commencement of the action:

> *The first lorry passed our position. I heard a shot, followed by a bomb explosion from the Column O/C's position.*[19]

Timothy Keohane, also in position with No.2 Section, stated the following:

> *The first lorry then drove past us and fire was opened on it by the section to the east at Tom Barry's post.*[20]

From those opening narratives it is less than clear as to how the attack on the lead lorry commenced. This isn't surprising, as in the case of those volunteers with No.2 Section their attention would be focused on the second vehicle, and with the passage of time specific details in their statements may have become confused. What is apparent is that the lorry was engaged by a combination of rifle and pistol fire and a grenade. We assume that there were only two Mills bombs with the column, and it may be taken that Barry had them and that he threw the grenade. Barry declares as much, referring to himself in the third person when he says "the Commander also had two Mills bombs."[21] This is supported by Barry saying that the commander would start the attack.[22] Let us, therefore , presume that Barry initiated the attack on the first lorry by throwing a Mills grenade at the cab of the truck.

Some assumptions are now necessary. Firstly, given the fact that the grenade exploded in the cab of the truck it is likely that the cab absorbed the majority of the explosion. It is reasonable to assume that the explosion from the grenade would have killed anyone in the cab of the Crossley Tender. With the driver out of action, the lorry would have either remained where it was or slowly continued on its path. Secondly, it is also reasonable to assume that not all occupants were killed by the shrapnel from the grenade. The lower cab as a contained unit on the truck would have absorbed a lot of the fragmentation, so it is again reasonable to assume that there were ADRIC survivors from this initial engagement. Thirdly, we are assuming that each Crossley carried nine ADRIC personnel.[23]

The Mills No.36 grenade was the standard military grenade of the time. It has been described as, "the most effective grenade used by any army and remained in service until the 1970s."[24] It had a four-second delay from the time that its pin was withdrawn to the time that it would explode. The Mills was very reliable and had seen extensive service with the British Army during the First World War where it was a formidable "trench-clearer." Due to its reliability it would have functioned as designed practically every time it was used.

Interestingly, Barry describes the Mills as landing in the cab of the truck beside the driver. If it had landed in the cab, it is probable that given the lethal radius of the grenade that the driver would have been killed outright. The thirty-five-yard range from the stone wall (where Barry may have been located) is the maximum range at which the grenade could have been accurately thrown.[25] The following extract from a British Army training pamphlet describes the high explosive grenade in the following terms:

1. *The grenade can be thrown by hand a distance of 25 to **35 yards**. Large fragments may have sufficient velocity to inflict wounds up to 100 yards or more, particularly if the burst is on stony ground. The thrower should therefore be protected from the explosion.*

2. *Grenades are particularly useful:-*
   - *In street fighting, for clearing houses, etc.*
   - **In uncivilized theatres of war,** *against an enemy who takes cover in caves or behind rocks, etc. (emphasis added)*
   - *In trench to trench fighting.[26]*

It should also be recognized that Barry's version of events differs somewhat when he further recounted his recollection of the commencement of the ambush in 1974:

Briefly what happened was that when the first lorry, slowing gently as it approached the fully uniformed and equipped IRA officer standing on the low ditch, reached some twenty yards from the command post it was met simultaneously with a Mills bomb and a burst of rifle-fire from the command post party.[27]

It may be assumed that the seven occupants in the rear of the lorry escaped the worst effects but may have been concussed or disoriented by the percussion effect of the grenade's explosion. It can also be expected that the riflemen of No.1 Section began engaging the occupants, but this must have only been momentary because very quickly after the grenade attack Barry describes the three occupants of the command position joining him on the road.

By his own account, Barry, having disabled the first lorry, now appears on the road with a number of other volunteers to take advantage of the surprise and momentum that the IRA had achieved. He was seeking to capitalise on the shock effect of the opening salvo and was now prepared to engage the survivors in a hand-to-hand struggle. Supporting fire would not have been possible at this stage, as the risk of hitting Barry and his team would have been too great. The ricochets caused by the rifles being fired from the elevated positions, where No.1 Section were deployed, down onto the hard surface would have also produced an unacceptable risk to Barry's team, although whether an untrained volunteer would have been aware of this collateral risk to Barry and his team is questionable, if not remote.

Tactically, Barry was leaving nothing to chance. He had handpicked those he knew would be fully committed to carrying the assault through. He knew the truck would have to come to a standstill and he must also have realised the shock-value that the initial attack would have on the occupants of the lorry. This advantage, however, would be fleeting, and the success of the ambush would depend on how well Barry could use it. Exploiting this advantage came with an enormous risk. With Barry's squad being so close to the action, the column had everything to lose. If the ADRIC managed to establish a position or gain a foothold or to take the initiative from the IRA, the end result for the IRA would be catastrophic. Barry could not risk this happening. It is possible that he lacked confidence in the ability of No.1 Section to eliminate the first lorry and its occupants, which might explain why he chose to locate the command post at such an unusual location at the extremity of the ambush position. The fact that Barry and his squad would appear to have accounted for most of the casualties at the first truck demonstrates the relative ineffectiveness of the IRA fire and thereby supports Barry's decision to position himself on the road.

Once on the road in close proximity to the ADRIC, Barry's team moved to deal with the survivors from the grenade attack. There is no composite picture of how Barry's team conducted this phase of the attack, but we can presume that in order to take full advantage of the opportunity presented by the grenade, Barry and his team literally threw themselves into the fray. The distance to be traversed by Barry's team in order to engage closely with the ADRIC members was quite short, a matter of yards. The only inhibiting factor was the stationary Crossley Tender which presented its own difficulties in terms of its simple presence and the protection it gave to the ADRIC members who would have used it as cover against the rifle fire from the high ground at No.1 Section's position. There is very little cohesion evident in terms of fire and manoeuvre or direction of attack other than an "up and at 'em" attitude.

Barry placed himself to the front of the assault, passing over ADRIC casualties, with at least one of the attacking party to his rear, John ("Flyer") Nyhan, killing one ADRIC member who had risen to engage Barry from behind. Barry also describes one of the ADRIC patrol being bayoneted. Bayoneting of wounded combatants as described in the narrative had not been an unusual practice during close-quarter engagements during the First World War. In the case of trench-clearing operations, such extreme ruthlessness was necessary and was provided for as a standard operating procedure, where the lead attacker would incapacitate the enemy and "the second bayonet man kills the wounded . . . you cannot afford to be encumbered by wounded enemies lying at your feet."[28] Such bayoneting was therefore to be expected as it had developed into an accepted close-combat drill.

What did this engagement look like from No. 1 and No. 3 Sections? It must have appeared chaotic, bitter and exceptionally violent. Remember that none of the volunteer participants would have been exposed to anything like this before. For most, this was the ultimate baptism of fire. To an uninitiated volunteer novice, with insufficient or simply non-existent combat exposure or experience, the picture must have been horrific, with dead bodies strewn about the area and some wounded and dying groaning or crying for help or mercy, as the case may be. It is possible that some of the fire from either of these positions could have contributed to the ADRIC casualty count, but it is improbable given the likelihood of the IRA hitting one of their own. Seen through the Lee-Enfield rifle's narrow aperture of the back sight and the bladed foresight, it would have been too difficult to distinguish friend from foe as light conditions at this stage would now be challenging the ability to see and differentiate clearly.

No.3 Section is described as having six riflemen deployed along a chain of rocks to the south of the road. The rocks, although set back between fifty and eighty yards from the road, overlooked the ambush site and were well protected by a stream and bog to the front. Their instructions were to deny or prevent the Auxiliaries from gaining firing positions south of the road. This was a tactically wise decision, and their subsequent deployment was intelligent and necessary. As a consequence, however, of Barry's team appearing on the road, these riflemen were effectively redundant, as the risk to Barry's team from their fire was too great. The riflemen of No.3 Section were also at risk from fire originating from the attack on the first truck, so there would have been a tendency for these volunteers to remain behind cover unless an opportunity target to the south of the road presented itself.

ADRIC reaction

It is possible to reconstruct to an extent the moment that Barry threw the grenade and the likely reactions of the ADRIC members in the lead lorry. Barry describes the truck slowly coming to a halt as he stood on the side of the road in his military attire. It is probable that all the occupants of the truck would have been looking in his direction and curious about who this uniformed figure was in such a remote location. We are not told if Barry had the grenade in his hand or, if he had, whether the pin had been withdrawn or not. I am presuming that the pin was still in the grenade, as Barry would have been aware that once the pin was pulled there was no putting it back.

From the time Barry decided to attack the truck we can allow him four to five seconds for producing the grenade, withdrawing the pin, steadying himself and then accurately throwing the grenade. Given the open nature of the Crossley Tender, the occupants would have realised what was coming their way as Barry threw the grenade, their suspicions already having been aroused by encountering a uniformed individual in such an unlikely location. The grenade had a delay of four seconds from the time the lever was released. This was more than enough time for the occupants in the rear of the truck to evacuate or extract themselves by jumping over the side of the truck and quickly moving away from the threat to take cover. This would have been the immediate reaction to this event. Professional soldiers with combat experience would have been well aware of the threat from a Mills grenade and would not have hung around for the consequences. Mills grenades, as previously described, were tools of the trade for trench operations in the Great War, and the patrol would have been acutely aware of the danger posed by such a munition. Having thrown the grenade a distance of thirty-five yards, and given that the danger radius of the grenade is up to a hundred yards, it is highly probable that Barry would have taken cover himself, most likely by prostrating himself on the road as the grenade exploded.

The patrol, having been surprised but now deploying and reacting, would now seek to do a number of things. The first basic instinct would be to protect themselves. The instinct to stay alive is a powerful, adrenalin-fuelled motivator. The survivors would have either chambered a round in the rifles they were carrying, or those who may have lost the rifle in the lorry would have drawn their side arms, a Webley .455. The reaction from the trained soldier would be to seek to reclaim the initiative and counter the IRA's initial advantage by responding quickly and effectively to this unexpected attack. Barry's team had the advantage in terms of surprise, initial momentum, and situational awareness and was now seeking to capitalise on this advantage. The surviving Auxiliaries would be faced with Barry and his team moving quickly to them over a distance of approximately fifteen yards. This would be more than enough time for the ADRIC to engage them with either rifle or revolver. Given the short ranges and the possibility of more rapid fire from a revolver, it is more likely that Barry's team were engaged with revolvers rather than rifle. The revolver would have allowed for six shots to be discharged in quick succession as against the ten more measured shots from the Lee-Enfield. Each shot from the Lee-Enfield would have necessitated the extraction and ejection of the spent cartridge by means of the bolt being withdrawn to the rear and a new cartridge being chambered by means of the bolt being pushed home, thus housing the new cartridge from the magazine. Both sides would have been completely focused on the task at hand; survival was key and adrenalin levels would have risen to meet this requirement. The engagement must have been ferocious and terrifying for those involved. Every moment was potentially their last. The overpowering desire of the party faced with this threat would be to hit their target. Faced with the sight of Barry's squad advancing towards them, the normal reaction of the ADRIC members would be to lay down a wall of defensive fire to stop them, drive them back and seek to gain an initiative.

Commentary

When Barry's squad closed in on the surviving ADRIC members what ensued was a well-armed brawl, which all close-quarter combat engagements ultimately become, but in this instance a brawl with a remarkable outcome. Within minutes all the ADRIC combatants were, to use Barry's own words, "…dead or dying", while none of the IRA attacking party either on the high ground overlooking the lead lorry or as part of the area denial team of No.3 Section to the south of the road or, even more surprisingly, the members of Barry's close-quarter group, suffered an injury. Not even a minor injury.

Barry's account of the action is full of martial imagery which portrays the fighting spirit of the IRA team but little about how they actually went about the conduct of this phase of the operation. The image of a dying ADRIC member rising to fire at Barry and being subsequently bayoneted, while another volunteer is hit in the mouth by the burst artery from another ADRIC member, and simultaneously Barry marvelling at the fighting qualities of his team is all more suggestive of a dramatised reconstruction suited to a theatrical performance than an actual portrayal or depiction of what actually transpired. If the descriptive aspects associated with the volunteers' personal fighting qualities are ignored, we are left with a version of events that quite frankly tests credibility.

Barry was fortunate in how the attack was so successfully initiated. His ruse of appearing on the road in uniform had the desired effect of slowing the vehicle down, which enabled him to attack it with the grenade. He would appear to have accurately thrown the grenade at the limit of its range and was doubly fortunate in that the grenade landed in the cab of the Crossley Tender, thus achieving a dual effect of killing the driver and disabling the vehicle.

It is extraordinary that the occupants of the truck would have been annihilated in such a fashion without at least wounding some of the attacking party. It raises the question, did the patrol put up any resistance here? Another reaction, which is quite understandable and predictable, would have been for the survivors of the grenade attack to fail to react or at least to offer or seek a surrender.

Given their close proximity to the grenade's explosion, it is not unreasonable to expect that some of the occupants would have suffered some level of concussion or nervous shock and were therefore incapable of offering any form of opposition to the attack. They would have been literally stunned into a state of inactivity. Is it possible that they surrendered, were disarmed and quickly handed to No.1 Section in the lane beside the command post? Or does Barry's account, which in this author's view is possible but not probable, really portray what happened here? Is it possible that the occupants of the first lorry were stunned by the sudden, completely unexpected explosion from the grenade and the short volley of supporting fire from the volunteers on the higher ground? Was the initial attack so unexpected and sudden that they sought to surrender to preserve their lives and buy time in the knowledge that they would ultimately be released or that the arrival of the supporting truck would soon change the situation for the better?

There are difficulties with reconciling Barry's account of this initial aspect of the ambush when measured against the terrain features.

Barry states that his team of three fighters were positioned out of sight behind the command post wall on the north side of the road. An examination of this position, which we can presume has not altered that much over the years, reveals a tight, constricted location. The position consists of a small stone wall behind which are approximately two metres of a drop to a small stream which would accommodate the three volunteers but would not facilitate, in relative terms, a quick entrance onto the road. It is not clear whether Barry was standing at this wall or forward of it, although one of the pictures in *Guerilla Days* does show Barry standing on the low wall. Barry describes the truck continuing towards him in the aftermath of the explosion, with the Auxiliaries engaging the IRA with revolver fire. It is remarkable that Barry escaped injury at this juncture given his own estimation that the truck only stopped a few yards from the wall. Barry must have been at point-blank range. One should also consider that after Barry had initiated the attack the members of Barry's team would have been appearing on the road as the ADRIC members were returning fire and seeking targets.

One of the more puzzling aspects of Barry's recollection of events during this phase is that his version of what transpired is not supported by one of the hand-picked fighters who were with him at the command post. Jim ("Spud") Murphy's brief account of the engagement details a much simpler picture, where those in the command post behind the wall engaged the front of the lorry from a range of twenty-five yards with rifle fire and thereby killed the driver and the occupants of the cab. According to Murphy it was only when it came to a halt, five yards from the wall, that Tom Barry threw the grenade, which landed not in the cab of the truck but rather in the centre of the vehicle.[29] Murphy does not detail any of the close-quarter combat that Barry describes, which is strange given Barry's view that he (Murphy) was a principle participant in the action.

It is possible at this stage to take two views on Barry's conduct. He was both extremely brave and quite literally led his men from the front, or was reckless about his own safety and by extension reckless about the column's survival. The costly consequences of platoon leaders leading from the front was realised by the American Army in its operations against the Germans in the Second World War:

> *Too much emphasis had been placed on leadership…leaders got the idea that they must always be in front. We lost many platoon leaders for that reason.*[30]

Had Barry been killed or injured we are not aware of a contingency plan whereby a nominated column member would take control of the action.

Michael McCarthy from the Dunmanway Battalion may have been a notional second-in-command but, as we will see, it is likely that he was either killed or very seriously injured shortly after the action commenced. Was there another member who would be prepared and capable of taking on this authority and responsibility? As the only column member with a formal military training Barry's direction and leadership were vital to the success of the operation. Barry was accompanied by some of the most experienced volunteers that were available to the column, but none had his level of training. If the IRA were to lose such experienced personnel then its ability to replace such individuals from locally available resources was severely limited.

Having engaged at such close quarters, Barry would have lost any situational awareness of what was happening beyond the direct engagement he was fighting in. He says as much himself when he declares, "It was not possible to see the efforts of the IRA except those near me."[31] This supports a view that the small unit commander's proper location in battle is at a vantage point from which he can see the fight, not in a command post. Given the close proximity of the combatants it is unlikely that any supporting fire from the other sections would have been of assistance. The attackers would have run an unacceptably high risk of killing some of their own. We can assume that all members would have realised at this stage that Barry and a number of their colleagues were intertwined with the ADRIC as the action was being played out in front of them. The outcome of this particular engagement without any effective supporting fire would lie in the hands of *four* volunteers according to Barry or *five* according to Paddy O'Brien who states that "Sonny" Dave Crowley was also with Barry. That this squad managed to kill all the occupants of the lead vehicle without suffering any casualties, given the nature of the fighting, is remarkable. There is no evidence to suggest whether any of these Auxiliaries were wounded or had tried to surrender. It can be accepted that they fought, but it is uncertain as to how long they fought for and whether their efforts achieved anything. It is assumed that all ADRIC members at this area of the ambush site were killed.

For reconstruction purposes we will make some further assumptions. We can assume that out of the nine occupants that were in the first truck, two were killed by the grenade explosion and one may have been killed by the opening fusillade, leaving six ADRIC combatants to face Barry's team. The characterization of the Auxiliaries as "cursing and yelling" while the IRA remained "tight lipped as loosely and coldly they outfought them" evokes a powerful imagery which appeals to a particular idealistic notion of a rabble British force ("terrorist officers" as described by the commemorative plaque at Kilmichael) being disposed of by the disciplined and highly effective IRA unit. The depiction, however, is not a realistic description of how such a small-scale yet highly intensive and violent engagement would ordinarily play out. Even with all its imagery, Barry's version of events is vague. He is content to outline the outcome as opposed to the events that occasioned the outcome. Is it credible that Barry's team "rose to the occasion" in the manner described? It would have been quite unexpected that Barry's team would have been so ruthlessly calm with the uncertainties that now confronted them. The training that armies expose their personnel to in order to deal with such uncertainties was absent in the IRA, and their own personal survival must have been foremost in all the combatants' actions. We are not informed as to any command and control measures, and given the fact that Barry uses nicknames ("Flyer" and "Spud") when describing his "hand-picked fighters" it is safe to assume that any subsequent success in battle would be attributed more to a group dynamic, a "band of brothers" looking after the welfare of each other, than to the existence of a particular plan. Barry picking such fighters should not be seen as unusual as he understood the enormity of the challenge facing the column. It also demonstrates the common frailties in any military group. Even among trained personnel, only a few can be counted to subjugate their own personal safety to the greater cause or are capable of participating in acts of ultra-violence which such close encounters present. It is difficult to reconcile the fact that none of Barry's team were killed or even wounded at this stage by the reactive or suppressing fire on the part of the Auxiliaries, given the proximity (hand-to-hand) of the combatants to each other.

There is little reference to any ADRIC members suffering anything other than a catastrophic injury. All were dead or dying. This is unusual for a number of reasons. Firstly, other than the Mills grenade, the action was conducted exclusively through the use of small arms. There was no artillery or machine gun support or even an improvised explosive device which would have lent more credence to such mortality statistics. To support the argument that such mortality figures with no survivors is unusual, one should consider the following description of the battlefield casualties suffered in one of the bloodiest and most intensive battles of the First World War:

On the first day of the Somme, July 1, 1916, the attacking British troops suffered 38,230 casualties and 19,240 killed: a ratio of just under 2 to 1. An attacking British infantry-man on that day had about a one in five chance of being killed.[32]

Given such statistics in a "total war" environment, it is simply not plau-

sible that some of the Auxiliaries failed to survive this aspect of the ambush or that any of Barry's team escaped suffering even an injury. Whatever
about the Auxiliaries who were killed outright in the course of the assault,
how could Barry in the absence of a close inspection have determined that
the others were dying? Barry refers to the occupants of the first lorry as
having in the course of five minutes "been exterminated."[33] But even had
some members of the ADRIC survived, their prospects were bleak. From a
practical perspective and given the numbers that Barry had at his disposal
to continue with the attack, he would not have been in a position to take
prisoners and he certainly could not take the chance of leaving ADRIC
personnel alive to his rear when he subsequently went to the assistance of
those volunteers who were engaging with the second lorry at the entrance
to the ambush site.

Barry has outlined his attack on the survivors in graphic terms. His conduct here concurs with John Keegan's view that,

> *Battle, for the ordinary soldier, is a very small scale situation which will
> throw up its own leaders and will be fought by its own rules – alas, often by
> its own ethics.*[34]

However, there are a number of circumstances which would question
the accuracy of what Barry sought to portray. It is worth noting that there
was no attempt to take prisoners. No quarter was offered nor given. Barry
had informed his men before the attack that the ambush would be a fight to
the finish; it would be a case of kill or be killed. This was how the first stage
of the attack played out.

Barry refers to stopping to replenish his ammunition stocks and picking
up a rifle from a dead ADRIC member. Let us consider why he would have
sought to do that. Other than the grenade, what had he attacked the patrol
with in the first place? Barry refers to replenishing his ammunition, but how
much ammunition could he have expended if the assault on the survivors
had been so sudden? Barry refers to an "automatic" being part of the IRA's
arsenal. This was more than likely a Mauser pistol ("Peter the Painter"), and
the ADRIC would not have been carrying ammunition with a compatible
calibre.

There were potentially only seven Auxiliaries to be dealt with and the
narrative accounts for all of them. The fact that the engagement was conducted at such close quarters with rifle butts and bayonet negates any suggestion that both parties engaged in any form of a sustained fire-fight. At
least one of Barry's team, John ("Flyer") Nyhan, was armed with a rifle with

a bayonet attached. It is not clear when the bayonet was fixed. Had it been fixed before the arrival of the ADRIC then it would have been quite cumbersome in negotiating the wall he was located behind. The volunteer was probably also unaware of the effect of an attached bayonet on the ballistic performance of the weapon, although once a bayonet is fixed there is a realization that the interaction between the combatants will be close and personal, and because of the extremely close range at which the ADRIC were engaged its effect on the ballistic performance would have been negligible.

It is questionable that there was any need for Barry's team to engage in such close-quarter combat. No.1 Section dominated the high ground to the north of the position from where the first lorry was attacked. They would have been very difficult to dislodge and had excellent observation and fields of fire onto the road below. With Barry's team on the road their effectiveness was greatly diminished.

The same can be said of the riflemen of No.3 Section located on the south of the road who were similarly prevented from engaging the ADRIC by Barry's team being so closely engaged. Had Barry's team remained behind the wall then more than twenty riflemen could have engaged the lorry, thereby creating a killing zone centred on the lorry with very effective interlocking arcs of fire. By engaging with the Auxiliaries in hand-to-hand combat Barry effectively made both No. 1 and No. 3 Sections of his ambushing party redundant. They ultimately became spectators to the action on the road.

The remaining members of No.3 Section, six in all, were described as being an "insurance group" to be used as a counter to a situation if more than two lorries were to arrive. They would be considered a reserve element. Given their location, to the rear of No.2 Section, and the fact that they were never engaged, they can be discounted as contributing anything to the action other than a limited form of psychological assurance. It is worth considering what the outcome would have been had a third lorry arrived. With such limited stocks of ammunition the only conceivable course of action would have been for the reserve element to contain the additional troops. As there was no possibility of engaging at close quarters, the additional ADRIC would eventually suppress this element due primarily to having more ammunition at their disposal. The consequences for the ambush party would have been very uncertain.

Phase 1 was now completed with nine Auxiliaries dead and the IRA still unscathed.

Phase 3 (H-hour): attack on the second lorry

IRA actions

No.2 Section had been allotted the task of dealing with the second vehicle. The section was deployed on the high ground at the entrance to the site on the Macroom side of the ambush position. Barry describes the attack on the two lorries as happening almost simultaneously, and whereas the lead vehicle was quickly incapacitated the same cannot be said for the following truck, which at the time of the attack on the lead vehicle is described as being approximately 150 yards to the rear.

No.3 Section's greatest contribution to the ambush could have been the field of fire it had in relation to the second truck. Given their deployment and the lack of any major obstacles between them and the second lorry, they would have had excellent observation on the conduct of the operation there; however, their instructions were to prevent the Auxiliaries from gaining any position south of the road, so it is unlikely that they would have engaged in any supporting or harassing fire on the occupants of the second truck. Barry had warned them about the potential danger from their crossfire. Once again, because of the rocky nature of the terrain where No.2 Section were deployed and the equivalent heights above the road at which both No. 2 and No. 3 Sections were positioned, any shots fired from the No. 3 position would be fired at a shallow angle of incidence. In practical terms what this meant was that the flight of the bullet would graze (or "skim") the surface like a stone skimming the surface of water. Regardless of the type of surface, a bullet of any calibre will ricochet at the same angle of incidence. In other words, a shallow angle strike will ricochet at a shallow angle and very little energy will be lost.[35] Had members of No.3 Section decided to engage the ADRIC at the second lorry, the ricochet possibility would have posed a substantial threat to those volunteers at No.2 Section. The Kilmichael Historical Society in their account of the attack on the second lorry lends support to the belief that No.3 Section did in fact actively engage in the fire-fight:

> *The second lorry was about 150 yards behind and the driver, having realised that they were ambushed, tried unsuccessfully to turn back but the vehicle got stuck on the side of the road. The Auxiliaries jumped out, threw themselves on the road and commenced firing from the cover of the lorry. The IRA opened fire from the rear. At this stage all units got involved and an all-out assault was mounted, It was a short but grim fight.*[36]

ADRIC reaction

For the ADRIC members in the second truck it can be assumed that they were aware of the attack on the first truck from the grenade explosion and ensuing rifle fire. It would appear that the driver of this second truck attempted to turn it, having possibly reversed seventy yards out of the engagement area, but he was ultimately unsuccessful. Once the truck had stopped and attempted to turn, it would have been engaged by the volunteers at No.2 Section on the Macroom side.

It is most likely that as part of an anti-ambush drill that the ADRIC would have deployed, immediately assessed the situation, and begun fighting back instantly. Any suggestion that the ADRIC just presented themselves as stationary targets, having been stunned into inaction, cannot be countenanced. British Army training, as a result of lessons learned nearly twenty years earlier during the Boer War, had resulted in increased levels of individual proficiency, with soldiers now more adept at both fire and movement in the attack and in regulated fire from defensive positions. Edward Spiers refers to British Army training exercises – in which the ADRIC members as commissioned officers would most likely have taken part – as characterized by troops being exercised "recurrently by squads or sections attacking each other in company training often without orders from officers and non-commissioned officers so that the ranks would act increasingly of their own initiative." C.J. Chivers outlines the developments in tactical awareness and response that had followed the First World War, whereby troops under fire "had learned to spread out, scattering the targets they presented and limiting the danger to the group."[37]

This increased emphasis on independent action during engagements helps us to envision how each ADRIC member would have gone on the offensive. Spiers additionally highlights the comments of a Commandant De Thompson who declared when observing infantry training during the British Army exercise of 1913, "they make wonderful use of ground, advance as a rule by short rushes and always at the double and almost invariably fire from a lying down position."[38]

In embracing an offensive doctrine encompassing initiative, freedom of action with fire and manoeuvre, it is possible to envisage the now deployed ADRIC as formidable foes. Unlike their comrades in the first lorry, they had not been on the receiving end of the percussive effect of a grenade attack. Given the nature of the terrain it would not be difficult to make an educated guess as to where the attacking IRA members were located. Those volunteers firing rifles from behind or around cover would be far more difficult to observe, as the cordite in rifle ammunition was comparatively smokeless when measured against the black powder of a shotgun round. Those firing shotguns would be more visible, since the flash of the shotgun on a dark evening would be quite conspicuous and the firers would be much more easily located.

Commentary

Having closely studied the ground in the immediate vicinity of where the second truck is reported to have finally stopped, I was struck by the sheer cover the truck would have been afforded by the rising ground immediately to the rear of the monument. This is very significant. The ground consists of a hard outcrop which would have obscured sight of the truck from Barry's combat team, all the members of No.1 Section, and even some from No.2 Section. Those members of No.3 Section who were positioned across the road would have had a field of view but a restricted field of fire and they also ran the risk of engaging their own members had they intervened. Interestingly, Tom Barry writing under the pseudonym "Eyewitness" in *An Cosantóir* in the 1940s, describes the Auxiliaries being "deployed with the large rocky hillock on the eastern edge of the road effectively protecting them from the fire of No.3 Section."[39] The ADRIC at this position were in a better position than their comrades in the lead lorry, but their options were limited. They would have had no choice but to fight back to the best of their ability or else be killed.

The engagement with the second truck would have been far more prolonged, since the initial element of surprise was not as applicable to this action, and significantly the ADRIC members here, as already mentioned, had not been exposed to a grenade attack. None of the units, ADRIC or IRA, would have been able to influence, co-ordinate, or exercise any control over any elements other than purely local as there were no communications between any of the dispersed units. The ADRIC, due to their better training and prior combat experience, would have assessed the situation and made a decision to either break out or break through the ambush or even surrender. All decisions would have to be immediate. It is possible to assume that the British forces would have rehearsed an "immediate action" drill which would have consisted of dismounting the Crossley Tender and engaging identified positions. We are also presuming that all the ADRIC would have been prepared to fight. What can be certain is that there would have been levels of panic, confusion, and fear. It is entirely plausible that some would have chosen to stand their ground while others, more aware of the potential hopelessness of their situation and unsure about the numbers engaging them, were willing to surrender in the hope that nothing worse than being stripped of their arms and material would befall them. The fire-arms exchanges at this particular juncture would have been intense, with the ADRIC returning heavy fire to the best of their ability.

Given the fact that the ADRIC members had previous service as com-missioned officers, it is not unlikely that many of them would have been shouting orders and giving directions, but it is unlikely that any of this was in any way cohesive. Their situation was desperate, they were unaware of the number of combatants engaging them, and fire was likely to be coming from a number of different directions. Their own fields of view, if we are to accept that they fought from the area where the lorry was finally disabled, would have been restricted by the same outcrop that was covering them.

Phase 4 (H hour + 8 mins): Barry's team move to assist with the attack on the second truck

This stage of the operation was possibly the most sustained, as the timings suggest that the fire-fight lasted between twenty and thirty minutes. This would concur with an overall timing assessment of the operation as lasting between thirty and forty-five minutes. Given the intensity and duration of the combat, an issue of thirty-five rounds of ammunition per volunteer was hopelessly inadequate to maintain such combat levels as it would average an ammunition expenditure of less than two rounds per minute. It is not real-istic to suggest that an intense fire-fight could have lasted for this duration with the paucity of ammunition available to the volunteers.

Having dispatched the occupants of the first lorry, Barry and his com-bat team would have been experiencing a challenging level of fatigue as a result of the physical effort that close combat demands.[40] Their first priority would have been to physically recover, to catch their breath and prepare for whatever was coming next. They could not have been aware of what was happening at the second truck other than the attack by No.2 Section had commenced and was continuing while the ADRIC were countering the attack with their own anti-ambush efforts. The thoughts going through the commander's head would have been primarily focussed on whether the ADRIC had deployed immediately, where they were now located, and how the members of No.2 Section were progressing with the conduct of their engagement.

We have already considered the threat that able ADRIC members from the first lorry would have posed to Barry's men. It is worth reconsidering that if Barry made a decision to advance towards the second truck, he could not run the risk of being engaged from the rear. He would have had to ensure that all the enemy to his rear were either dead or secured by other members of the ambush party. We are not told what ensued, but on the basis that the team would have had to replenish their ammunition stocks and possibly take possession of the ADRIC rifles it is a likely assumption that all were either dead or incapacitated to such an extent that they did not pose a threat for the remainder of the operation.

Having replenished their ammunition and more than likely taken possession of a Lee-Enfield rifle each, Barry's combat team now worked its way forward along the road either in file (where one followed the other) or in extended line (where the team extended across the road). This movement is corroborated by the testimony of Edward Young who was located on the southern side of the ambush position and who describes Barry's team as advancing along the road "shooting as they came."[41] In modern tactical doctrine, where the team is already engaged in combat, a grouping of this size would either move using cover and movement, where half the team would provide cover (not fire) to the movement of the other half for what are termed "bounds" of approximately twenty metres. In other words, one team would move twenty metres and take up a covering position and cover the movement of the other team who would pass and then move a further twenty metres in a "leap-frog" style movement. Fire and manoeuvre is a little different in that the squad would already be engaging the enemy and thereby signalling their avenue of approach. One team would fire at the enemy while concurrently the other team would advance, and once they had reached their bound would commence firing at the enemy and allow the original fire party to move forward under their covering fire. This is referred to as "shooting in" and requires absolute cohesion where the troops have very definite bounds so that they don't out-run each other or cross each other's fields of fire. Unless it was tightly controlled it could result in an unacceptably high level of expenditure of ammunition.

In his account of this part of the action, Barry states that they ran in single file along the side of the road, but we are not given any indication as to how he conducted this part of the move. If they were advancing in single file then it is difficult to corroborate Edward Young's testimony that they were shooting at the same time. It is unlikely that they were shooting, as this would have alerted the ADRIC to their approach. Accepting that Young may have been mistaken in his recollection of events, and given the low light levels and the cover afforded by the ground where the monument is now located, it is possible that the ADRIC members of the second lorry didn't notice Barry's advance. However, it would become a different matter once his team started opening fire. Due to the slightly rising gradient in the road, the volunteers would have had to fire from either a kneeling or standing position, thus presenting an easier target to the ADRIC members, who were more than likely firing from the much more stable prone position. Firing from a standing position is the least stable of the standard firing positions, even in the calmest environments, owing to the firer's high centre of gravity and small support area that the firer's leading arm provides. When one considers these challenges as well as the fact that the volunteers would have been under considerable physical pressure after their previous physical exertions, one can appreciate that firing the rifle for effect was more a case of good fortune than anything else. Firing under such strenuous conditions, in which the shooter maintains a sight picture of the enemy through a small rear aperture sight while trying to control his breath, is a skill that is only acquired with considerable coaching and practice. Many experienced shooters never master this challenge, and in my experience it is one of those principle skills that sets marksmen apart from experienced shooters.

By advancing towards the enemy and firing at the same time from the standing position, the IRA team would have provided the ADRIC with a much larger target profile than if they had been firing from the prone position. If we assume that the ADRIC were engaging the advancing IRA from the prone position at a distance of between fifty to seventy-five yards, it is astonishing to believe that none of the IRA advancing party was hit, particularly if the ADRIC were to hear Barry shouting to the men of No.2 Section to keep firing.

The challenges for the IRA become apparent when one considers the combat limitations in terms of marksmanship and general co-ordination. The amount of ammunition carried by each volunteer without access to replenishment was inadequate to sustain the level of fire for the duration and in the circumstances as described by Barry. By the time Barry's team had arrived to relieve the situation, it is most likely that those volunteers from No.2 Section who had actually engaged the ADRIC would have either expended their ammunition or their ammunition levels would have been critically low.

It is at this point that we must consider the issue of the alleged false surrender by the ADRIC.

The false-surrender controversy

Barry describes the circumstances pertaining to the "surrender" as follows:

We had gone about 50 yards when we heard the Auxiliaries shout "We surrender." We kept running along the grassy edge as they repeated the sur-

render cry and actually saw some Auxiliaries throw away their rifles. Firing stopped but we continued, still unobserved, to jog towards them. Then we saw three of our comrades on No. 2 section, one crouched and two upright. Suddenly the Auxiliaries were firing again with revolvers. One of our three men spun around before he fell, and Pat Deasy staggered before he too went down.

When this occurred we had reached a point about 25 yards behind the enemy party and we dropped down as I gave the order, "Rapid fire and do not stop until I tell you"…the enemy sandwiched between two fires, were again shouting, "We surrender."

Having seen more than enough of their surrender tactics, I shouted the order, "Keep firing on them. Keep firing on them No. 2 Section. Everybody keep firing on them until the Cease Fire."[42]

One of the few accounts mentioning a surrender is given in the testimony of Timothy Keohane. He recalls the events in a significantly different manner:

At this stage Tom Barry blew a blast on his whistle as a signal that all men should get on the road. At the same time he moved with his section along the road from the east to take the survivors in the rear. Tom Barry then called on the enemy to surrender and some of them put up their hands, but when our party were moving on to the road the Auxiliaries again opened fire. Two of our men (John Lordan and Jack Hennessy, I think) were wounded by this fire. Pat Deasy had been wounded, while Jim O'Sullivan and Mick McCarthy (V/C Dunmanway Battn.) had been killed prior to this happening.

The O/C (Tom Barry) immediately ordered an all-out attack, and after a few sharp bursts the enemy forces were silenced.[43]

Jack Hennessy, who was a member of No. 2 Section, outlines a dramatic version of events as he engaged with the second lorry:

At this time the second lorry was just opposite our position. The Auxies jumped out and tried to find cover. The lorry driver held his seat and attempted to back the lorry out of the position. I was engaging the Auxies on the road. I was wearing a tin hat. I had fired about ten rounds and had got five bullets through the hat when the sixth bullet wounded me in the scalp. Vice Comdt. McCarthy had got a bullet through the head and lay dead. I continued to load and fire but the blood dripping from my forehead fouled the breech of my rifle. I dropped my rifle and took Michael McCarthy's. Many of the Auxies lay on the road dead or dying. Our orders were to fix bayonets and charge on to the road when we heard three blasts of the O/Cs whistle. I heard the three blasts and got up from my position, shouting "hands up." At the same time one of the Auxies about five yards from me drew his revolver. He had thrown down his rifle. I pulled on him and shot him dead. I got back to cover, where I remained for a few minutes firing at living and dead Auxies on the road. The Column O/C sounded his whistle again. Nearly all the Auxies had been wiped out. When I reached the road a wounded Auxie moved his hand towards his revolver. I put my bayonet through him under the ribs. Another Auxie tried to pull on John Lordan, who was too near to use his bayonet and he struck the Auxie with the butt of his rifle. The butt broke on the Auxies skull.[44]

Michael O'Driscoll was also with No.2 Section and he recalls the engagement with the second lorry as follows:

The Second lorry was just approaching our position and had not quite reached it when the driver stopped and tried to reverse. We opened up. The Auxies jumped out and sought cover replying to our fire. The fight was general along the road. Jim Sullivan who was alongside me was killed. As far as I could judge, a bullet struck his rifle and part of the bolt was driven into his face. Michael McCarthy, our section commander, was also killed. Pat Deasy, another of our section, was seriously wounded.

Tom Barry had dealt with the first lorry and he led a party along the grass verge of the road to come up behind the Auxies fighting us. Soon the fighting was over. We were ordered out on the road.[45]

Patrick O'Brien, who was involved with the attack on the first lorry, describes Barry's involvement with the second lorry as follows:

Barry rushed on to the second tender where firing was going on, and where three of our men had been shot, one being killed outright and two seriously wounded. The driver of the second tender had not been hit as he had not driven right into the position when the attack on the first one commenced. He was manoeuvring it, trying to turn it, while the Auxiliaries in it had jumped out and were trying to get into position. The fight was short however and only one of the enemy succeeded in getting away from the scene. He was shot later in the day in Macroom. All the others were fatal casualties, except one who survived his wounds.[46]

Once again, Barry's version of events as to the actions of his team moving to assist the volunteers is not supported by another principle participant, Jim ("Spud") Murphy. Murphy describes his involvement:

> *By this time, the second lorry had entered the western end of the position and was attacked by the men of (No.2 Section). Some of the men of the second lorry got out on the road and took up positions by the fence and started firing back on the men in (No.2 Section). We were ordered out on the road – Tom Barry first – and we followed. We got down on our knees and we opened fire on the men that got out of the lorry at the other end (west) of the position. After an exchange of fire lasting about ten minutes they were all killed with the exception of one man who jumped into the bog and ran about 50 yards before being shot.[47]*

The ADRIC members in the second lorry could not have been fully aware of what was happening or had happened at the first lorry, and again we must assume they would either try and rescue them or link up in an un-coordinated counter-attack. Their first priority, however, would be to win the fire-fight and regain the initiative from the attacking party, which is why we can assume a heavy engagement with a resultant increased rate of fire. Is it possible to assume that the ADRIC members of the second lorry were totally distracted about what was happening further along the road while they engaged the volunteers of the No.2 Section? With the levels of noise at this part of the ambush, they would not have been able to appreciate the fact that no further engagements were taking place at the first truck.

There is a level of confusion and uncertainty as to where the ADRIC were located at this stage of the engagement. It would appear that they de-ployed immediately after being attacked and began exchanging fire with the volunteers of No.2 Section. It is unlikely that they remained in the lorry as the driver sought to reverse out of the killing area. Their immediate action drills would have informed any decision on their part as to the appropriate response, and that response would have been to use whatever ground was available to effectively counter the IRA attack.

That the ADRIC being engaged by No.2 Section were more central-ly located in the engagement area is supported by the testimony of Jim ("Spud") Murphy, whose account, as outlined, is at variance with that of Barry. Murphy describes simply deploying on the road at the location of the attack on the first lorry and engaging, at short range, the ADRIC who had deployed from the second lorry. Murphy's recollection of events may be plausible, as from here it would only be possible to engage targets locat-ed more centrally within the killing area. It would not have been possible to engage targets at the final location of the second lorry, due to the cover afforded by the terrain features at the entrance to the ambush position.

Commentary

It is during this phase of the operation that the controversy emerges. Did the ADRIC members indicate to the IRA attackers that they wanted to surrender? Did the IRA call on the ADRIC to surrender? Confusion abounds, with Barry suggesting that the offer to surrender originated with the ADRIC members, while other column members recollect the IRA calling on the ADRIC to lay down their arms.

How difficult could it have been to determine the origin of such a crucial piece of information? The confusion could be explained by the extreme noise levels experienced by both sides during the course of the engagement. Verbal communication in the presence of sustained gunfire is extremely difficult. The noise from gunfire is described as impulse noise – a noise of short duration and high intensity with a characteristic waveform. Such impulse noise from rifle gunfire can create a sound pressure level of between 100 and 110 decibels (up to 152 decibels for some modern assault rifles). To put this in context, it compares to sound levels greater than those emitted by a pneumatic drill or the average disco. The percentage hearing disability that such levels of noise intensity produce is 100%.[48] A simple experiment of trying to communicate with someone over a distance of thirty-five yards either in a disco or with a set of headphones at full volume gives a good indication of the challenges that the combatants had in terms of communicating with someone outside their immediate vicinity. These challenges were the reason why whistle blasts were chosen to indicate particular actions. Barry would have been well aware of the difficulty in trying to communicate with his troops by shouting orders over gunfire. They simply would not have heard him. Therefore it is unlikely that any of the combatants could declare with certainty exactly what they had heard. This is further reinforced by studies that suggest that temporary hearing impairment is possible even after short exposures to such levels of noise interference.[49]

Barry's account suggests that the volunteers rose from their positions when they heard the ADRIC members offering to surrender. Having just detailed how difficult it could prove to be heard above the gunfire, further consideration should be given to an alternative reason why they showed themselves. Two of the volunteers recall hearing Barry's whistle blasts indicating particular actions, possibly resulting in the volunteers presenting themselves as opportunity targets to the ADRIC. It is worth considering whether Barry's actions in blowing the whistle caused the volunteers to show themselves rather than the alleged shouts of "we surrender" from the ADRIC. Would it be a normal reaction to emerge from their firing positions as described? Even if the volunteers had stood up, the natural inclination would be to continue to "cover-off" the enemy with the rifles and to be prepared to re-engage them if they attempted to recover their discarded weapons or to draw their revolvers. If it was the case that the ADRIC did engage the IRA, then they managed to hit their targets at the maximum realistic range of their revolvers' capability. Consider this in light of the inability of the members of the first lorry to hit any IRA target, even at point blank range. This disparity in revolver marksmanship between the occupants of the first and second lorries is not easily explained.

The timing of the deaths of McCarthy and O'Sullivan and the wounding of Deasy are relevant factors to be considered for a number of reasons. Barry refers to two volunteers being killed as a result of the ADRIC false surrender:

> Then we saw three of our comrades on No. 2 section stand up, one crouched and two upright. Suddenly the Auxiliaries were firing again with revolvers. One of our three men spun around before he fell, and Pat Deasy staggered before he, too, went down.[50]

The identity of the volunteer who "spun around before he fell" is not disclosed, but it could only have been either Jim O'Sullivan or Michael Mc-Carthy. Barry has stated that two volunteers were killed when the ADRIC opened fire with their revolvers. He confirms this when he states:

> I ran the short distance to where I had seen our men fall and scrambled up the rocky height. Michael McCarthy, Dunmanway and Jim O'Sullivan, Knockwaddra, Rossmore, lay dead and, a few yards away Pat Deasy was dying.

Later in his narrative, Barry doesn't offer any further clarity when he reflects on the IRA casualties:

> Our dead! Two of them might be alive now had I warned them of the bogus surrender trick which is as old as war itself. Why did I not warn them? I could not think of everything. Liam will be cut up but he will understand. Pat would come. What will Mick's and Jim's people say?[51]

A question therefore remains as to what "two" Barry was referring to? Was it Michael McCarthy and Jim O'Sullivan who would appear to have been the only two IRA men killed outright with Deasy dying of his wounds later? Or was it Pat Deasy and one of the other two that Barry was referring to?

Meda Ryan provides support to the suggestion that Jim O'Sullivan was one of those killed as a result of the false surrender. Ryan states:

> *Dan Hourihan, who was beside Jim O'Sullivan, told me, "I'll never forget it — same as 'twas only yesterday. After they shouted that surrender, it was silence! Jim lifted himself. Thought it was over. God rest his soul."*[52]

Ryan also refers to the fact that Jim O'Sullivan's nieces, Joan and Margaret, grew up with the story from participants that "he heard the surrender, got up and was fatally wounded."[53]

On the basis of these recollections it is popularly assumed that Jim O'Sullivan was killed as a result of the false surrender.

Michael O'Driscoll, who testified as being alongside Jim O'Sullivan when he died, fails to mention anything of a false surrender and his incidental remark describing the rifle bolt being driven into the face of O'Sullivan would indicate that O'Sullivan was still in the prone firing position with the bolt close to his face and therefore his head was exposed. This particular injury is discussed later and is very pertinent to the study. O'Driscoll's testimony further suggests that McCarthy and Deasy had suffered wounds before the arrival of Barry's team.

Jack Hennessy describes Michael McCarthy as having been shot in the head in the course of the engagement but being dead by the time Barry arrived on the scene. Hennessy fails to mention the ADRIC members offering to surrender. This should not be considered an oversight on his part, as he describes in detail instructing the ADRIC from a distance of five yards to put their hands up and the subsequent response when an ADRIC member, having thrown down his rifle, then drew his revolver.

At this juncture and in the interests of balance it should be stated that Peter Hart contests this version of events and in particular how McCarthy and O'Sullivan met their deaths. Hart does not accept that any false surrender occurred and his view of the action that unfolded at No.2 Section's position is as follows:

> *The second lorry was about a hundred yards behind the first when the ambush began. The driver reacted immediately and tried to turn around. The road was narrow, however, and he reversed into a bog and became stuck. At*

this point the second section of guerillas began firing but they were some distance from their targets and did not have quite the same advantage of surprise as Barry's section. Consequently, most of the Auxiliaries survived the first volley and were able to get out and down on the road or under the lorry. These men proved difficult to suppress and were able to return fire. Two Volunteers, Jim O'Sullivan and Michael McCarthy, were hit in the head and killed where they lay.[54]

Hart develops this point quite forcefully in a supporting footnote:

All of the men interviewed agree on this point: McCarthy and O'Sullivan did not stand up and did not die because of a fake surrender. Two of these veterans considered Barry's account to be an insult to the memory of these men.[55]

Jack Hennessy, who we have established was heavily engaged in the fighting, provides a dramatic account of what unfolded. Hennessy would appear to have been the most fortunate of all, surviving at least six shots to what he describes as his "tin hat." Hennessy was probably wearing the British Army standard helmet of the time known as the "Brodie." The Brodie was designed to provide some protection against secondary shrapnel impacts from above and therefore its ballistic protection performance was confined to low-level velocity impacts either from handguns such as the Webley or even grenade fragments. It would not have protected the wearer against a high velocity rifle round. It provided no cover to the lower parts of the head.

That the helmet is alleged to have taken five rounds without effect on the firer needs to be treated with a measure of caution. Hennessy also refers to his rifle becoming ineffective due to blood from an injury he sustained fouling the breech. It is difficult to fathom how Hennessy had come to this conclusion without stripping the mechanism. Rather than impeding the performance of the rifle, the blood in that short period of time would be more likely to have acted as a lubricant. It is more likely that the rifle was either jammed due to an inefficient feed of a new round to the chamber of the rifle or that the breech locked due to an insufficient extraction of the spent cartridge or indeed dirt impeding the action of the mechanism. It is also possible that the difficulty that Hennessy was having with his weapon may have been as a result of an inherent defect with the weapon rather than as a result of Hennessy's injury. This will become more apparent when we further probe the cause of Jim O'Sullivan's death.

Jim O'Sullivan has been described as suffering a fatal wound to his head

The memorial erected at Kilmichael to Jim O'Sullivan. According to the conventional narrative, he was shot dead in a false surrender by the Auxiliaries.

as a result of his rifle being hit by a round that caused the rifle's bolt to be driven into his face. We recount exactly O'Driscoll's testimony: ". . . Jim Sullivan who was alongside me was killed. As far as I could judge, a bullet struck his rifle and part of the bolt was driven into his face." Small as this level of detail is, it is an exceptionally important piece of information depending on what type of rifle O'Sullivan was firing. The description of the injury is so specific and unusual in its detail that we can accept it as reflecting exactly what Michael O'Driscoll saw. O'Driscoll's credibility as a witness is also evidenced by the investigating officer's "S" file:

> *The witness was recommended by the Bde O/C, Mr. Liam Deasy as one who could give first hand evidence of certain operations.*[56]

The bolt that Michael O'Driscoll describes as likely to have caused the death of Jim O'Sullivan could only have come from one of two rifle types. Let us therefore consider Jim O'Sullivan's injury from two perspectives: firstly on the basis that he was firing a Lee-Enfield, and secondly that he was using the Ross rifle.

O'Sullivan firing a Lee-Enfield rifle

If O'Sullivan was equipped with the Lee-Enfield then it is unlikely that his death can be attributed to the rifle bolt as described. When ready to fire, the bolt is fully locked, secured, and streamlined with the body of the rifle. To remove the bolt it must first be rotated anti-clockwise to disengage from the firing position, then be withdrawn to the rear, and the bolt head (at the front of the bolt) must then be manipulated through another turning action

Irish Army soldier with a Lee-Enfield rifle shooting from a lying position.

in order to remove it from the rifle's mechanism. The bolt is a critical part of the rifle's mechanism and is designed to be extremely secure as it has to facilitate the action of the striker (firing pin), withstand considerable pressure, and assist in the maintenance of a gas–tight seal in order to propel the round from the rifle at maximum velocity.

Consider the accompanying photograph on this page, which is a very useful front view of an Irish soldier adopting the lying position with a later version of the Lee-Enfield. Note the highly streamlined design features and the absence of protruding parts (rear sight excepted) for ease of use and to reduce the risk of the rifle snagging on vegetation and similar objects. The Lee-Enfield was almost "soldier proof" in that it could withstand significant levels of abuse and still function operationally. Of interest to this analysis is that fact that unless the bolt is locked in the firing position it was not possible to fire the weapon.

From a frontal view, as can be seen in the photograph, it is not possible to see the bolt. Therefore it is not possible to hit the bolt without first hitting something else in its way. It will also be noted that the bolt is just under the rear sight and is in line with the "shooting eye" on the right side of the head. The right side of the face is further protected by it resting against the stock butt of the rifle. It is also protected by the position of the right hand forward of the face around the stock and trigger. The left side of the face and the upper head is exposed.

While accepting that O'Sullivan must have suffered an injury to his face, which would have been obvious to his comrades, and that he may have suffered the injury as a result of a bullet strike, we need to consider what possibilities would contribute to such an outcome. For the reasons I have just outlined, it is unlikely that the fatal shot was delivered from the front.

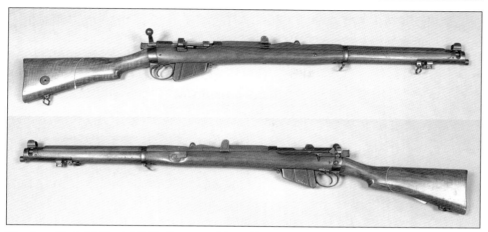

The Lee-Enfield No.1 MkIII rifle: considered by many shooting enthusiasts as the best bolt-action rifle ever manufactured.

Yes, it would be possible to impact O'Sullivan's face (left side) but due to the direct flight of the impacting round it would not have damaged the bolt. The bolt would not have been in the bullet's flight path. For obvious reasons we can rule out a shot directly from the rear. We are left with two further possibilities: the shot coming from either O'Sullivan's right (Macroom side) or left (Dunmanway side). Dealing with the "Macroom side" first, this can be discounted as there were no ADRIC members to the right-hand side of O'Sullivan's position. Finally, we are left with the probability that O'Sullivan was hit from the left, but even here we have a number of options. Before we analyse these, consider the following description of the impact on a firer whose Lee–Enfield mechanism was hit while he was in the firing position. The details of the incident, which happened in France in 1915, are provided by a Corkman, Sergeant J.F. Lucy of the 2nd Battalion, Royal Irish Rifles:

> *One of my men, Brown, had his rifle shattered by an enemy bullet as he was firing and scores of metal dust splinters penetrated his face, hands and chest. He looked in a dreadful mess, but he was not badly wounded, and he moved back out of the line quite unconcerned, judging by the way he kept wondering what part of his rifle the enemy had hit.*[57]

This incident supports the view that even after the impact of a high velocity bullet, the general integrity of the weapon's mechanism remains intact. It appears that the soldier was still able to examine his weapon, and even then it was not clear what part of the rifle had been impacted.

If O'Sullivan's rifle was hit first in the area of the bolt, it is reasonable to expect that, given the kinetic energy associated with a .303 bullet travelling at 2,750 feet per second, the weapon would either be knocked from his hands or splinter at its weakest point. As well as damaging the rifle, a lateral impact from the left-hand side would tend to push the rifle away from the firer and certainly not facilitate the bolt entering O'Sullivan's face. A plausible explanation could be that the bullet hit O'Sullivan around the lower jaw area first (Paddy O'Brien describes Jim O'Sullivan as having been shot in the jaw [58]) and then continued its journey through his face to finally impact the area where the wooden butt stock intersects the steel mechanism, thus throwing the majority of the debris caused by the impact away from O'Sullivan. However, due to the location and nature of the injury it looks like the wound was caused by a part of the rifle, in this case the most likely part being the bolt. The fact that O'Sullivan was aiming his rifle at a target to his front and at lower elevation would have caused him to drop his shoulder and thereby present a larger aspect of the side of his head as a target. Only the left-hand side of his jaw was exposed, the right being fully protected by the butt of the rifle. In summary, if we accept that O'Sullivan was firing the Lee-Enfield rifle, then he was more than likely shot by a rifle round from a position on his left-hand side, slightly to his rear and possibly from a lower elevation. There is information to suggest that the ADRIC members Pallester and Taylor had managed to outflank No.2 Section and their location in that area would be consistent with how O'Sullivan may have been killed. The damage as described could only have come from a rifle round as a revolver impact would not have had the kinetic energy to cause the damage as outlined.

O'Sullivan firing a Canadian Ross rifle

In addition to the Lee-Enfield rifle we have also established the possibility of up to forty-four Canadian Ross rifles being available to the volunteers in the column; ten had been secured in a raid on the Coastguard station at Howe's Strand, Courtmacsherry, in June 1920 and twelve more in a further raid on the same station a number of days later. At least eleven Ross rifles were taken from Ballycrovane Coastguard station on the Beara Peninsula, while ten Ross rifles had also been taken from a naval vessel a year earlier by a unit of the IRA from Bantry. Because of the paucity of rifles available to the IRA, it is a near certainty that the Ross rifle was present in the column's armoury and was used by members of the column in the course of the engagement. The rifle clearly had several serious defects, as mentoned in a previous chapter, and outlined in detail in Appendix II. These defects most likely had a direct bearing on how Jim O'Sullivan died, thus calling into

The Ross rifle.

question much of the traditional narrative of what happened to O'Sullivan in the course of the ambush..

The most obvious defect with the Ross rifle concerned its bolt mechanism. It is clear that if Jim O'Sullivan had been firing a Ross with an incorrectly assembled bolt then the bolt of the weapon would have been propelled to the rear into O'Sullivan's face and this would have occurred with the firing of the first shot. O'Sullivan's early death in the engagement is consistent with such an event, as Jack Hennessy tells us that O'Sullivan was dead by the time Barry's team arrived. It is possible that O'Sullivan may have been left-handed; had he been firing from the right side, the bolt would have injured him in the vicinity of the eye and he may have either survived or lived for a little longer.

One further point needs to be made relating to the bolt. The bolt on the Ross operated as a "straight pull." That means that rather than the bolt having to be rotated out of its locked position, as was the case with the Lee-Enfield, the Ross bolt was simply pulled to the rear by the firer to extract a spent cartridge and pushed forward to feed a new cartridge to the barrel chamber. In terms of rifle design, the Ross bolt was even more streamlined than the Lee-Enfield, reducing to negligible proportions the chances of the bolt being hit and dislodged by an impacting bullet.

In the absence of any other bullet wound or visible cause of death, and given the probability that O'Sullivan had been firing the Ross rifle, the evidence suggests that rather than O'Sullivan sustaining his fatal injury as a result of an ADRIC member firing a revolver or rifle shot at him, he was most likely killed when the bolt of his rifle propelled to the rear into his face and head because it had been incorrectly assembled.

What could have caused the bolt to have been incorrectly assembled? It is unclear whether the rifle had been stripped and assembled by the IRA. The rifles captured in Bantry "were carefully oiled" and would have had to be stripped and cleaned. Could it be that the bolts on these rifles were either incorrectly assembled by the British in the knowledge that they would come into the possession of the IRA, or that the weapons would be cleaned by the IRA prior to use and incorrectly assembled with disastrous conse-

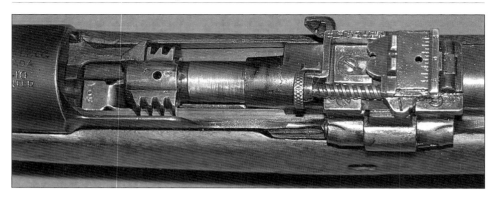

The bolt mechanism of the Ross rifle which if incorrectly assembled could still fire a bullet but would propel the bolt to the rear with catastrophic consequences for the firer.

quences either way for the users?.

In addition to the bolt design defect, there was another factor that could have accounted for the bolt being accelerated back into Jim O'Sullivan's face. In the course of research I was presented with correspondence that supports a possibility that the ammunition O'Sullivan was using may have been tampered with or booby-trapped.

A letter from Major General G.F. Boyd, Commanding Officer of the Dublin District, to GHQ dated 24 April 1920 states:

> *I understand that a certain amount of ammunition of a highly dangerous explosive nature has been issued to the intelligence staff of Divisions by GHQ for the purposes of being gradually distributed to Sinn Feiners of extreme views with an object which is obvious.*
>
> *Up to the present I have always been opposed to such a policy as being un-British and likely to lead to reprisals.*
>
> *Before allowing any more of this ammunition to be distributed in my district I should like to be assured that this policy is approved by the Commander in Chief.[59]*

This is obviously a very pertinent piece of information. Note that the letter refers to "intelligence staff of Divisions", not just the Dublin District. It is highly likely that the intelligence staff of the 6th Division, whose area of responsibility included West Cork, were also involved in the "gradual distribution" referred to.

There is also evidence to suggest that the British authorities did not only supply tampered small arms ammunition but that they may have also tampered with the explosive material available to the IRA.

Some of the major operations of the West Cork Flying Column were severely hampered by the quality of explosives and detonating material they were using for their operations. In simple terms, they were having major difficulties in getting their explosives to initiate – in other words, to explode. Instances of bombs and mines failing to explode feature regularly in *Guerilla Days*. Barry's prior experience of a mine failing to explode at the Toureen ambush may have weighed heavily on his decision not to use one at Kilmichael. That may have been a particularly good decision on his part.

In order to access or destroy the fortified barracks they were attacking, Barry needed to use explosives. To do this the flying column engaged in the manufacture of what would now be considered Improvised Explosive Devices (IEDs). As the following operations show, the explosive failures hampered IRA operations and saved a considerable number of British and Irish lives:

On 22 October 1920 in the course of an ambush at Toureen, Barry threw a bomb manufactured by the IRA into a British lorry, but it failed to explode.

At the same ambush a mine that had been laid in anticipation of disabling the lead lorry failed to explode. The IRA had been using an electric detonator.

On 3 January 1921, a mine laid by the IRA against the door of the Black and Tan post at Kilbrittain failed to detonate. They had been using an electric detonator.

On 15 January 1921, the IRA returned for another attempt at destroying the Kilbrittain post. This time, instead of using an electric detonator, they used an ordinary detonator and safety fuse. Once again the device failed to function.

On 26 January 1921, having reverted to using an electric detonator, a mine was placed at the door of Innishannon barracks. The mine failed to detonate.

On 12 February 1921 in the course of an attack on Drimoleague barracks, they had a success of sorts in that the mine partially detonated. Barry describes a plunger being used, which means the IRA was again using an electric detonator. The fact that the "explosion" failed to even damage the box in which it was carried suggests that although the detonator exploded, it failed to impart a sufficient level of power (velocity of detonation) to initiate the main explosive filling.

Barry has described the mine used in the attack on Kilbrittain as consisting, "of thirty pounds of gelignite and guncotton encased in a wooden box. It had an electric detonator, connected by forty yards of electric cable to an exploder."[60]

Considering each of these components individually it is possible to isolate where the problem with initiating the explosives may have originated.

Gelignite is *blasting gelatine,* the most violent of all the glycerine explosives, with the addition of potassium nitrate and wood meal. Although the purpose of the latter two substances is to make the gelatine component milder, gelignite remains a very violent explosive and sensitive to handle. Crucially for the IRA, who had rudimentary storage facilities, it is practically unaffected by water.

Guncotton comes in two forms: wet slabs and dry cylindrical primers. In its dry state guncotton is very sensitive and needs to be handled with caution. Wet guncotton is much less sensitive and will require the action of a detonator augmented by a primer to make it explode. Both the wet and dry forms are unaffected by damp.

Had the IRA been using gelignite and guncotton, then any form of initiation should have caused the material to explode. The firing of high velocity rounds into the mine would certainly have caused it to explode, which leads one to consider whether in fact the IRA were using explosives or indeed whether any of the IRA had managed to hit the box.

The problem, however, was most likely to have been the detonators that the IRA were using. When they finally initiated a mine during the attack on Rosscarbery barracks, for instance, it was by using two ordinary (non-electric) detonators. The electric detonators are much safer and more reliable than the ordinary detonators, so why were they experiencing such difficulties with the electric detonators? Is it possible that the British were supplying the IRA with inert or faulty material?

Suggestions that British intelligence was not only interfering with IRA munitions in 1920 but also with the demolition and blasting explosives at the IRA's disposal is apparent in the witness statement of Francis Davis, who served with a flying column in north Longford. Davis attributed the failure of a mine being used in an ambush to the electric detonators in the following terms:

The mines failed to explode…I rushed down and tried to make them explode – but without result. The detonators used were "dud ones" which had been pawned off by some individual on our GHQ, I believe, at the instance

The ruins of Howe's Strand Coastguard station – raided twice for rifles.

of the British Government…(subsequently) a despatch arrived from GHQ warning us not to use the detonators as they had found out that they were "duds", and ordering us to destroy them.[61]

The fact that a total of thirty-three Ross rifles were taken from the Coastguard stations at Ballycrovane and at Howe's Strand on two occasions with "surprisingly little military or police activity" and that the Royal Navy, by conveniently docking in Bantry against local RIC advice, had "facilitated" more Ross rifles coming into the IRA's possession supports a suspicion that the British Naval Intelligence Division (NID) may have been involved. Rather than being due to carelessness on the part of the Navy, Royal Marines and Coastguard, the making available of so many Ross rifles had the hallmark of a well-considered intelligence operation. The two leading British intelligence departments engaged with Irish affairs at this time were the Special Branch of the Metropolitan Police and the NID. Responsibility for the Coastguard stations would have fallen to the NID.

Up to 1919, the NID was headed by Rear-Admiral Reginald "Blinker" Hall who has been described as "the most successful intelligence chief of the First World War."[62] His influence on Naval intelligence operations was

Rear-Admiral Reginald 'Blinker' Hall: the IRA's necessity for rifles was an intelligence opportunity that would have been difficult for the British not to take advantage of.

to last decades.[63]

By any standards, Hall was a fascinating character. He was described by Ruth Skrine, his secretary as follows:

> *The Machiavelli in him was cruel…but the school-boy was always around the corner, and the love of the dangerous game he, and all of us, were playing would bubble out, and the fun and hazard of it all would fill him with infectious delight. "Adventures are for the adventurous" he would chant, rubbing his hands and grinning like a crafty little French Abbé.*[64]

His intelligence coups are legendary. Hall is credited with bringing America into the First World War by intercepting what became known as the Zimmerman Cable, a coded cable to the Mexican government offering German support should the Mexicans decided to attack the US. It was an intelligence masterpiece. Closer to home he was responsible for intercepting and decoding communications leading to the interception of the *Aud,* thus preventing the importation of German rifles for the 1916 Rising and leading to the arrest of Roger Casement.

The mischievous and vengeful side to Hall is most apparent in two separate incidents. The first of these, described brilliantly by David Ramsey in his 2008 biography of Hall, involved the mining of Waterford harbour by a German mine-layer. When Hall was informed that the harbour had been heavily mined, he banned all shipping from entering the harbour for two weeks. He then arranged for a message to be intercepted by the Germans, which declared that the harbour had been quickly cleared of all mines by Royal Navy minesweepers. Days later the German U-boat mine-layer returned and was promptly blown up by one its own mines. Hall took enormous delight from the fact that the rescued captain of the U-boat bitterly complained that the British minesweepers had failed to do their jobs properly! The German captain was oblivious to the fact that he had been tricked.

The second incident is described in Patrick Beesley's 1982 biography of Hall, *Room 40: British naval intelligence 1914-18*. According to Beesley, who was himself in military intelligence during the Second World War and met Hall in 1936, "the story may well be apocryphal but it is revealing that it is one which Hall himself was fond of telling."[65] The story began with a magistrate's failure to convict a German spy who had been found taking pictures of British factories. The judge felt that the pictures were of "no military significance" and duly acquitted the German. Hall was furious and arranged for an intelligence report signed by the German spy to be sent to Germany, which gave the address of the judge's country house as another factory. Soon afterwards Zeppelins arrived and subjected the house to a rain of bombs in which the judge narrowly escaped being killed. Hall subsequently found himself at a dinner sitting next to the judge who outlined the tale to him; Hall delighted in informing him that his house was obviously of "no military significance."

Hall turned his talents to address the growing difficulties in Ireland. Throughout his tenure, he is described as maintaining a constant surveillance over the activities of the Irish extremists with considerable success.[66] His imagination knew no limits, as evidenced by his chartering of a yacht, *Sayonara*, to sail Irish waters, crewed with Royal Navy personnel but disguised as an American vessel with an owner who was overtly anti-British. The ruse was so successful that the local RIC and even the Royal Navy had the vessel under close scrutiny. This achieved the desired result:

> *The scrutiny did not go unnoticed by the Irish rebels, who assumed that the yacht and its crew had come to the West Coast to support and encourage them and were more than ready to contact and befriend Hall's agents.*[67]

Hall would have been aware of the importance of targeting the IRA without alienating the population. The IRA's necessity for rifles was an intelligence opportunity that would have been difficult for the British not to take advantage of. A surgical instrument, not a blunt one, was required. The capture of ten Ross rifles from the naval vessel in Bantry deserves further comment, particularly when read in the light of Flor Crowley's testimony that the vessel was alongside against the advice of the RIC. Crowley states:

> *. . . the sergeant (RIC) in charge of that party swore bitter oaths against the*

*ship's company and officers who had ignored the police warning and tied
their boat at the pier, and so in their culpable carelessness had played directly
into the hands of the IRA.*[68]

It is clear from Major General G.F. Boyd's letter, quoted earlier, that
British intelligence were engaged in these kinds of operation. If British intelligence intended a policy of either sabotaging weapons or ammunition to
be really effective then Boyd's phrase "gradually distributed" is very relevant.
Gradual distribution would consist of doctoring a weapon here and there or
placing a booby-trapped round of ammunition in an otherwise serviceable
batch which would remain unnoticed. The ultimate objective of such an
operation would be to kill IRA men without the IRA ever realising that
they were being killed by the actions of the British.

While interfering with ammunition could be as simple as removing the
propellant from a round so that it wouldn't fire, in the case of the ammunition that Boyd refers to, the procedure would have been to remove the
propellant and to replace it with a quantity of high explosive. The velocity
of detonation from such a charge would be more than sufficient to propel
the bolt of a Ross rifle to the rear with enough momentum to kill the firer instantly. The damage that the small explosion would do to the breach
might, to an untrained eye, look like something caused by a bullet impact.

Vice-Commandant Michael McCarthy appears to have been hit once
by a shot to the head. We are not given any further information, but if
we are to accept Jack Hennessy's testimony he seems to have been in an
area that was experiencing very heavy accurate fire, and all aimed at the
region of the head. This fire was more likely to originate either from the
front and/or the-left hand side. Michael McCarthy's death could have been
caused by a number of possibilities.[69] Being close to the road, he was in
range of revolver fire from the front and side. A weapon defect is ruled out,
as Hennessy describes picking up McCarthy's weapon and continuing the
engagement once his own rifle had jammed. It is possible to posit a more
controversial view that the risk to McCarthy was not only from the ADRIC
but also from those volunteers who were deployed with him, who did not
have enough training in weapon handling or marksmanship. McCarthy's
position was directly in the line of fire from No.3 Section on the other side
of the road. Crucially, McCarthy's death not alone deprived No.2 Section of
a rifleman, for McCarthy was also the section's commander. The remaining
members of No.2 Section were now leaderless.

In the case of Jack Hennessy, notwithstanding my earlier comments concerning the five shots that hit his helmet, this level of accurate fire was

It can be seen from this image that the mechanism of the rifle is considerably forward of the shooter's head, thus negating the possibility of blood from a head wound fouling the mechanism as described in Jack Hennessy's statement.

unlikely to have come from one of the ADRIC patrol members due to the restricted view that those on the road would have had of the volunteers. That being said, the wound that Hennessy suffered was more than likely fired from the front and probably grazed the right-hand side of his forehead as, from his description, the blood from his wound fouled the breech of his rifle. It is difficult to see how the blood from Hennessy's wound could have affected his rifle's mechanism as described. From the image on this page it can be seen that the breech is well forward of the firer's head. The blood would have to pump at a high rate in order to bridge the distance between the wound and the breech mechanism. I consider this to be unlikely.

We must also consider the possibility that Hennessy was also firing a Ross rifle. Hennessy's weapon was more likely to have had its mechanism jammed by any number of reasons, but not through the action of blood fouling the breech. Interestingly, Hennessy refers to continuously firing and loading his rifle. While the Lee-Enfield had a ten-round magazine, the Ross had a five-round magazine, which would explain why Hennessy remembers loading the weapon so often. Additionally, Hennessy was engaged in rapid firing, and we have seen that the Ross was susceptible to jamming when engaging in such firing practices. This jamming problem was a painful lesson that the Canadians, and now possibly Hennessy, learned the hard way:

Etched permanently in to the minds of Canadian soldiers were all-too-vivid scenes of advancing Huns who couldn't be stopped because of seized up rifles; of desperate men hammering frozen Ross bolts with entrenching tools, or jumping on them with mud-logged boots, tears of exasperation running down their cheeks.[70]

The jamming problems Hennessy was having with his rifle had been identified in France five years earlier. Due to these reported difficulties that the Ross was presenting to Canadian soldiers, it was decided to conduct a number of trials to ascertain the source of the problem. As a result of such tests, the Canadian Army had established by June 1915 that the only ammunition suitable for rapid fire with the Ross was that manufactured by the Dominion Arsenal. The Dominion ammunition was different from the standard .303 ammunition in that it was of a slightly smaller calibre than the British equivalent by a matter of .010 of an inch. Although this differential was very small, it had a crucial impact on the performance of the rifle. The difference in ammunition size would not have been discernible to an inexperienced eye, but when the Ross was rapidly fired using the British .303 equivalent, the cartridge would swell in the tighter and hotter chamber, thus making it much more difficult to extract the spent cartridge, and this was the primary reason why so many Ross rifles had been jamming for Canadian troops who had been using British ammunition during the First World War. The Dominion Arsenal ammunition was used in the successful field trials that the Canadians had held before the general issuing of the rifle, and thus the problems only began to emerge once the troops started using the standard British .303 round. Hennessy could only have been using .303 British ammunition as even the British had difficulties in securing enough Canadian ammunition to conduct their own field trials, as can be seen in Appendix II.

It is highly unlikely that the IRA would have been aware of this difference and the importance of not engaging in rapid fire using the British .303 round.

Deployed to McCarthy's and Hennessy's front were ADRIC members Jones and Barnes. Jones is of particular interest to us at this point. A notice in a local English newspaper following his death gives some indication of what combat potential he possessed:

Before the War he was a gamekeeper in Cambridgeshire and joined the 11th Suffolk Regiment as a private within a few weeks of the outbreak of hostilities. Almost immediately he was promoted to the rank of sergeant and in that capacity he accompanied his regiment early in the winter of 1914 to France, where except for brief intervals in England, consequent upon wounds received in battle, he served until long after the armistice. He took part in the fierce struggles which raged around the town of Albert in 1915 and was wounded in the head. Two years later he was again wounded and was sent home for the second time. A month before the armistice he was raised to

110

commissioned rank being gazetted as a second lieutenant to the Duke of Wellington's Regiment.[71]

Being a woodsman, Albert Jones had more than an average knowledge of how to use ground to his advantage and an equivalent level of good marksmanship that one would associate with game-keeping. What is additionally significant is that Jones had quickly attained the rank of sergeant, an indication of his military capability. He had served as an infantry NCO for the duration of the war, only being promoted to officer rank in October 1918. He had been wounded in action, survived and was battle experienced. This was a significant advantage he had over his attackers. If we are to accept the theory that Jim O'Sullivan was killed by the action of his own rifle and not by enemy fire, it is not beyond the bounds of possibility that Jones may well have killed Michael McCarthy and injured Jack Hennessy. The medical examination report for Jones conducted in the aftermath of the ambush discloses that he was hit at least seven times in various parts of the body. Ned Young, who was positioned on the opposite side of the road and therefore to the rear of the ADRIC patrol, described in his statement to the Bureau of Military History seeing an ADRIC member firing from underneath the lorry at IRA men on the high ground opposite the lorry.[72] One wonders whether Young meant "beyond" the lorry? If he did, then that ADRIC member was most likely to have been Jones as he would have been more exposed to Young than the other ADRIC member, Barnes, found closer to the lorry in this location. As Jones was probably more actively engaging the attackers than Barnes, he would have therefore been drawing a greater rate of return fire, a theory supported by the number of bullet wounds he had received – almost twice that of Barnes. Young describes opening fire on the ADRIC member from the rear and probably killing him, as he describes the fire subsequently ceasing from that ADRIC member's position.[73]

Pat Deasy is described as having been hit twice in the body. There is no information to suggest where on the body, but he was lying in close proximity to O'Sullivan. Barry describes him as being "a few yards away" from O'Sullivan's body.[74] Deasy may have been hit by either Pallester or Taylor, as they would have had a fuller sight of his torso than Jones. It is not certain what ammunition types killed Deasy or McCarthy.

John Lordon is the other volunteer who received wounds in the course of the engagement, but no detail is given about these.[75] There is a suggestion that he was located at the temporary small wall constructed at road level beneath the high ground. This is consistent with the possibility that he clubbed Pallester with his rifle butt as Pallester would have been the

ADRIC member closest to him, and the wounds that were inflicted upon Pallester accorded with Hennessy's description of Lordon's action.

No.2 Section had taken a significant number of casualties for a section that comprised ten volunteers, with fifty per cent either dead or injured. Recall that Barry declares that the two/three volunteers were wounded by revolver fire after the ADRIC had called a false surrender:

> *Then we saw three of our comrades on No.2 section, one crouched and two upright. Suddenly the auxiliaries were firing again with revolvers. One of our three men spun around before he fell, and Pat Deasy staggered before he too went down.*[76]

The distance from the road to what might be considered the most likely firing positions where No.2 Section was deployed is approximately twenty-five yards. It would appear, therefore, that the IRA casualties were hit at the revolver's maximum range. According to the .455 Webley manual the revolver should be fired as follows:

> *The occasions on service when a pistol is likely to be used are rare but, when necessity does arise, it is essential that shots should be delivered accurately and very quickly. The pistol should, therefore, normally be used at close range, i.e. 25 yds or under, and the instinctive action of a man suddenly confronted with an opponent within this distance is to fire instantly by sense of direction.*[77]

It is not at all certain that a target will be engaged successfully at twenty-five yards, and I would again refer the reader to the Webley experiment on pages 132-136 to provide a further insight as to the weapon's capabilities and limitations.

If all the IRA injuries were as a result of ADRIC fire, it is more likely the case that they suffered their injuries as a result of rifle fire from the ADRIC members as outlined rather than revolvers as suggested by Barry.

Pallester and Taylor would also appear to have been subjected to particularly harsh treatment in terms of the wounds inflicted. Could this have been as a result of having caused so much damage to No.2 Section?

Phase 5: (H hour + 35 to 45 mins): After the action

With the deaths of the ADRIC members from the rear lorry, the combat was now over. The inexperience and lack of training among the volunteers was now most evident. Barry describes the column members as being in a state of shock. The column would have been extremely vulnerable to an attack from British forces. If we accept that there had been a prolonged fire-fight then the volunteers' ammunition levels would have been running very low if not entirely expended.

In order to recover his troops and to inject some measure of efficiency into the column, he ordered his men to reload their weapons and proceeded to drill them up and down the "corpse-strewn, blood-stained road." Arrangements were made to collect the arms and ammunition from the ADRIC, and the dead and wounded IRA were carried from the scene. As a final act of defiance the lorries were set ablaze.

Given the levels of inexperience among the volunteers and the lack of any battle inoculation training it is not surprising that the volunteers were so stunned and traumatised. The effect of battleshock is dealt with in further detail in Chapter 8. Barry's response was perfectly correct. He needed to recover the troops quickly, and the best way to achieve that was by re-estab-lishing a group bond, which is the aim of close-arms drill, and to get them to react on order. The presenting arms to their dead comrades not alone rendered honours but also and more importantly had the rifle moving in their hands. He re-acquainted them with their weapons. It is very unlikely that they stayed in the area for any length of time, and soon after he moved the column to a safer area to recuperate. The action was complete. The col-umn moved away victorious, having achieved its mission.

Once the column had reached a safe area we get an interesting insight into Barry's state of mind and a confirmation that, despite the military suc-cess, he was still an inexperienced junior officer. This is apparent from the fact that he began to blame himself for the deaths of the volunteers. This was an emotional challenge which we are not certain that Barry was capable of coping with. Such reactions are, however, normal:

> *One of the greatest emotional challenges for inexperienced officers came in the aftermath of battle. They tended to brood over feelings of direct personal responsibility for each casualty. Training publications took a hard line in dis-pelling their anxieties. Junior officers were to "steel" themselves against losing men and to realise that casualties are an expected product of war and must be accepted as such.*[78]

Barry was hospitalised in Cork City shortly after and this may have as-sisted in his recovery from the trauma and feelings of and responsibilities he was experiencing.

CHAPTER 6

After-action assessment

FOR THE PURPOSES of analysis the engagement was split into a number of distinct phases, each of which was examined on the basis of the existing narratives. The purpose of the overall assessment now is to consider the viability of what was described when compared and contrasted with a number of principles that are critical to mission success.

The uncertainty and confusion associated with war has already been highlighted, yet military planners feel that for a successful operation there are fundamental principles that need to be adhered to. These principles are collectively referred to as the "Principles of War". The US Army field manual *FM-3: Military Operations* defines these principles as follows:

Principle	Definition
Objective	Direct every military operation towards a clearly defined, decisive, and attainable objective.
Offensive	Seize, retain, and exploit the initiative.
Mass	Mass the effects of overwhelming combat power at the decisive place and time.
Economy of Force	Employ all combat power available in the most effective way possible; allocate minimum essential combat power to secondary efforts.
Manoeuvre	Place the enemy in a position of disadvantage through the flexible application of combat power.
Unity of Command	For every objective, seek unity of command and unity of effort.
Security	Never permit the enemy to acquire unexpected advantage.
Surprise	Strike the enemy at a time, at a place, or in a manner for which he is unprepared.
Simplicity	Prepare clear, uncomplicated plans and concise orders to ensure thorough understanding.

In addition to considering the operation against these nine principles which are applicable to all operations, in tactical terms Kilmichael can be considered a special operation – an operation that was distinct from the standard military engagements that were a feature of the conflict before 28 Nov 1920. For such a special operation William McRaven has identified six fundamentals that are essential to success, and which draw heavily on the principles as outlined. McRaven suggests that the plan for a special operation should be:

A simple plan, carefully concealed, realistically rehearsed and executed with surprise, speed and purpose.[1]

Based on that description he splits the operation into three phases associated with the principles as follows:

Planning Phase: *Simplicity*
Preparation Phase: *Security, Repetition*
Execution Phase: *Surprise, Speed, Purpose*

The analysis and overall assessment will now be conducted against this framework.

Planning (simplicity)

The decisions Barry made about where his force would be deployed require comment. The most striking weakness in his deployment scheme was the decision to position his command post, which would necessarily include him as commander, on the extremity of the engagement area. The entrance to the lane-way at which the command post was located offered very little in the way of exercising command and control over the attacking party. Once he had positioned his column, Barry would not be able to control any aspect of the deployed sections' actions, including, most importantly, the reserve element. The plan was therefore unnecessarily uncertain, with success dependent upon all the sections working more or less independently of each other with little consideration for contingencies.

The command post was directly in line with the approach of the enemy, and in the event that the first lorry was not stopped, it would offer the first opportunity target for the ADRIC patrol to counter-attack. Crucially, it placed Barry as the commander and leader along with probably the best fighters in the column to the forefront of the action. Given the untrained and untested nature of the majority of the column members, the risk to losing Barry represented an unacceptable risk to the column as a whole. The location of the command post would also impede the opportunities for No. 1 Section and No. 3 (across the road) to engage the ADRIC without running an unacceptable risk of hitting the command post members. Once members of the command post party were on the road and engaged in close-quarter combat, there would not have been an opportunity to provide supporting fire. The only conceivable advantage to the location of the command post was that it enabled Barry to hopefully slow down the first lorry, initiate the attack, throw the Mills grenade, get involved in the assault on the lorry through to a conclusion, and then continue the engagement by leading a relief party to recover a deteriorating situation with the second lorry. However, by locating the command post where he did, Barry was seriously exposed from start to finish. Had he failed to stop the lorry, and if a member of the ADRIC patrol had managed to fire a composed shot, then Barry was at serious risk of becoming a casualty. The extent of the danger that Barry exposed himself and his command post team to cannot be overstated when one considers the ADRIC members' combat potential. For those reasons an objective assessment of the location of the command post would have to consider it as poor. It would have been much better if it had been located centrally or occupied higher ground where No.1 Section was located. This would have allowed Barry an appreciation of how the ambush was unfolding, referred to in military parlance as a "situational awareness", and would have at least allowed him to control the activities of those personnel in that area of the ambush site. Once the engagement began, Barry could only influence those within his immediate vicinity. Rather than being in a position to command all aspects of the ambush, his impact on the conduct of those operations he was not directly engaged in was severely limited.

The location and role assigned to the reserve element was strange. Located to the rear of No.2 Section at the entrance to the ambush site and assigned a role to engage with any unexpected arrivals, it was a reserve element in name only. In tactical doctrine, a reserve is a flexible element available to the commander to be deployed as necessary. Its utility is that it is a force immediately capable of being deployed to counter a threat or support other elements within the area of operations. For an engagement of this size, the reserve was only capable of being deployed once. By assigning it a role prior to the commencement of operations, the reserve was effectively deployed and in reality was a flank security unit. By locating the command post at the opposite end of the ambush site, Barry could not have any further contact with the reserve until the attack was completed. The reserve should have been available to the commander throughout the engagement. It should have been more centrally situated and therefore deployable throughout the ambush site.

As the Kilmichael ambush is being considered at a tactical level, it is important to appreciate that the encounter would have been engulfed by what is termed the "fog of war." There are a number of factors which create this "fog"; these include, firstly, the physical challenges of the surrounding environment, which can impede contact between the commander and his troops; secondly, low light levels, which would have been characteristic of an early wet November evening; and, thirdly, the space over which the troops were deployed and the consequent difficulty in maintaining effective communications with the deployed sections. The noise levels associated with the engagement, as we have already outlined, would have presented their own difficulties, rendering vocal commands and instruction between the deployed sections difficult, if not impossible.

It remains unclear whether the volunteers understood what was to occur once the engagement began. Barry would appear to have acted flexibly and as he deemed necessary at the time. It is obvious that No.2 Section were not in a position to defeat the occupants of the second lorry, and it would seem that only Barry's direct intervention saved them from defeat as the ADRIC were beginning to gain the upper hand. Barry's squad moving along the road effectively negated the efforts of those volunteers deployed with No.3 Section who were most likely reduced to spectators once the initial volleys had been fired.

There is a military axiom which provides that no plan survives the first contact. Once the engagement commenced, this would seem to have been the case. The plan was too dependent on Barry's direct involvement. It was poorly conceived, and in the absence of a thorough understanding by its members as to their role, the column was put at an unacceptable risk. From a planning perspective the operation failed to adhere to the simplicity requirement. It is unlikely that Barry engaged in a proper troop-leading process of analysing his mission, developing a simple plan and making adequate preparations for the operation.

Preparation (security and repetition)

The column members were inadequately prepared and insufficiently equipped for the operation. What is clear from the number of rounds issued is that the column would not be capable of sustaining a prolonged engagement unless its members were practised and experienced in fire discipline. Each ADRIC member was issued with both rifle and revolver ammunition and had more than three times what each IRA volunteer was carrying. Standard infantry training at that time suggests that a soldier was capable of firing approximately sixteen aimed shots per minute. Hackett, writing in 1983, states, " . . . in the eighty years between Clausewitz and 1911 the rate of rifle fire had increased from three rounds per minute to sixteen."[2] More recently, Martin Van Creveld has revised that figure and suggested that lessons from the Boer War taught the British Army the value that marksmanship combined with rapid fire could have. This, Van Crevald says, was a lesson which the British "took to heart by training their men to deliver 'twelve rounds a minute aimed' as the saying went."[3] With each volunteer in possession of thirty-five rounds and in the absence of any fire discipline measures, it would therefore be possible for the ambush party to expend their ammunition within three minutes. Fire discipline is a tactical consideration to ensure that the force does not deplete its ammunition to the extent that its members either run out of ammunition or are not in a position to take advantage of opportunities and exploit their success. For the successful conduct of the operation, fire discipline was absolutely vital. Neither Barry's nor Deasy's accounts mention this aspect, and if it had not been considered then the column ran the risk of expending its stock of ammunition. It is not unreasonable to assume that young, largely untrained volunteers would expend ammunition in the excitement of being involved in action for the first time. Testimony refers to the volunteers "pouring lead" into the ADRIC, and while the metaphor is accepted as imparting a dramatic effect to the action, it is also suggestive of the volunteers simply firing at will without any fire discipline or control. It needs to be recognised that such independent firing has its own advantages, in that the volunteers would be able to select their own targets, fire at their own rate, and administer all aspects of their weapon control, such as adjustment of sights, to engage more distant targets; this was possibly only applicable to the volunteers deployed with No.3 Section and definitely applicable to the flank/reserve element who would have to engage the arrival of unexpected troops from the Macroom direction should the need have arisen.

In trained military units it is the responsibility of platoon and section leaders to study the ground before them and consider the practical effects of the fire they can bring to bear on the area. This is known as "fire planning" and is aimed at securing a maximum return for the weapons available. There are no details from Kilmichael about any arcs of fire being chosen, or whether any members of the column were given specific fire tasks. In the absence of a specific fire plan it is assumed that section leaders used their own initiative. However, the lack of a co-ordinated fire plan would greatly reduce the combined effect of the column's fire-power. It is also unclear if Barry considered the fire power of the column and how it would be given best effect other than in an unspecified support role.

The hazards associated with potential cross-fire were very real because of the levels of weapon handling and the limited military skill-set of the rank and file. The volunteers were deployed in very close proximity to each other, and once Barry's group became active in the killing zone the operation became much more complicated. I do not doubt that they were capable and motivated, but their sheer lack of training has to be considered. The fire and manoeuvre tactics adopted by Barry's men as they advanced in the killing zone towards the engagement at the west end of the ambush site is a skill only mastered by continuous repetition and full awareness of what is happening by all the participating elements. Each attacking member would have to have his own line of advance to enable his fellow attacker to provide supporting fire and, more crucially, not to cross in front of that firer and thereby risk being hit by one of his own. Flanking troops would have to be aware of the "lift and shift" required to ensure that their suppressing/supporting fire would not result in what in modern military parlance is referred to as a "Blue-on-Blue" incident, where the volunteers of No.3 Section deployed on the southern side, had they been firing, would inadvertently engage Barry and his advancing riflemen.

Barry was aware of the possibility of the volunteers engaging each other and he gave a warning order to the effect that volunteers were to be conscious of where they were aiming. What is clear is that Barry expected the engagement to be fought at very close quarters. Revolvers and shotguns would have been ideal for such short-range engagements where volumes of fire as opposed to aimed shots would carry the day.

Charles Townsend describes military ambushes as "sophisticated operations which require extensive preparations as well as skilful execution."[4] The preparation phase for the ambush can be assessed as poor. Even though Barry maintained internal tight security, the fact that Lieutenant Pat Deasy followed the column and a number of volunteers simply turned up and nearly jeopardised the entire operation would indicate that the external security procedures were seriously inadequate. In the absence of any information regarding rehearsals for the operation, we can assess the preparation phase of the operation as not meeting a required minimum standard.

Execution (surprise, speed and purpose)

The element of surprise is achieved where the enemy is attacked at a time or place or in a manner for which he is unprepared. The ambush achieved this. Barry's ruse of appearing on the road in an officer's tunic slowed the patrol. As an act of deception it was extremely effective as it distracted the enemy at a crucial moment. It also introduced a level of confusion as the patrol members, once the attack commenced, would momentarily hesitate in attacking what they thought was a British officer.

Surprise was also achieved by the timing of the attack, though Barry had not factored this into his plan. Darkness was falling and the patrol had been deployed throughout the day. We can assume on a cold November evening that levels of alertness and concentration would be low and thus the element of surprise was more easily achieved.

Achieving the ambush's objective in as fast a time as possible was crucial to mission success. Given the paucity of training and low levels of ammunition available, Barry could not risk a protracted engagement. Barry had to consider that the enemy would fight back and he knew that as professional soldiers they had the ability to counter-attack. The longer the engagement lasted, the more vulnerable the column would be; speed, therefore, was of the essence. Barry moved quickly, and from his account it would appear that the first lorry was wiped out in five minutes; however, the same cannot be said of the attack on the second lorry. Having failed to incapacitate the second lorry, it is clear that No.2 Section stayed firmly in their firing positions and engaged in a prolonged fire-fight, thus failing to achieve the element of speed. They lost the benefit of the surprise achieved earlier, and it is more probably the case that they would have been defeated but for the intervention of Barry's group who rescued them.

The purpose of the mission had been made clear to all volunteers: the patrol was to be wiped out. In that sense, with only one surviving patrol member, the mission achieved its purpose. How the patrol was wiped out . however, remains uncertain.

Summary

One of the most important considerations in military planning is to ground the plan on the probable or plausible operational circumstances that the force in question would face and that the planner must also be aware of the expected manner of each side's conduct of operations. The operation has to be cautiously planned and must have realistically achievable aims and the necessary resources in place to accomplish the mission. In this regard, Kilmichael displays little preparatory planning; the operation was loaded with risks, any of which could have been fatal to the success of the ambush and indeed the column's very existence. Barry's plan should therefore have sought to manage or minimise those risks.

Consequently, an inherent weakness either in Barry's plan, or to confirm Barry's lack of confidence in the combat capabilities of the column, is that the ADRIC patrol acted as Barry assumed they would. The first lorry was stopped opposite No.1 Section's position while the second lorry was engaged in front of No.2 Section's position. When we consider Barry's exhibited courses of action, rather than them being step-based, where particular events would trigger particular pre-determined reactions, they are more suggestive of a commander improvising with on-the-spot responses. The ADRIC were stopped as Barry hoped they would be and they deployed and fought as expected, but rather than each lorry being engaged and dealt with by the individual sections it would appear from Barry's narrative that his personal intervention at all stages was critical to the success of the mission. Barry should have been aware or at least capable of analysing the combat capability of the column in advance of the operation and therefore have allotted sufficient resources in terms of material and personnel to both No. 1 and No.2 Sections so that they could accomplish their tasks without each being so dependent on his intervention. This should have been the case as the column had the advantage of being able to organise itself before the mission. Superiority, in terms of organisational structure, is determined at the point of contact. The attacker is pre-positioned while the attacked can be disorganised and separated.

On the basis of Barry's depiction of events we are left with considering the Kilmichael ambush as a conjunctive event, defined as a series of stages where the previous stage must be successful for the next one to begin. In simple terms, each phase of the operation is dependent on the one that preceded it, and the probability of accomplishing an overall objective gets smaller with the addition of more objectives.

Developing this concept a stage further, it is possible to assess the mathematical probability of Barry being successful given the conjunctive nature of the linked stages of the operation. An example might be helpful: in a three-stage operation and with an optimistic probability figure of 75% success being allowed for each stage, the overall probability of the entire operation being successful is assessed as .75 X .75 X .75, which becomes a much less convincing 42% probability of success. If we were to allow a much more realistic probability of success for the second stage, the attack on the second lorry by No.2 Section, say of 40%, the overall success probability reduces to 22% (.75 X .40 X .75), in other words a 78% probability of failure. Based on these figures the operation as described by Barry was more likely to fail than succeed. To accomplish the mission, each phase required a competent level of military performance that was beyond the capabilities of the volunteers present that day. (A more exhaustive mathematical analysis of the engagement can be found in Chapter 10)

These figures are compounded when one considers that Barry was faced with making quick decisions in an uncertain and complicated military environment. His decisions were intuitive, instant, and made in the absence of any overall situational awareness. He would have been under intense physical and psychological pressure. The volunteers, despite their motivation and willingness to make the ultimate sacrifice, were still bereft of the essential tools to accomplish the task. Without adequate stocks of ammunition, reliable armaments, training, and preparation, it is wholly unrealistic to expect that they could defeat the ADRIC in the manner as presented by Barry.

A rational conclusion suggests that the killing of the ADRIC members was likely to have been other than through a tactical engagement in the conventional sense.

In support of such a conclusion, one needs to consider the overall expenditure of ammunition. One of the principal indicators of the scale and intensity of a battle is the amount of ammunition expended by the combatants. We are told that each volunteer rifleman had thirty-five rounds of ammunition at the beginning of the engagement.[5] No detail is provided about the amount of ammunition that the IRA used during the action, but given the intensity of the conflict we would expect the IRA to have seriously depleted, if not exhausted, their ammunition supply quickly. The same would be expected of the ADRIC. No figures have been supplied to determine definitively how much ammunition the ADRIC had at their disposal, but based on the uniform scale of issue which would have applied to the ADRIC it is possible to make a reasonable guesstimate, as quartermasters are notoriously tied to standardisation and consistency when it comes to issuing arms and ammunition. In this regard the British Army have traditionally led the way. Also of assistance is that each member of the ADRIC patrol, according to Barry, was armed with a rifle, two revolvers, and "two Mills bombs hung at the waist from their Sam Browne belts."[6]

According to Barry, at the conclusion of the engagement the column had secured eighteen rifles, thirty revolvers and ammunition, Mills bombs, and 1,800 rounds of rifle ammunition.[7] This last figure deserves closer consideration. The figure of 1,800 rounds of rifle ammunition represented 100 rounds of ammunition for each ADRIC member. Based on Ernest McCall's figures of each ADRIC member having forty rounds of ammunition, this would have represented 2.5 times the scale of issue.[8] These figures are difficult to comprehend given the British Army's almost neurotic approach to standardisation, especially as it related to the issue of ammunition. The source that McCall uses for this figure of forty rounds is not apparent from his text.

A stronger argument can be made that each ADRIC member would have been issued with at least fifty rounds of ammunition. This is based on the British Army's *Text Book of Ammunition* which provides that when packing .303-inch Mk VII ammunition, the same ammunition that was used in the engagement, five rounds were placed in a charger and ten chargers were in a bandolier.[9] This is consistent with the bandoliers visible in photographs of ADRIC members at that time. Each bandolier therefore held fifty rounds. It would be unusual to think that ten rounds would have been removed from each bandolier prior to issue. William Sheehan's account of the British 5th Division's operations in Ireland, referring to an ADRIC patrol being ambushed in Longford, states that each ADRIC patrol member had fifty rounds.[10] Therefore if each ADRIC member was wearing a bandolier (50 x 18= 900 rounds) and had a spare belt (another 900 rounds in total) then this would account for the 1,800 rounds that the column subsequently acquired. Accepting those figures, it would therefore appear that the ADRIC members in the course of the exchange, to a man, didn't use their rifles. This is surprising, particularly if we are to accept the intensity of the ambush, its duration, and the nature of the engagement. It would appear, based on Barry's own figures, that there was a collective decision not to use the most powerful weapon at their disposal, their rifles. This is, however, consistent with Barry only ever describing the ADRIC members as engaging the volunteers with revolvers. Even in the course of the alleged false surrender, Barry describes the ADRIC as killing the IRA men with revolver fire.

The fact that none of the ADRIC members, based on the ammunition secured after the event, appeared to have used their rifles is highly unusual. The surprise is even greater given the additional fact that each ADRIC member had at least one grenade in his possession, yet it would appear that none of them used a grenade against the ambushers. They would have been well aware of the utility of a grenade in such close proximity to the enemy. Experience during the Great War would have taught the ADRIC the benefits of the grenade and revolver combined when engaging enemy at short range, but such experience would appear to have escaped all of them at a time when they needed it most.

This focus on ammunition expenditure and weapons secured can re-open another debate with a fresher perspective. That debate relates to the authenticity of the report allegedly prepared by Barry in the immediate aftermath of the engagement. That report, dealt with earlier in the text, details specifically the quantity of arms and ammunition that the IRA captured in the aftermath of the engagement. The haul is described as follows: 14 rifles, 5 bayonets, 17 revolvers, 719 rounds of .303, and 136 rounds of .45. The arms and ammunition recovered would reflect, more realistically, the fact that an engagement had occurred. Given that there were 18 ADRIC personnel involved one might expect that the column would have recovered eighteen rifles, but it would not be unusual for the drivers to be armed only with revolvers. There is also the possibility that the officer in charge of the patrol would only take a revolver. That would account for three rifles. It was dark by the time the engagement was complete so it is possible that a rifle or rifles remained at the scene to be later recovered. It is also possible that Gutherie escaped with his rifle, but what became of that subsequently we may never know. Revolvers were unlikely to be lost as they were attached to the uniform by virtue of a lanyard. The detail in the contested report would appear to be a much more realistic inventory of what the ADRIC were armed with. Rather than two revolvers, it is likely that each member of the patrol had a single revolver. With eighteen members of the patrol and only seventeen revolvers accounted for, the discrepancy is easily explained, since Gutherie, after being captured by the IRA a number of miles from the ambush site, near Inchageela, was shot with his own revolver.

The scale of issue for revolver ammunition was twelve rounds per patrol member. Rounds were carried in pouches containing twelve rounds.[11] As the patrol was on active operational service, it is probable that all members had their revolvers loaded, ready for immediate action. Leaving Gutherie out of the calculations for both revolvers and rifles, the total number of .45 ammunition that Barry could have secured was therefore 17 ADRIC x 12 rounds = 204. The report lists 136 rounds as captured, which implies 68 rounds were expended in the course of the engagement. If 719 rounds of .303 were recovered and allowing Gutherie and the two drivers to be excluded, then 15 ADRIC x 50 rounds = 750 rounds of .303, implying only 31 rounds of .303 were fired by the patrol. Note, however, that Barry states that after the attack on the first truck, his team stopped to replenish their stocks from the dead ADRIC members. This would invariably have been rifle ammunition, and since each magazine carried ten rounds of ammunition it is quite possible that Barry's team accounted for the majority of the 31 rounds of used ADRIC .303 ammunition.

In summary, whatever figures are taken as representing the true account of the ammunition expended, it would appear that the ADRIC members failed to use their rifles, or if they had, and therefore accepting that by replenishment the IRA had reloaded with revolver ammunition as opposed to rifle, then the ADRIC rifle fire was restricted to no more than three or four rounds. This is extraordinary and does not support a view that the engagement was a fire-fight of any protracted duration. It is, however, illustrative of how short the engagement was. Taking revolver and rifle ammunition into account, the ADRIC patrol had (204 (.455) + 750 (.303)) 954 rounds at its disposal. It expended (68(.455) + 31(.303)) 99 rounds or just over 10% of its ammunition and these figures also exclude the IRA replenishing their stocks.

From the moment the ADRIC patrol was ambushed its members were each faced with a limited number of options. Separated in terms of distance and with no form of communication between both vehicles, a combined response was not feasible. The reaction would vary depending on how each individual perceived what an appropriate response should be. The responses to the attack would vary from a determination to counter the threat, as evidenced by the actions of the infantry officers, to seeking to extract themselves as seen in the case of Lieutenant Gutherie, to seeking to surrender because of the hopelessness of the situation they found themselves in; on the balance of probabilities, the last option was most likely the one taken by the majority of the patrol members.

The amount of ammunition expended is a prime indicator of what the majority decided was the best course of action. In light of these figures for ammunition expenditure, it would appear that the engagement was over in minutes. This doesn't mean that all the ADRIC members had been killed. It simply means that the ADRIC weapons were no longer firing. How the ADRIC met their deaths is still uncertain.

CHAPTER 7

Marksmanship, weapons handling, and an experiment

T HE INDIVIDUAL RIFLEMAN, whether IRA volunteer or ADRIC member, was the backbone of both the combatant parties. The importance of each rifleman being able to use his weapon to the best of its abilities was crucial to the outcome. Brigadier General Merritt Edson describes the importance of rifle fire in the following terms:

> *It is rifle fire that ultimately takes ground, and it is rifle fire that holds it after it is taken, by throwing back enemy counter-attack. The man with the rifle is the man who wins wars; and accurate fire from individual riflemen is the most effective factor on any battlefield.*[1]

Given the critical impact that one would expect the standard of rifle marksmanship to have had on the result, it is worth considering the weapons used, the training received, and the marksmanship capabilities of the combatants.

Although we can be certain as to the weapons issued to the ADRIC members, we are less sure as to the quantity and weapons type that the IRA possessed. It would appear that the column was armed with a mixture of rifles, shotguns and revolvers. The shotguns and revolvers can be discarded for ranges beyond thirty yards; therefore, without the ballistic potency/kinetic effect of rifle fire, the IRA could not have in any sense achieved their mission. It is therefore worth considering the weapon in further detail.

It is more than likely that the rifles which the IRA members were using that day were a mix of the Canadian Ross rifle Mk III and the Lee-Enfield Short Pattern–Mark III magazine rifle. I deal in detail with the difficulties associated with the Ross rifle later. The fact that they may have been used would suggest either an ignorance on the part of the IRA about their suitability for the type of engagement envisaged or else rifles were at a premium and the IRA may not have had another option.

The same cannot be said for the Lee-Enfield. This rifle has become associated with the British Army of both world wars and is undoubtedly the most recognizable of the various rifles that were also in use at that time. The Lee-Enfield has also, to some extent, become strongly associated with the Kilmichael ambush due to the fact that the rifles engraved on the monu-

The author taking aim with a Lee-Enfield rifle. Note the bolt drawn to the rear and the finger extended over the trigger guard.

ment are Lee-Enfields. In terms of rifle development, the Short Magazine Lee-Enfield (SMLE) rifle was a great improvement on its predecessors. It had a magazine that held ten rounds and its bolt was designed to accommodate rapid firing. Martin Pegler in his history of the Lee-Enfield rifle describes how a sergeant of the Rifle Brigade fired twenty-five aimed shots in one minute, all of which struck an 8 x 6 inch target at 200 yards.[2] While such a feat of marksmanship was exceptional to that particular firer, the rifle in the right hands had awesome potential. The SMLE's reputation as a combat rifle has been described in the following terms:

> *It served in both world wars. Indeed many British soldiers in 1939-1945 went to great lengths to acquire one instead of its wartime replacement, the Rifle No. 4: there was nothing wrong with the No. 4 but the SMLE was a legend in its own time. Utterly reliable with the smoothest bolt-action ever made, the SMLE was sneered at by the purists for not being a Mauser, but it silenced all its critics in 1914: German units on the receiving end thought they were under machine gun fire.[3]*

Any of the ADRIC members carrying a rifle had the SMLE. It is far from certain that this was the case with the IRA. Accepting, however, that each side had access to such weapons, the most compelling consideration that would suggest an outcome different from that portrayed by Barry is the difference in weapons training and marksmanship possessed by both com-

CHAPTER 8

Injuries, physical and psychological

I N THIS CHAPTER we will consider the nature of the injuries inflicted by both sides. In the case of the ADRIC members, we have the benefit of the record produced by the Court of Inquiry which is reproduced in full in Appendix I. There is also detailed but lesser known information available in relation to the IRA casualties, which will allow us to gain a fuller understanding of the action.

The physical injuries are well documented, but much less considered has been the psychological trauma that would leave its own scars. There is now a much greater awareness of the causes and effect of traumatic stress injuries which generally present themselves in the aftermath of violent actions – thus the title, Post Traumatic Stress Disorder (PTSD). We are therefore in a better position to understand the potential psychological impact of the engagement on the participants.

The physical Injuries

The method and means by which the ADRIC members were killed has been the subject of considerable comment, and there is little doubt that the nature of the wounds inflicted, as described in the course of the Court of Inquiry, would have been used by British propaganda elements to create an impression of savagery and ruthlessness on the part of the IRA. Terms such as "hacked" and "mutilated" are commonly encountered in the literature, as too is the use of axes, to suggest that excessive, unacceptable, and cruel methods had been employed to dispatch the ADRIC members. This would have suited the British propaganda purposes at the time and would have accorded with a policy of describing the IRA as a "murder gang." In order to test the veracity of what the British propaganda machine was alleging, the details of the injuries inflicted require a re-examination. The examination of the dead ADRIC members was performed by Dr Jeremiah Kelleher, a medical practitioner based in Macroom where "C" Company had been stationed. It is worth nothing that Dr Kelleher doesn't refer to having conducted an "autopsy" but rather a "superficial examination." This would suggest that the nature of the wounds were not examined in any great depth, and conclusions may therefore have been reached based on the appearance of the wound rather than probing the extent of the injury. Before discussing

MURDERED CADETS.

MUTILATION WITH AXES.

MINISTERS' DEFEAT IN THE LORDS.

The bodies of the 16 murdered cadets of the R.I.C. Auxiliary Division will be brought to Pembroke Dock from Ireland to-day on board a destroyer. In each case there will be a military funeral.

The Government were defeated in the House of Lords last evening on the Home Rule Bill. An amendment to set up a Second Chamber in the proposed Parliament for Southern Ireland, though resisted by the Lord Chancellor, was carried by a 3 to 1 majority.

The bodies of the 16 members of the Auxiliary of the R.I.C., who were ambushed and killed at Kilmichael on Sunday have been lying since Monday at Castle Macroom, the headquarters of the company to which they belonged. To-day they will be removed to Cork, where a funeral procession will take place. The General Officer Commanding the troops in the Cork area has asked that all shops and other business premises in the city shall be closed from 11 a.m. to 2 p.m., as a mark of respect for the dead.

This afternoon the bodies will be placed on board a destroyer and brought to Pembroke Dock, where they will arrive at about 9 o'clock this evening. A guard of honour of 16 members of the R.I.C. Auxiliary will sail in the destroyer. The relatives of the dead officers and cadets have been communicated with by the authorities, and it has been arranged that in each case a military funeral will be held. According to present arrangements, the coffins will pass into the control of the relatives at Pembroke. One member of the guard of honour will attend each funeral. The coffins will be removed direct from Pembroke to the places of burial. Three only of these are in London or its vicinity. The funeral of Major F. Hugo, O.B.E., M.C. (late Indian Army), will take place at Southgate; that of Cadet W. T. Barnes, D.F.C. (late R.A.F.), at Sutton; and that of Temporary Constable A. F. Poole (late Royal West Kent Regiment), at King's Cross.

Lord French has sent the following telegram to General Tudor, who is in charge of the R.I.C.:—

Please convey to all ranks of your men my deepest sympathy with them in the loss of so many gallant comrades, who were all personally distinguished on many battlefields. I cannot express my sorrow that such fine careers should be ended at the hands of despicable murderers of the lowest type.—FRENCH, Viceroy.

The following account of the ambush, prepared by a senior officer of police in the Cork neighbourhood from the evidence available, was issued yesterday:—

District Inspector Crake took out a patrol in the ordinary course of duty. They were going in search of a man wanted in the Dunmanway direction, and

had been previously working in cooperation with the Essex Regiment at Dunmanway. When dusk was falling, at about 5 p.m., the patrol was proceeding along the Macroom-Dunmanway road and reached a point where the road curves. Low stone walls flank the road and there are narrow strips of tussocky bogland, rising to boulder-covered slopes of high ground on either side.

It is surmised from an examination of the site and from inquiries that the attackers, who were all clad in khaki and trench coats, and wore steel helmets, had drawn their motor lorry across the road and were mistaken by the first car of cadets for military. The first car halted, and the cadets, unsuspecting, got out and approached the motor lorry. The second car, which had been travelling 100 yards behind, now came up. Something aroused the suspicion of the cadets who had got out of the first car. Shooting began, and three were killed instantaneously. Others began to run back to the first car. The cadets in the second car ran along the road to the help of their comrades. Then from a depression in the hillside behind the second car came a devastating fire at close range. The cadets were shot down by concealed men from the walls, and all around a direct fire from the ambushers' lorry also swept down the road. After firing had continued for some time, and many men were wounded, overwhelming forces of the ambushers came out and forcibly disarmed the survivors.

There followed a brutal massacre, the policy of the murder gang being apparently to allow no survivor to disclose their methods. The dead and wounded were hacked about the head with axes, shot guns were fired into their bodies, and they were savagely mutilated. The one survivor, who was wounded, was hit about the head and left for dead. He had also two bullet wounds. The bodies were rifled, and even the clothes taken. The ambushing party departed in lorries. Terrible treachery on the part of local inhabitants is indicated by the fact that, although many people attending Mass on Sunday morning were diverted from their route by the murder gang, no word was sent to the police, and the ambush sat there until dusk.

From *The Times*: it suited British propaganda purposes to promote the idea of 'savagery' on the part of the IRA volunteers.

the content of those examinations, it should be noted that questions have been raised over the integrity of his findings. There are suggestions that Dr Kelleher may have had difficulty in maintaining the required level of professional objectivity. A.J. Byrne describes Dr Kelleher as being a leading loyalist in the town, and a presumption of his anti-republican feelings is reinforced by the fact that his son, an RIC constable, had been killed a number of months earlier by the IRA in Cavan. If there was a question mark over his political leanings, then the same could possibly be said about his competency to examine and explain the nature of the wounds he was asked to report on. It is not certain what level of training or exposure Dr Kelleher, a country town general practitioner, had to investigating fatalities as a result of military gunfire. None is presumed.

But was there a basis by which such wounds could have been categorised by Dr Kelleher, correctly or incorrectly? An important distinction should be drawn between what the injuries appeared as and what could have caused them to present as they did. To be aware of such a distinction would assist in addressing the misunderstandings that exist about the nature of injuries and how those injuries may have been inflicted. In the case of Dr Kelleher's testimony, the nature and cause of some of the injuries can be explained by an understanding of the ballistic action and effect of both the .303 and .455 ammunition types that were used.

The Court of Inquiry report reproduced in Appendix I deals in much greater detail with the injuries received by each casualty. For the purposes of our examination, rather than dealing with each ADRIC member individually we will consider the general nature of wounds that can be caused by high and low-velocity weapons. Such a study is commonly referred to as the study of wound ballistics.

Dr Kelleher refers to wounds being caused by an "explosive bullet." A definitive view as to what would account for such injuries necessitates an understanding of wound ballistics, which at that time was in its infancy as a forensic science. On the basis that he may only have possessed a basic appreciation of such injuries, his description of the wounds being caused by an explosive bullet may have been a prescient observation on his part. The effects of bullet strikes on living flesh had been studied by the military ever since wounds caused by rifled firearms became noticeable for their "explosive effect."[1] In-depth investigation of such effects was cumbersome and difficult. Even small arms "low-velocity" events happen quite quickly, and an understanding of the performance of a bullet has traditionally been restricted by the non-availability of measuring equipment capable of capturing images at high speeds. Modern technological developments, having now addressed the research obstacles, have allowed the effect of a bullet travelling through the human body to be studied and understood in much greater detail. Such studies of wound ballistics are a relatively recent development, greatly assisted by the availability of instrumentation such as ultra-high speed photography, sometimes referred to as "microflash photography", and lasers and computer modelling. It is now possible to study the action of a bullet as it passes through a medium replicating the human body. The medium most often used for such studies is gelatine.

The wounds which a bullet will cause are heavily influenced by the velocity at which it is travelling and the constituent of the bullet itself. The velocity of the bullet creates energy which, on entering the body, creates a stress wave. For low-velocity, or subsonic bullets, the stress wave is, in relative terms, small and generally results in the wave effect not disturbing areas other than those in the immediate vicinity of the path of the bullet.

For high-velocity bullets, the effects are much more pronounced and extensive. The higher velocity creates a compression wave which moves much further away from the path of the round. As the bullet continues on its path it creates a temporary cavity. It is this cavity, referred to as cavitation, which contributes to the severe wounding that is often associated with high-velocity injuries. The injuries can be extensive, often occurring at areas beyond the immediate path of the projectile. Farrar and Leeming, ballistic scientists at the Royal Military College of Science at Shrivenham in the UK, describe the effect of such cavitation as follows:

Cavitation takes place mainly after the passage of the missile, and accounts for the explosive nature of high velocity missile wounds. The greater the energy that is imparted to the tissues, the greater is the size of the temporary cavity and the more extensive the damage.[2]

Robert Rinker succinctly explains the effect of such a high-velocity impact in the following terms:

The faster the bullet, the stronger the waves propagated through the body. The wound, then, is not a mere puncture but an explosive release of the wave before the bullet has reached the surface... The higher the velocity the more explosive the effect.[3]

Extending this knowledge to his examination, Dr Kelleher when referring to wounds that he attributed to "explosive bullets" was describing the wounds in terms of what was visible to him and such observations we now know are consistent with high-velocity injuries received from rifle fire. This is not to suggest that there was some ulterior motive to how Dr Kelleher described the injuries. He was not alone in falsely attributing such injuries to the use of explosive bullets. The lack of understanding, even on the part of military doctors, about the explosive nature of a high-velocity wound is evident in the following description from a British soldier who suffered such a wound in the Battle of Elanslaagte during the Boer War:

> *The doctors all said at first that I had been hit by a shell, but that is impossible, for the enemy only had two guns, and we had taken both of them when I was hit. The doctors now say that it must have been a very heavy explosive bullet…it has made a very big jagged hole in my shoulder which you could put your hand into.*[4]

While there was explosive ammunition available for the Lee-Enfield it is highly unlikely that it was used here as such ammunition was in its infancy and was being developed as an experimental round. The only other plausible explanation for the reference to "explosive bullets" could have been the presence of either incendiary or tracer rounds, but they would not have exploded in the body.

Dr Kelleher detailed the number of rounds that each ADRIC fatality suffered. Note that some of the fatalities were reported as having received only one bullet impact while others had considerably more. This is dependent on whether the impacts were received as a result of rifle or revolver fire. For example, a high-velocity strike to the head from a rifle round is invariably fatal as the brain is primarily water-like and violently expands in all directions in the micro seconds that the high velocity bullet moves through it. Head shots are quickly fatal as they interrupt essential bodily functions such as respiration and circulation.

The effects of lower velocity shots, such as those from the Webley revolver, are dependent on penetration. The deeper it penetrates, the more likely that it will hit a vital area. If it fails to hit a vital area, then the body has the opportunity to recover quickly and it may take a number of subsequent hits to ultimately kill the intended target. Evidence to this effect is widely available in the generally accessible ballistics texts. Accounts of police officers in the US having to shoot adrenalin-fuelled or drug-influenced criminals up to six times with .357 magnum ammunition (very powerful) are legion and offer a plausible explanation as to why some of the ADRIC members were displaying multiple gun-shot impacts. It may well have been the case that a number of shots were required to kill those who put up a struggle.

Further explanations as to the nature of the wounds, described as "lacerated wounds", or evidence to counter a suggestion that an injury was inflicted by an axe can be provided by a number of sources. Firstly, we are aware that bayonets were in the possession of the IRA and that would account for some "bayonet-like" wounds. Secondly, we should be aware that the wound caused by a low-velocity round, due to the nature of its limited expansion, can resemble a knife wound. The lower velocity bullet, as a result of its lower energy when travelling through the body, will only slightly widen its path, broadening it to resemble a wound more characteristic of a knife than a bullet strike.

The final explanation for what might appear to be a lacerating wound is provided by the action of a high-velocity round which, when travelling through the body at an oblique angle, produces an injury that can be mistaken for a laceration. Farrar and Leeming believe that "if the bullet enters, or more commonly leaves the skin sideways-on to some degree, *then the hole in the skin will be large and ragged*, but the internal damage may be no more [emphasis added]." This then offers a credible explanation for a wound appearing like a laceration or mutilation.

There is some discussion evident as to the use of "expanding" or "dum-dum" bullets, as they are more commonly referred to.[5] I don't intend to deal with them in much detail as there may have been dum-dums used at Kilmichael. It is impossible to declare their non-use or rule out their presence. A dum-dum is easily made by simply cutting the point off the standard .303 round. On impact, the front of the bullet crushes and splits back with the lead of the bullet peeling back further and expanding. Expanding bullets, even though their use had been banned under Declaration III of The Hague Convention of 1899[6], were still commonly used during the First World War because the ordinary rifleman was able to make the necessary cuts to the bullet. It is not beyond the bounds of possibility that they may have been used. It is therefore understandable that troops who didn't understand the nature or characteristics of the injuries may well conclude that such injuries could only have been caused by dum-dums or even to attribute them to ammunition types that weren't even in existence. Martin Pegler in his Lee-Enfield rifle study reveals the general lack of awareness of the effect of high-velocity ammunition:

A number of myths about modern high-velocity ammunition arose among the troops occupying the trenches…The Germans were accused of using dum-dum ammunition-bullets that had their noses filed down or snipped off to deliver more serious wounds (named after the Dum Dum arsenal in

India). Yet the men often simply failed to understand the terrible effects of close-range bullet strikes on the human body- and most trench shooting was characterized by its closeness, sometimes no more than 50 yd.[7]

While this lack of understanding may have applied to the British soldiers, the same cannot be said of the German troops that opposed them. Ernst Junger, a German soldier who fought throughout the war and authored the acclaimed *Storm of Steel*, makes the following observation about wounds they had inflicted after his unit engaged Indian troops with rifle fire from the Siegfried line in 1917:

*They were delicate and in a bad way. At such short range, an infantry bullet has an **explosive effect**. Some of them had been hit a second time as they lay there, and in such a way that the bullets had passed longitudinally, down the length of their bodies [emphasis added].[8]*

What is more significant and more plausible to counter suggestions of the presence of dum-dums or explosive bullets is an ammunition defect that was associated with the .303 round that was then in service. The .303 round that concerns us at Kilmichael was the "Mk VII Ball." The Mk VII is described as follows:

*Bullets for the Mk VII cartridge had an aluminium-or fibre-filled tip, with a base of conventional lead alloy. This made the bullet longer than normal for its weight. It also produced a stable projectile in flight that would tumble easily on contact, **thus increasing wounding potential** [emphasis added].[9]*

Such a design characteristic would account for the explosive-like injuries that Dr Kelleher's examination refers to. Farrar and Leeming refer to the design as having another unintended consequence in that the round tended to break up on contact:

The British .303 inch Ball Mark 7 created an unintentionally severe wound. In the design the nose filling consisted of a metal plug. The nose tended to break off and could cause in a wound, break-up of the bullet with consequent serious wounding effects. The intention behind this design however had simply been to improve the external ballistics of the bullet by placing the centre of gravity as far back as possible.[10]

The .303 inch Ball Mark 7 round, that Farrar and Leeming refer to, was the standard round issued to British forces between 1911 and 1939 and was therefore in wide circulation at that time as the standard issue British cartridge. Once again without realising the ballistic nature of the cause, the Germans were aware of the wounding effect of this ammunition and explained it in the following terms:

> *On 07 April, on the right flank, Fusilier Kramer, received head wounds from some bullet fragments. This type of wounding was very common, because the English munitions were so soft as to fragment on contact.*[11]

Based on these insights, it is not improbable that Dr Kelleher was observing the "explosive" nature of the wounds that such ammunition we now know capable of producing.

Because of the nature of the ammunition and weaponry available to the IRA, it is clear that the only explosive munition employed in the course of the ambush was the grenade used by Barry against the occupants of the first lorry. It is reasonable to presume that there were no explosive ammunition types available for the Lee-Enfield of Ross rifles or for the Webley revolver in West Cork at that time. Consequently, when Kelleher refers to "explosive bullet wounds" he is referring to the "explosive" feature of the wound rather than the nature of the ammunition type.

The wounds to the axilla areas are difficult to account for in terms of a wound likely to have been acquired in the "normal" course of a firefight. This difficulty is compounded when one considers that in the course of Dr Kelleher's examination, four ADRIC members' bodies displayed this unusual wound. In the course of considering this particular injury I came across only one description that was vaguely similar. Major General Julian C. Smith describes the injuries that Japanese troops inflicted on US Marines engaged in clearing Tarawa Atoll during the Second World War as follows:

> *The Japs all withdrew to the northern end of the atoll and made a final stand. The ranges in the last steps of the attack were very short and the Japs, who were among the best trained Japanese troops, were unexpectedly good shots. Quite a number of our men were shot through the head when they lifted their heads looking for the enemy. Also an amazingly large number were shot through the right arm or shoulder while in the act of throwing grenades.*[12]

We have established that the level of advanced marksmanship required to administer such a precise, almost surgical, impact could not have been present among the attacking volunteer body. This leaves us with few realistic alternatives to explain how such an unusual wound was inflicted and also to explain how four members suffered the same type of wound. There is a plausible explanation which could credibly account for this – the shot impacted the area of the armpit from the side at very close range while the victims' arms were in the air, thus exposing the area. In all probability the ADRIC who suffered that wound were shot while their arms were in the air, most likely having surrendered.

With regards to the blunt trauma injuries, an instrument such as the butt of a rifle would account for these, and this is supported by testimony which describes John Lordon as administering such a blow to one of the ADRIC, most likely Pallister, who would have been in close proximity to him.

The injuries as described by Dr Kelleher suggest that the ADRIC were killed by a variety of means including grenade, rifles, revolvers, shotguns, and bayonets. A persuasive case can be made that the ADRIC members were killed at very close range, as this would explain the multiple bullet strikes which are likely to have been revolver shots.

The lacerating wounds and the "axe wound" can be explained by the ammunition effects that have just been detailed. It is unlikely that the bodies were mutilated as there is insufficient evidence to support that claim, and the injuries are also capable of being accounted for by the effect of the ammunition. The effect, however, would only present if the shot entered the body longitudinally or "sideways-on", which leaves a possibility that the bodies were also shot once they were in the lying position.

In the case of the IRA casualties there is a strong suggestion that volunteer Jim O'Sullivan died as a result of the blow-back from the Ross rifle bolt, causing him a catastrophic head injury. O'Sullivan is likely to have fired only one round from his rifle. This has been dealt with earlier in the text.

Michael McCarthy is described in *Guerilla Days* as having been killed during the ambush, but a more recent paper from the Kilmichael Historical Society suggests that he was still alive at the end of the engagement and only died in the course of being evacuated to a house owned by the Buttimer family in Gortroe. Pat Deasy is described as dying at 10pm "on a mattress in front of the fire at Buttimer's kitchen."[13] There is little further information available as to the nature of their wounds or the calibre of the ammunition that killed them. All three were buried temporarily in Gortroe bog as it was feared the authorities would be looking for signs of a burial in the local graveyards, with a subsequent round-up of suspects. They were finally laid to rest on the Thursday night in Castletown-Kinneigh, four days after the ambush.

The psychological injuries

Much has been written about the reactions of military units when encountering hostile fire for the first occasion, and many fine narratives exist depicting the individual reactions of soldiers when exposed to hostile fire for the first time. These narratives in general concern the reaction of trained personnel. In that regard, Kilmichael is somewhat different as the same reactions would not be expected from trained and untrained personnel. The difference between the two opposing forces, as already highlighted, was not limited to training but also to operational experience. Other than a few exceptions, the IRA were generally novices, with little training and a modicum of previous combat experience.

Although there are a number of uncertainties about the events as they transpired in the course of the ambush, there are certainties that we can rely upon in assisting our understanding of the engagement. What is certain is the mixture of reactions that would have been shown by the volunteers to coming under fire and witnessing what subsequently occurred. Battlefield behaviour is predictable and has been studied to the extent that such behaviour can be retrofitted to the action at Kilmichael and help to give an insight into how the volunteers may have reacted on an individual basis.

Von Clausewitz recognised the extensive effect that the elements of warfare will have upon troops and the almost paralysing effect it can have on those exposed to it for the first time:

> *Indeed he must be a very extraordinary man who, under these impressions [battlefield experiences] for the first time, does not lose the power of making any instantaneous decisions . . . an ordinary character never attains to complete coolness . . .and so we perceive that here again ordinary qualities will not suffice...*[14] *[Author's insert]*

The majority of volunteers were under "these impressions for the first time", with most military experience restricted to attendance at a training camp and being, as acknowledged in Barry's words, "mostly quite untrained." While Barry pays tribute to their subsequent performance he does allude to the fact that there were exceptions.[15] Barry doesn't develop this point any further, but the impact of what the volunteers were to experience for the first time becomes apparent in the immediate aftermath of the engagement.

The potential psychological injuries of what the combatants, both IRA and ADRIC, were exposed to have been described by a variety of terms such as "shell shock", "battle stress", or "combat fatigue." In modern parlance, and referred to earlier, it is now more commonly referred to as "Post-Traumatic

Stress Disorder" and better known by the acronym PTSD. One of the earliest clinical descriptions of "shell shock" was provided by Dr Aldren Turner who had been engaged by the War Office to investigate this phenomenon, which was referred to by the British Army as "a new disorder." Turner described shell shock as,

> . . . a form or temporary "nervous breakdown" scarcely justifying the name of neurasthenia, which would seem to be characteristic of the present war . . . ascribed to a sudden or alarming psychical cause such as witnessing a ghastly sight or a harassing experience . . . the patient becomes "nervy", unduly emotional and shaky. . .[16]

This early attempt at providing a definition has been reviewed and changed as observations and awareness in combat psychiatry improved in subsequent conflicts. A report associated with the Walter Reed Army Institute of Research in Washington DC, based on the Israeli experience of dealing with psychiatric casualties in combat, provides an insight into how this field of neuropsychiatry has developed. The report details how the Israeli Defence Forces (IDF), based on their experiences in the Arab Israeli war of 1973 and their subsequent engagement in Lebanon in 1982, have introduced a distinction between "battle shock" (more commonly referred to in the IDF as "combat reaction") and "battle fatigue":

> Battle shock, defined as a simple emotional reaction to the stress of battle, developed after hours or days of intense combat. In contrast, battle fatigue developed after weeks or months of combat.[17]

For our analysis we will confine ourselves to considering the potential impact of battle shock on the combatants. Using the Israeli description, in particular the fact that the condition would seem to develop "after hours or days of intense combat", would suggest that the engagement at Kilmichael didn't last long enough for battle shock to have an impact on the combatants during the engagement. Said differently, battle shock, using the Israeli definition, would appear to manifest itself after a number of hours, by which time the engagement had finished.

Bearing in mind, however, that as the volunteers were exposed to such violence for the very first time with no battle inoculation and the Israeli experience was based on the recorded instances with trained personnel, then it is possible that some of the volunteers experienced battle shock within the time-frame of the engagement. What are useful, therefore, are additional insights provided by Soviet military psychiatry expertise which recognises the immediate impact of shock, ferocity, and surprise on combatants' effectiveness. A soldier who was too frightened to move or suffered tremors and consequently had difficulty in processing information, or was reluctant to fire his weapon, was simply reacting to normal battlefield conditions:

> *Soviet soldiers who exhibited certain battle shock symptoms were regarded as making a very functional adjustment to their environment. Soldiers who wished to escape the horrors of the battlefield were regarded as essentially normal and sane people who were prepared to go to great lengths to escape their environment.*[18]

Recognising that such reactions are normal allows us to consider the probability of the combatants being susceptible to and possibly displaying battle shock symptoms as very real.

The engagement was short, lasting for less than an hour, and brutal in the extreme when measured against the standards of that time. Accepting that the majority of volunteers had no previous battle experience, it is possible to envisage what their reaction to the action may have been. The best depiction is provided by Barry who writes, " . . . some showed the strain of the ordeal through which they had passed, and a few appeared on the point of collapse because of shock."[19] This was a discerning observation on Barry's part. He appears to have recognised the battle shock symptoms as being more widely present throughout the column rather than in isolated cases.

Barry's observation that members of the column were suffering from battle shock is also supported by testimony from an IRA officer at that time who described the impact the Kilmichael ambush had on the members from the Dunmanway battalion as follows:

> *The 3rd Dunmanway Battalion had been falling away rather badly since the Kilmichael ambush. A number of men out of the battalion had fought at Kilmichael, but the strain had affected their nerves to such an extent that a number of battalion officers were practically useless from that time on, and no resistance was being shown to the enemy.*[20]

Although Barry does not mention any injury to himself in the course of the engagement, interestingly he refers subsequently to having experienced a sharp pain in his chest during his attack on the patrol, possibly reflecting the immense physical and mental pressure he must have been under:

During the action on the previous Sunday at Kilmichael, so sharp was the sudden spasm of pain that struck me, I thought I had been wounded in the chest. Several similar, but lesser pains had occurred afterwards, but did not appear serious.[21]

Further evidence of the psychological impact of the operation on the members of the column is vividly captured in Barry's testimony when he describes having to recover his own unit by conducting an arms drill among the corpses and debris. This was more a preventative rather than restorative measure. Barry could not risk a further deterioration among his men. It is obvious that the column would not have been in a position to counter a further attack and it also suggests that the defeat of the ADRIC patrol had more or less exhausted the column's combat capacity.

One of the natural reactions to dealing with the aftermath of a traumatic event of this magnitude is not to talk about it, or even to try to forget it ever happened. Such a response is plainly evident in the testimonies provided by two volunteers present that day. What is noticeable about the accounts of their parts in the ambush is the brevity of their responses to fairly open-ended questions. When their testimonies are read in full it is obvious that they had no compunction about providing details of other engagements – but not Kilmichael. The relevant sections are reproduced here:

The statement of Volunteer John Roche:[22]

Question: Tell us about Kilmichael- the first attack on Kilmichael?
Answer: Tom Barry was in charge and put us into position in the morning. Two lorries came about mid-day. Our column was about 35 strong. The fight lasted for something over an hour.
Question: All Auxiliaries?
Answer: Yes
Question: Did you wait for them at the Police Barracks?
Answer: No- an ambush on a country road.

The statement of Volunteer Jerome O'Hea:[23]

Nov 1920. Joined Cork No. III Brigade column. Engaged with column in ambush of Tans at Kilmichael.
Question: Ambush at Kilmichael?
Answer: I was there.
Question: What had you?

Answer: *I had a rifle.*

The question remains as to when those volunteers began to display the effects that the trauma of the conflict was having on them. The anecdotal accounts, whilst supporting a view that battle shock was present in the column, do not reveal the moments within the lifetime of the action that the affected volunteers psychologically collapsed. This is an important omission as we are left with considering whether the shock was a response to the general turmoil of a combat situation or whether the column members experienced an event of such concentrated violence that they were quite literally stunned into a state of ineffectiveness?

The final casualty of the Kilmichael ambush was possibly the ADRIC "C" Company commander, Lieutenant Colonel Buxton Smith, who is reported as taking the unusual step of relinquishing his command by reverting to T/Cadet[24] before finally resigning from the ADRIC, becoming destitute and committing suicide on Wandsworth Common in 1922.

CHAPTER 9

What one map reveals, and the laws of war

N O GRANITE MEMORIAL exists to commemorate the ADRIC, but that's not to say that they don't continue to be remembered. In fact, a memorial of sorts exists and can be seen in Barrett's Bar, the only public house in the village of Coppeen, just a few miles east of Kilmichael. This memorial is in the shape of a map detailing the location of the ADRIC dead and wasn't commissioned by a committee or commemorative society but was created by an engineer ADRIC officer who was instructed in the immediate aftermath to record the site of the engagement. A replica of the original, it was given in the 1950s by the Grainger family to A.J.S. Brady, author of *The Briar of Life*, a memoir of life in early 20th century West Cork. T.P Grainger had been the solicitor for the only ADRIC survivor, Temp Cadet Forde, and had secured his client £10,000 as compensation, taking a sum of £100 as legal fees, which appears to have caused Forde some distress. The map is a remarkable depiction of the aftermath of the action and, similar to a painting, introduces a visual language, whispering from graves. The map depicts another version of events, a version that begs to be interpreted and debated.

The map was prepared the day after the ambush by a Lieutenant Fleming of "C" Company, ADRIC. As in any battlefield, the bodies of the fallen ADRIC lay where they met their deaths. Fleming's task was to reflect the scene as accurately as possible, noting the identity and location of each body. The map is a sketch, and while some topographical features are lacking in both scale and detail, the depictions of the main action areas are quite accurate. A point to note is that Fleming dated the map as 25 January 1921. We can presume, therefore, that this map is based on rough sketches prepared in the immediate aftermath of the ambush while bodies were being recovered, with the finished product being completed later.

The map, in this writer's opinion, would have been prepared for three main reasons. The first would have been to establish what had happened and to assist any efforts to secure a conviction against the perpetrators. Secondly, the deaths would require investigation by a military court of inquiry, which would rely on the map as an exhibit to inform an understanding as to what may have transpired. Thirdly, it would be required to ensure that dependants would qualify for any "death-in-service" benefits such as pensions. The

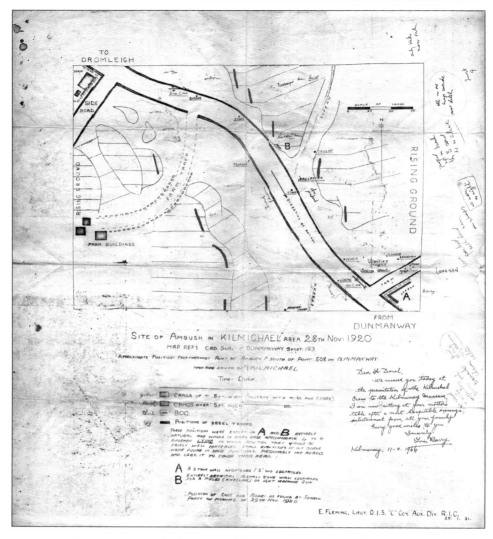

A copy of the map drawn by Lieutenant Fleming in the immediate aftermath of the ambush, with an annotation by Tom Barry in the lower right corner. On the opposite page is a schematic presentation of the map.

only surviving ADRIC member, Forde, probably relied on the map in his compensation claim, and thus its presence in the files of the Grainger firm of solicitors, to be "discovered" in the 1950s.

There are many aspects to the map which assist in our analysis. One of the more important is that it reflects the IRA positions as determined by the location of spent casings and cartridges. The areas where the ambush party lay in wait would have also portrayed a number of tell-tale signs such

raises the question as to whether the column, if its members had killed the ADRIC as accused, had engaged in war crimes.

The laws of war

It remains to be considered whether the actions at the Kilmichael ambush were subject to the laws of war. Legislating for irregular warfare has always proved problematic and even in the 21st century it still presents challenges. The difficulties arise from the fact that the law of armed conflict was drafted with symmetrical interstate conflicts in mind.[3] The War of Independence was an asymmetrical conflict in which state actors, in the shape of the British security forces, fought non-state actors in the guise of rebels or insurgents.

In this section we will consider a brief historical overview of the development of the laws of war, which will be followed by a consideration of the legal status of the conflict, the "asymmetrical" volunteers of the column engaged in the conflict, and whether they could be categorised as lawful or unlawful belligerents. In the event that the ADRIC had surrendered, what protections should they have been afforded? The examination will then consider if the column's conduct accorded with the requirements as set out in the legal provisions applicable at that time.

Historical development

The Geneva Convention of 1906 and The Hague Convention of 1907 had set rules and standards for particular aspects of war on land and at sea. Born out of the experience of a Genevan businessman, Jean-Henri Dunant, who had witnessed the paucity of treatment afforded to the wounded after the Battle of Solferino in 1859, the first Geneva Convention was an attempt to legalise or order the treatment that should be given to wounded combatants. Of particular significance to this study are those rules pertaining to the treatment of the sick and the wounded.

Defining the irregular fighter

One of the first practical attempts at regulating irregular warfare is evident during the American Civil War. The actions of Confederate irregular fighters and the appropriate military response to their actions was a difficulty faced by commanders of the Union armies. The Union military was unsure as to how these irregular forces should be categorised. In order to introduce a measure of legal certainty, a lawyer, Francis Lieber, was retained by the Union to settle the question. His opinion, more commonly known as "The

Lieber Code" and published as *Guerilla Parties, considered with reference to the Laws and Usages of War,* set out to introduce a level of clarity that was missing at that time. Lieber commenced his opinion by setting out a definition for what was understood to constitute a *guerilla party*:

> *It is universally understood in this country at the present time that a guerilla party means an irregular band of armed men, carrying on an irregular war, not being able, according to their character as a guerilla party, to carry on what the law terms a regular war.*[4]

Lieber further suggests that guerillas were connected,

> *. . . with the idea of necessitated murder, because guerilla bands cannot encumber themselves with prisoners of war; they have, therefore, frequently, perhaps generally, killed their prisoners.*

Lieber in his description of what constitutes a guerilla force still suggests that to avail of the protections of the laws of war, the guerilla force would have to be an adjunct to the main army engaged in the conflict. He further expands on this point by declaring:

> *The law of war, however would not extend . . . to small bodies of armed country people, near the lines, whose very smallness shows that they must resort to occasional fighting and the occasional assuming of peaceful habits…*

The struggle for independence, a war or insurrection?

Field Marshal Bernard Montgomery, who had served an earlier part of his military career in Cork, described the War of Independence in the following terms:

> *I was sent as Brigade Major to the 17th Infantry Brigade in Cork and went straight into another war- the struggle against Sinn Fein in Southern Ireland. In many ways this war was far worse than the Great War which had ended in 1918. It developed into a murder campaign in which, in the end, the soldiers became very skilful and more than held their own. But such a war is thoroughly bad for officers and men; it tends to lower their standards of decency and chivalry, and I was glad when it was over.*[5]

Montgomery described the conflict as a war but equally he referred to the existence of a "murder campaign." That such confusion existed is not surprising because of the nature of the engagements which varied from general disobedience and obstruction to small-unit tactical actions against Crown forces. The British Army was aware of this potential for confusion and its *Manual of Military Law* devotes a chapter to the "Law of Riot and Insurrection." Under British military law an insurrection was distinguished from a riot as follows:

> *An insurrection differs from a riot in this-that a riot has in view some enterprise of a private nature, while an insurrection savours of high treason and contemplates some enterprise of a general and public nature. An insurrection, in short, involves an intention to "levy war against the King" as it is technically called; or otherwise to act in general defiance of the government of the country.*[6]

The IRA's acts of violence were associated with a political purpose and therefore aligned readily with what could be considered a rebellion or insurrection. The consequences of being tried and found guilty of participation in an insurrection were ominous, as "a participator in an insurrection may be held guilty of treason and capitally punished."[7] The attitude of the Crown is most obvious the following open letter to the IRA:

TO MEMBERS OF THE IRA

Read this and if you still decide to be led astray by your leaders in the belief that you are "soldiers", and entitled to be treated as soldiers, you will have only yourselves to blame. Only armed forces who fulfil certain conditions can avail themselves of the rights conferred by the Laws and customs of war. These conditions are;-

1. *They must be commanded by a person responsible for his subordinates.*
2. *They must wear affixed distinctive sign or uniform RECOGNISABLE FROM A DISTANCE.*
3. *They must carry arms OPENLY.*
4. *They must conduct their operations in accordance with the customs of war.*

These laws and customs of war were not drawn up by England for the purpose of fighting the IRA. They were drawn up by all the great nations including America, in order that the war between white men should be carried out in a sportsmanlike manner, and not like fights between savage tribes. Your leaders tell you that you are "soldiers" belonging to an army. They tell you that you cannot wear uniform and come out into the open and fight, because the English are too strong for you, but yet they tell you that if you are captured you are entitled to be treated as "prisoners of war" under the Laws of war. Your leaders are only lying to you for their own ends. They rarely get captured. They know a man dressed in civilian clothes who tries to kill other persons whether soldiers, police or civilians, is nothing more than a common murderer.

There are among you men who fought in the late war. Ask them what would have happened to men dressed in civilian clothes who suddenly shot, or threw bombs at soldiers in one of the villages behind the lines. They will tell you that such persons would have been shot immediately on capture, and all civilised nations would have approved.

Your leaders are encouraging you to do that for which any civilised nation would execute you. Do not be deceived. If you go on murdering disguised as civilians you will in the end pay the penalty either fighting or on the scaffold. Make your leaders tell you the truth, and then make up your minds but with your eyes open.[8]

What was it that led to the development of this "murder campaign"? Was it the inequalities in arms, material, personnel, and general resources between the Crown forces and the IRA, an inequality that was so characteristic of the War of Independence? The conflict in West Cork was no exception to such inequalities. Given such an imbalance or asymmetry in military capacity, the IRA was never going to find itself in the position of achieving a complete military victory over the combined military and para-military resources that were arrayed against it. Given the scale of what was being contemplated at Kilmichael, allied with not being in a position to avail of the status of a prisoner of war, left the IRA volunteers in a particularly vulnerable situation. They faced death either as a result of the actions of the ADRIC or a court martial.

Would it be realistic, given those circumstances, to expect the IRA to conduct its activities in accordance with the customs of war applicable at the time? Robin Geib suggests that "military imbalances of this scope evidently carry incentives for the inferior party to level out its inferiority by circumventing accepted rules of warfare."[9] If we were to extend this reasoning to the IRA then they could have been further incentivized to such circumvention by the action of their adversaries who had established a considerable reputation for "departing from the rules" by their indiscriminate attacks on the non-combatant civilian population and their use of legally questionable detention and interrogation techniques. Such actions on the part of the ADRIC may have triggered a violent reciprocity on the part of the IRA, and it is evident from Barry's narrative that he intended a response that would not alone be militarily significant but also symbolic in terms of delivering a message to the wider conflict.

Were members of the flying column lawful belligerents?

Article 1 of The Hague Convention of 1907 only defined what lawful belligerents were and, in addition to armies, included volunteer corps and militias. Whereas the IRA would lay claim to being the legitimate army of the Irish Republic, the *de jure* position remained that the Irish State wasn't in existence and the status of the IRA as an irregular force had little or no legal standing under the laws of armed conflict. The, as yet un-established, Irish State could not be considered as a "contracting power" and therefore was not a party to the convention.[10] It was not until 1977 and the adoption of two Protocols to the Geneva Convention that a definition was introduced to make provision for those armed forces representing a government or authority that was not recognised by the other party to the conflict.[11]

Similarly, the laws of war were not just restricted to conventional armies but also extended to militias and volunteer corps. The IRA could not have been covered by this extension either; under the associated regulation they would not qualify as belligerents as they may not have carried arms openly and certainly didn't wear a fixed, distinctive emblem that was recognizable at a distance.[12] It is also uncertain if Barry's command of the column fulfilled the requirement that he as the commander was responsible for the actions of his subordinates. In order to satisfy British military law in force at the time, Barry would have to show that he was,

> . . . *regularly or temporarily commissioned as an officer, or is a person of position and authority, or if the members are provided with certificates or badges granted by the government of the State to show they are officers, NCOs or soldiers, so that there may be no doubt that they are not partisans acting on their own responsibility.*[13]

The formalities associated with command were therefore predicated on another state being a party to the conflict. On a purely practical level, as has already been shown, membership of the column at any moment in time was liable to change, depending on the availability of personnel and the nature of the engagement that was being contemplated. The column, therefore, was composed of irregular fighters outside the protection of the laws of war in force at that time and therefore would not benefit from the special privileges of armed forces.

The treatment of prisoners

Barry was not in a position to take prisoners, but this may have suited a particular agenda. David Kilcullen lists four basic tactics that he describes as "standard for any insurgent movement."[14] He lists these as provocation, intimidation, protraction, and exhaustion. It is conceivable to consider Barry's possible actions as satisfying those four criteria.

Was the killing of the ADRIC an attempt to force the British to overreact and thereby harm their interests? The annihilation of the patrol would be expected to provoke an excessive response from the authorities and thus add to the general air of instability that pervaded West Cork at that time. Kilcullen reminds us that:

> *Insurgents throughout history have committed atrocities, carrying out extremely provocative events to prompt their opponents to react (or overreact).*

Military necessity

Under the Lieber Code, military necessity is defined as "…measures which are indispensable for securing the ends of the war, and which are lawful according to the modern law and usages of war."[15] Considered in the light of the plainly obvious military disparities between the opposing forces, one has to consider what was militarily necessary for the IRA in the course of this engagement. At a minimum, and due to the IRA's obvious deficiencies, they needed to completely defeat the ADRIC patrol as quickly as possible. Article 15 of the Lieber Code provides that in order to achieve this goal,

> *Military necessity admits of all direct destruction of life or limb of armed enemies . . . it allows for the capturing of every armed enemy . . . Men who take up arms against one another in public war do not cease on this account to be moral beings, responsible to one another and to God.*

Such a formulation allows for a broad interpretation of what is justifiable when dealing with an armed enemy; however, it is tempered by reminding combatants that there is a requirement to recognise and give effect to a humane approach in achieving those aims.

Summary

Based on the foregoing, it is obvious that the conduct of combat operations has to satisfy particular ethical proprieties. These are referred to as either the "Laws of War" or the more recently adopted description of "International

Humanitarian Law." These bodies of law set out strict rules. Those who engage in war are required to observe and abide by those rules. Whereas these rules extend to the commanders, as it is they who are ultimately responsible for the actions of the troops under their command, primary responsibility for adherence lies with the individual. As the Canadian writer Michael Ignatieff declares:

> *The decisive restraint on inhuman practice on the battlefield lies within the warrior himself, in his conception of what is honorable and dishonorable for a man to do with weapons.*[16]

In 1920 there were three recognised principles that determined the development of the laws of war. The first principle was that a belligerent was entitled to use any amount and any kind of force necessary for the purpose of war. The second principle relates to a principle of humanity which proclaimed that the level of violence permitted is only that which would be necessary to achieve the submission of the enemy. The third and final principle has been referred to as the principle of chivalry, which required a certain amount of fairness and respect between the opposing forces. The British authorities, through their reports and propaganda, sought to portray the IRA as murderers and they certainly never attached the claim of "war crime" to the actions of the IRA. To have done so would have legitimised the insurrection as a war. Without such a declaration of war by the British, it begs the question as to whether the IRA as an irregular grouping could be classified as lawful belligerents and whether they could have charges of war crimes levelled against them? While the British never acknowledged being engaged in a war, the same could not be said of the Irish. A declaration of sorts was published in *An t-Óglach* on 31 Jan 1919:

> *Dáil Éireann, in its message to the free nations of the world declares a state of war to exist between Ireland and England.*

Conduct can only be categorised as lawful or unlawful when measured against the legal instruments in force at a particular time. In 1920 the most current applicable codification of the laws of war was to be found in The Hague Convention. Based on the application of that code, the IRA volunteers were not recognized as lawful belligerents and therefore the question as to whether they committed "war crimes" does not arise. The IRA, despite their own beliefs, were not engaged in a war. The hostilities are more properly categorised as a rebellion or insurgency. Had the column come within the remit of the code then any prosecution taken against members of the column would have to satisfy the criminal standard of proof: that the execution of prisoners and wounded had been established beyond a reasonable doubt. Based on what has been presented with so far, that determination is for each reader to decide for him or herself.

CHAPTER 10

What the figures tell us

"The ultimate proof of an army's fighting abilities and effectiveness, however, is victory on the ground."[1]

ONE OF THE most difficult planning considerations prior to engaging in warfare is estimating the number of casualties that may be occasioned by the conflict. With Kilmichael, this difficulty is compounded by the fact that the action was more a pulse of activity than a sustained level of engagement. Kilmichael thus throws up its own unique features, which may not be as amenable to a matrix analysis as a tactical engagement of a longer duration; however, for the purposes of this study there are sufficient similarities which allow for a basic application of a useful methodology.

Von Clausewitz described war as similar to gambling, where the outcome is as dependent on luck as anything else. In essence he contended that it "most closely resembles a game of cards."[2] Despite war's chaotic and complex nature, however, attempts have been made to build a coherent framework that will allow predictions to be made about the effects and the level of casualties that follow from a conflict.

Lanchester's theory of warfare

Attempts at creating such a coherent framework have produced methods of mathematical analysis which help to predict the casualty rate of any prospective engagement. One such model was developed by a British mathematician by the name of Frederick Lanchester and is known as "Lanchester's Theory of Warfare" or "Lanchester's Square Law." It is a method of mathematical analysis based primarily on differential equations and allows an estimation of the casualty rates that may ensue when one force X encounters another force Y under "modern combat conditions."[3] At its simplest, Lanchester's model allows us to consider the size of the forces involved and the effectiveness of each in order to predict an outcome. There are criticisms of the model, particularly where the situation under analysis is complex, and it is also worth highlighting that doubts have been expressed as to the validity of the equations for actual combat.[4]

Susan Lindee, writing about the difficulties in predicting the actual numbers of casualties on a battlefield, declares that ". . . due to the many variations in field conditions, estimates of absolute numbers of casualties were likely to be subject to great error."[5] The weaknesses having been declared, the benefit of Lanchester's theory to this study should be understood as seeking not to predict the casualties that may occur, as these are known, but rather its utility in understanding how these casualties occurred in the first place. Choi feels that an advantage of Lanchester's theory is that it provides a "sense of direction, where we want to explore."[6] In support of its application to the events at Kilmichael, we are in possession of enough facts to allow its use to be considered.

The modern combat conditions that Lanchester refers to are:

1. *The forces are within weapons range of one another.*
2. *The effects of weapons rounds are independent.*
3. *Fire is uniformly distributed over the enemy targets.*
4. *Attrition coefficients are constant and known.*
5. *All of the forces are committed at the beginning and there are no reinforcements.*

Under the conditions as outlined, the Lanchester theory states that the casualty ratio should vary inversely as the force ratio. In other words, using the known force strengths at Kilmichael, the rate of attrition of both the ADRIC patrol and the IRA column should be proportional to the fire-power of the other.

Let X_1 be the numerical strength of the ADRIC patrol and Y_1 be the numerical strength of the IRA ambush party. Let m and b be coefficients that represent the combat effectiveness of the ADRIC and IRA forces respectively. In other words m and b reflect how good one side is at killing members of the other side. J.H. Engel provides a useful description of b and m as the casualty-producing rate of the average combatant in the force.[7] Then the rate of casualties for both parties is:

ADRIC force: $dX_1/dt = -bY_1$ (The change in numerical strength of the ADRIC patrol over a period of time is dependent upon the military effectiveness of the IRA multiplied by the number of IRA fighters directly engaged in the firing. It is a negative value, as the numerical strength of the force will be decreasing.)

IRA force: $dY_1/dt = -mX_1$ (The change in numerical strength of the IRA ambushers over a period of time is dependent upon the military effectiveness of the ADRIC force multiplied by the number of Auxiliaries directly engaged in the firing.)

If we develop this further and assume that the losses suffered by both parties are proportionally the same then:

$$(dX_1/dt)/X_1 = (dY_1/dt)/Y_1$$

Then substituting from the previous differential equations gives the following:

$$-bY_1/X_1 = -mX_1/Y_1$$

If we now cross-multiply we get the following:

$$-bY_1^2 = -mX_1^2$$

This suggests that the combat strength of both the IRA and the ADRIC forces would be equal when the squares of the numerical strengths multiplied by the value for combat effectiveness are the same (equal). If that was the case then both forces would expect to suffer the same level of casualties. However, the combat effectiveness of the opposing forces was far from equal. A poorly-equipped and untrained IRA force engaged a well-equipped and experienced patrol. Applying Lanchester's model we would expect the ADRIC patrol to inflict more casualties on the IRA than the IRA could inflict on them. The exact opposite though seems to have occurred. How can this be explained? As we will see later, there are a number of factors which would impact on this seemingly straightforward calculation and outcome. These have been described as the "intangible behavioural considerations" or "human factors."

There is little difficulty in determining the strengths of the forces involved as these are well known and accepted. What is also not in dispute is the number of casualties inflicted on both sides. The ADRIC patrol consisted of eighteen men travelling in two trucks, so it is reasonable to assume that nine personnel were located with each truck and that all ADRIC personnel were engaged directly in the fighting.

What is not clear is just how many IRA volunteers were directly involved in the combat action. Even though we are told that thirty-six personnel were involved, a considerable number of these were involved in either a supporting or protective roles through flank security, area denial, and as reinforcements. On that basis, the force ratios, when considered from the perspective of those actually engaged in the fighting, were more evenly matched than might appear at first glance. What is often overlooked, particularly when one considers the one-sided nature of the attrition rate, is that each one of the combatant participants was both a target and a shooter, in other words shooting and being shot at.

At the culmination of the action, sixteen Auxiliaries were dead, one was severely injured, and one escaped only to be captured and killed later. Three IRA men died as a result of ADRIC fire, two at the site and one later as a result of wounds suffered.

During Phase 2 (the attack on the first lorry), nine ADRIC troops were engaged by fourteen IRA volunteers. Ten of these volunteers are described as being with No.1 Section while four, including Tom Barry, were located at the command post. Based on this deployment, fourteen IRA volunteers accomplished a total victory with that part of the ADRIC patrol suffering nine dead and the IRA emerging unscathed. This suggest a combat effectiveness of .64 (9/14) for the IRA attacking forces, and by virtue of their failure to inflict any casualties on the attackers, a combat effectiveness of 0 (0/9) for the ADRIC forces in the first lorry. But can the combat effectiveness of the ADRIC force really be 0, given their background as professional trained soldiers? There is no suggestion that they were stunned into inaction, as many of the accounts describe the Auxiliaries reacting in a militarily appropriate fashion to the ambush. Upon being attacked they immediately started returning fire. "Eyewitness" describes the truck as continuing its course after being hit by the grenade, "with some of the Auxiliaries firing with revolvers." [8] The statements from the Bureau of Military History recount the ADRIC putting up a determined resistance. The positioning of the IRA ambush party at this juncture is very significant. However, there are a number of different accounts as to where the attackers were located and therefore it is difficult to gauge the potential effect of their fire-power. Certainly the position of No.1 Section gave them an excellent lateral or side-on (enfilade) field of fire, but the IRA would have been firing at a moving target. The same, however, could be said for the Auxiliaries who would have been returning fire with revolvers at a distance in excess of thirty yards from a moving truck, with negligible effect other than disrupting the actions of the IRA. They would have trained in the use of the revolver from a moving platform, be it horse or vehicle, and would have been aware of its limitations. Foremost in the ADRIC mind would have been the desire to return as much fire as possible to either suppress the attack or at a minimum disrupt the actions of the volunteers. The Webley revolver would have allowed the ADRIC patrol an increased rate of fire to be delivered from an awkward firing platform in the shortest possible time frame.

In the course of Phase 3, the attack on the second lorry, the opposing forces were numerically more evenly matched. Here nine ADRIC troops were engaged by ten IRA volunteers. To aid our understanding and analysis, the action here can be split into two events: the action prior to the arrival of Barry's squad (Phase 3) and then the action once Barry's squad was involved (Phase 4). We have already considered the controversy over whether the ADRIC inflicted IRA casualties after falsely offering to surrender or whether those casualties were suffered as a result of the ADRIC engaging in a conventional manner with the attacking force. It is not clear as to what transpired, but out of the ten IRA men that initially engaged the ADRIC party, three casualties were inflicted by the Auxiliaries' return fire. Even though, as "Eyewitness" suggests, "some of them must have been hit", it would appear that nine Auxiliaries deployed and engaged the attacking party. This indicates a different level of combat effectiveness for this group in that it would now appear that the ADRIC patrol, at least in the initial encounter at this site, suffered no recorded casualties yet inflicted three fatal casualties so that the combat efficiency of the IRA attacking party at this site was 0 while the ADRIC combat efficiency was .33 (3/9).

Once Barry's squad became engaged, the force ratios were more or less returned to their original state, with the IRA effective numbers being increased by 1. Three IRA casualties were now replaced by the arrival of four effective volunteers. The remainder of this engagement resulted in eight casualties (seven dead and one seriously wounded) and one ADRIC escaping who was subsequently summarily executed having been captured by IRA men not associated with the ambush. On the basis of having been killed in an action unrelated to the ambush, the escapee can be disregarded for the purposes of these calculations.

With the arrival of Barry's squad we witness an unexpected change in the combat effectiveness of both units. From an IRA perspective, eight ADRIC casualties are now inflicted by eleven IRA volunteers. Therefore the combat effectiveness of the IRA increases from 0 to .73 (8/11) and the ADRIC combat effectiveness drops from .33 to 0.

Is it possible to explain such a pendulum change in combat effectiveness over such a short time frame?

Returning to Lanchester's square law, where:

$$-bY_1^2 = -mX_1^2$$

Then given that the IRA's numerical strength was only slightly greater than the Auxiliaries, the large disparity in attrition rates can only be explained by a large disparity in combat effectiveness. What this means simply is that the IRA's combat effectiveness must have been considerably higher than the ADRIC's. Herein lies the difficulty, and it is worth considering what factors might have contributed to this.

A number of determinants have been identified as contributing to an attacker's battle success. Factors such as force ratio, posture (defensive or offensive), surprise, training, morale, logistics, intelligence, technology and leadership have been identified as major determinants.[9] Having already studied the force ratios, we will now consider the other elements.

Posture

When we refer to posture we are describing whether the combatants were in a defensive or offensive deployment. The postures of both ambushing positions were relatively the same, with the IRA force occupying the key and critical terrain from selected firing positions. From the IRA's positioning it is obvious that they occupied strong defensive positions but were orientated to launch an offensive action against the ADRIC patrol. Combatants in a defensive posture have between a 20% and 60% advantage in combat effectiveness when compared and contrasted against an attacking posture. However, it is not clear that the ADRIC force ever "attacked" the IRA force in the traditional sense. They more than likely adopted their own defensive posture, which would explain why Barry's squad had to advance onto the road at the first ambush position and attack them at close quarters and continue towards the second truck, in an offensive posture against a stronger deployed force who had more or less survived the opening salvo from the volunteers of No.2 Section, and were thus at the same disadvantage that would affect any attacking force yet suffered no casualties.

Surprise

It is a military truism that the party with the benefit of surprise is at a considerable advantage when engaged in offensive operations. We are told that the attacks on both lorries occurred at the same time. Therefore the element of surprise would have been the same for both ambushing sections. This element, where the ADRIC patrol was caught off-guard, seems to have been highly effective at the first truck yet yielded little result at the second truck other than to stop the vehicle and force the deployment of the occupants.

Training, morale, logistics, intelligence and technology

The ADRIC were better trained and more experienced than the IRA attackers.

As this section of the analysis seeks to reconcile the presumed lack of effectiveness on the part of the IRA with achieving such a successful outcome, it is helpful that Colin Gray makes the following observation about the importance of morale:

> *The fighting power, or combat effectiveness, of a military force is by no means solely determined by the quality of its leaders. Nonetheless, there are good reasons to believe that superior leadership is the single most significant contributor to what nearly all people agree is by far the most important ingredient in fighting power, morale.*[10]

As for morale, we have no information to suggest that it was higher or lower for either side. Logistics, in terms of continuity of supply, was not a factor, as the engagement was not protracted. The same numbers of ADRIC forces were involved at each site.

The IRA had better intelligence than the ADRIC, as they knew the route that the ADRIC party would take but were unsure of the strength of the patrol they would encounter. Barry could have made arrangements to establish the strength of the patrol he was to encounter. They were following an established pattern on known routes and it would have simply required someone to note the strength of the patrol that left Macroom Castle that day and to inform Barry. This lack of intelligence planning caused Barry to needlessly devote an "insurance group" of six riflemen for a contingency that never materialized. The ADRIC would have been prepared for an engagement but would have no knowledge about time or location. Some were prepared, however, to react immediately as evidenced by their actions once engaged by the IRA.

In terms of technology the ADRIC had the upper hand. Their individual scale of issue, with each having a rifle, a revolver, and Mills grenades was in excess of that available to the average volunteer fighter. As regards ammunition supply, the ADRIC were much better equipped for a prolonged engagement. The Ross rifle, the more than likely presence of which we have established was in the hands of the IRA, was not fit for purpose and the IRA volunteers were more likely than not using unsuitable ammunition for it.

Leadership

Gabriel and Savage declare astutely:

> *Military groups have often prevailed under circumstances that almost certainly should have resulted in their destruction. Under such conditions the*

evident cohesion of military groups under great stress appears linked to the quality of leadership most importantly as it operates at small-unit level.[11]

In this regard, was Barry's involvement critical to the success of the ambush? The predominant position that his leadership occupies in the course of the engagement must be acknowledged, but was Barry an exceptional leader? That can only be answered by considering if he did indeed lead his men and successfully conduct the battle *as a leader.* When did he become a leader to these volunteers whose personal loyalty to him was so unwavering to the extent that, as Diarmuid Begley describes, "all of whom would have followed him to hell and back"?[12] He hadn't been with his troops long enough to fully understand their capabilities or to even build the rapport that one would expect a commander should have before engaging in the level of combat he was contemplating. Ordinary volunteer membership of the flying column fluctuated as members were rotated in and out. Recall that a number of volunteers decided of their own initiative to simply join the action without the commander even being aware of their intention. As they were untested and unknown to him, Barry could not be certain how they would have reacted under combat conditions.

Was this the ultimate determinant when he decided to locate himself at the "front line" of the action, surrendering his command and control to ensure the attack was carried through with the best possibility of success? Barry, by placing himself to the fore of the engagement, took a maxim of command to the extreme:

The first and greatest imperative of command is to be present in person. Those who impose risk must be seen to share it.[13]

From the accounts it appears that he became enmeshed in the action, potentially sacrificing the immediate requirements of the other sections under his command. Was this the high expression of officer leadership where, despite his rank and status as the column commander, he was willing to share and even exceed the risks that his men would be exposed to? Begley describes him as "short tempered, uncompromising and ruthless."[14] Were these the personal qualities and traits that induced impatience on his part to simply get on with the job and get it done rather than a more considered view as to how his role as commander should be conducted?

If Barry hadn't the confidence in his deployed sections to succeed on their own, to what can we attribute this ineffectiveness or lack of combat efficiency on the part of those same sections? The level of training was wholly inadequate to accomplish by conventional means alone what was a complex mission. It is interesting to note that the US Army in Vietnam felt that for professional combat-exposed infantry, "aggressive and effective small unit operations required two months of on-the-job retraining."[15] The lack of adequate levels of training and prior combat experience is accepted, but there may have been other factors which are worthy of consideration.

In much of the historical commentary it is simply accepted that all of the combatants at each commander's disposal fought with equal vigour and commitment. To accept this or to disregard it as something not essential to an understanding of the engagement is to deny the importance of battle-field psychology in determining the eventual outcome. Each individual in combat will react differently to particular perceived dangers. There exists the well-known, adrenalin-fuelled, "fight or flight" reaction, but that pre-supposes the ability of the individual to take a proactive step to either en-gage or flee. What may be less perceived, and in this author's view probably more common, is the reaction of simply doing nothing. "Doing nothing" may serve a number of purposes; by keeping the head down, burying into the earth, the combatant is taking himself out of immediate danger. The decision here is to allow the other combatants to carry on the engagement without any assistance. This may satisfy the desire to survive an initial on-slaught when the action is of a general nature. When an individual, however, is being targeted personally there is a final possibility and that is to submit or surrender to the force that is seeking to kill you.

These reactions suggest that the ineffectiveness of troops in battle can be attributed to the natural reactions that soldiers exhibit when engaged in combat. Of equal importance in determining what that reaction will be is the physical proximity of the individual to his comrades. It is often the case that even in the most intense combat fire-fights soldiers can become men-tally isolated from their group. As the combat unfolded before them, each volunteer would have reacted in their own way, making their own deci-sions to survive the engagement. In the manic, confused, and disorientating environment the volunteer would experience a plethora of emotions not assisted by the threat and deafening noise associated with gunfire. Rounds of .455 and possibly .303 were impacting the soil and rocks around them. .303 and shotgun rounds were being fired in very close proximity with the attendant noise levels, black powder smoke and the smell of cordite. The volunteers would never have experienced anything like this. What had only minutes previously been a quiet, lonely and isolated road had now been transformed in to a killing zone, full of danger. The decision to simply lie as flat as possible would be a very natural reaction to such danger, and in the absence of effective junior squad leadership this would be expected.

The importance of junior leadership in co-ordinating the reaction to effective fire is well recognised. The absence of such junior leadership can be potentially catastrophic. It is very possible that given the paucity of training and total lack of exposure to such combat intensity that more than a few of the volunteers reacted primarily from a sense of self-preservation. Such reactions have been a hallmark of combat throughout the ages. S.L.A. Marshall, a well-known US military author, has controversially posited a remarkable view that during the Second World War it is possible that only 25% of combat troops engaged in battle actually fired their weapons:

. . . a commander of infantry will be well advised to believe that when he engages the enemy not more than one quarter of his men will ever strike a real blow unless they are compelled by almost overwhelming circumstance or unless all junior leaders constantly "ride herd" on troops with the specific mission of increasing their fire.

Marshall continues:

The 25% estimate stands for even well-trained and campaign seasoned troops. I mean that 75% will not fire or will not persist in firing against the enemy and his works. These men may face the danger but they will not fight.[16]

Marshall's thesis was informed by a methodology which involved interviewing troops shortly after an engagement to document how the troops had reacted in battle. This ranged from interviews conducted the next day following operations in the Pacific to several weeks in the case of the Normandy D-Day landings. A primary criticism of Marshall's work is that one of those that worked closely with him considered Marshall's interest to be centred on the human experience of battle rather than collecting information on fire-ratios.[17] This criticism accepted, it is still the case that Marshall is seen to have contributed to the field of military psychology by observing that a resistance to killing one's own species is also a key factor in human combat, and that when left to their own devices, the great majority of individual combatants throughout history appear to have been unable or unwilling to kill.[18] There are fascinating statistics available to show that after the Battle of Gettysburg during the American Civil War, 27,574 muskets were recovered on the battlefield. Of these, nearly 90% were loaded; 12,000 of these were found to be loaded more than once and 6,000 of these had between three to ten musket balls in the barrel.[19] One can only surmise that the reason behind this multiple loading is that the soldier didn't want to fire his weapon yet couldn't look inactive either. John Keegan narrates the account of an officer during the battle of the Somme who on spotting a German would hand his rifle to a sergeant to do the deed.[20] These statistics do not address the more obvious methods of not killing your fellow human being, which would be simply to aim high or low.

There is nothing to suggest that the combatants at Kilmichael were possessed of an additional trait that would enable them to conquer what appears to be a primordial aspect of human nature: that of not wanting to kill a fellow human.

This has consequences when we consider, force strengths apart, how many of the combatants actually engaged in the action by firing their weapons. By Barry's own estimation, no more than sixteen or seventeen of the volunteers were in a position which would have allowed them engage the ADRIC. Establishing where these volunteers were located may not be as difficult as it seems if we are to use Barry's information as to how his troops were deployed.

Firstly, it is reasonable to presume that the scouts played no part in the action as we are told they were unarmed and were there purely to signal the approach of the ADRIC patrol. It is also unlikely that the six volunteers that Barry had appointed to constitute a reserve element engaged the enemy. Due to its force protection and area denial role, it is unlikely that much fire emanated from those positioned south of the site with No.3 Section. We are therefore left with Barry's squad, all of whom we can accept fired their weapons as this would accord with Marshall's theory that firing increases greatly if a nearby leader demands that a soldier fire. There is also information available that points to Barry's team members having had previous experience of close-quarter engagements as part of assassination operations. Both James Murphy and "Flyer" Nyhan had jointly assassinated a Black and Tan Constable Murray in Clonakilty on 27 July 1920 and had planned an attack on an RIC inspector, which was called off due to the unexpected arrival of civilians who were in a position to identify the attackers.[21]

The absence of a leader figure at No.2 Section, with the killing of the section commander, Michael McCarthy, increases the possibility of some volunteers in that area not having engaged with the enemy.

Given these uncertainties, the question remains as to whether it is possible for analytical purposes to reproduce the actions as they occurred on the battlefield? Lanchester's theories seek to rationalize from a mathematical perspective what were in essence, chaotic events. There will always be a significant level of uncertainty as it is simply not possible to manage disorder. With respect to the events at Kilmichael, the real benefit in considering the action by the application of Lanchester's theory is that it forces us to consider all aspects of the engagement by considering the numbers involved and their relative performance over space and time. What is of assistance to our analysis is that we have good information from the disparate sources as to where the forces were deployed at the commencement of the action. The first truck was attacked at one end of the site whilst the second was attacked at the entrance. The IRA were deployed at their respective positions and for the most part remained stationary, that is other than Barry's team. Barry's small group was to have a disproportionate impact on the outcome. As already discussed, they would appear to have more or less inflicted the majority of fatalities on the occupants of the first lorry and then regained the initiative by rescuing the IRA at the second lorry and at a minimum contributing to the fatalities at that location, without they themselves suffering any injuries. Was this feasible?

Summary

It is questionable whether a quantitative analysis in the manner as just outlined can provide meaningful information and knowledge when so much is determined by the influence and effect of human variables which are so difficult to account for.

The feasibility of Barry's team being engaged throughout the course of the action, inflicting the majority of fatalities on the ADRIC patrol and not suffering even a minor injury is an unusual outcome.

When we apply Lanchester's model to the result of the engagement it is difficult to accept that the IRA were possessed of such combat efficiency that they wiped out the ADRIC patrol by purely conventional means and only suffered three fatalities given the required intensity of the action necessary to achieve such an outcome.

CHAPTER 11

Conclusion

"To fight with honour is to fight without fear, without hesitation, and by implica-
tion, without duplicity…those who fight each other bravely will be bound together
in mutual respect; and that if they perish at each other's hands, they will be brothers
in death."[1]

THERE ARE A number of purposes to this concluding chapter. It will initially set out what has been established in the preceding chapters and then seek to place this knowledge in a wider perspective. Friedrich Hayek, the Austrian economist, famously declared that facts without a theory serve no useful purpose; the chapter therefore presents a number of theories as to what may or may not have happened based on the reasoned interpretation and application of the findings so far.

The 'newer' knowledge

Recent detailed research focussing on the backgrounds of the individual members of the ADRIC has revealed the patrol consisted of soldiers who could hardly be described as "elite." They may have been professional soldiers, well equipped and well trained, but the reality of their individual circumstances indicates a patrol group likely to have had difficulties responding as a cohesive unit when confronted by the ambush party. The analysis has clearly shown that the ADRIC patrol displayed few of the martial qualities that the force was reputed to possess. Accepting that they were caught unaware, their reaction to the ambush was disjointed and confused. With some exceptions, the patrol put up a poor defence and were poorly led, ultimately resulting in their near total annihilation. The poor reaction to being attacked, otherwise known as a counter-ambush drill, is evidenced by the fact that the IRA recovered almost 90% of their enemies' ammunition. In other words, the ADRIC members only managed to expend 10% of their allotted fire-power, may not have fired their rifles, and not once made use of any of the Mills bombs that each member was equipped with – the Mills being the ideal response, particularly in the case of those in the rear lorry being attacked by No.2 Section.

The IRA volunteers were for the most part untrained but well led by Tom Barry. Even though Barry's location at the commencement of the action was far from ideal, he still managed to halt the ADRIC patrol in the killing area and accomplished his mission, albeit by uncertain means.

The commonly held view that the IRA ambush party were all armed with Lee-Enfield rifles is now in doubt. It is more likely the case that a number, perhaps the majority, of volunteers were using the Canadian Ross rifle. A strong probability has been established that Volunteer Jim O'Sullivan was more than likely killed by the bolt from his own Ross rifle and not from ADRIC fire. His death can be attributed to the known defect present in the weapon's mechanism. Evidence of identical injuries with the same weapon exists to support this finding. It is also the case that O'Sullivan most likely fired only one round in the course of the engagement, which caused the bolt to be driven backwards with such a devastating consequence for him.

Jack Hennessey was also likely to have been using a Ross rifle. This would explain why he was loading and reloading so often. The Lee-Enfield magazine carried ten rounds, while the Ross magazine carried five rounds and he was only issued with thirty-five rounds. Blood flowing from Hennessy's wound is very unlikely to have impeded or jammed the rifle's mechanism. It is more likely the case that his rapid firing with unsuitable ammunition caused the cartridge to swell, thus making it extremely difficult to extract the empty cartridge and thereby causing the rifle to jam.

It remains unclear whether Michael McCarthy died in the course of the engagement or shortly afterwards, although there is a substantial amount of detail, provided by the Kilmichael Historical Society, to suggest that he sustained his injuries during the action but died while being evacuated to a safe house.

Allegations that the bodies of the ADRIC were "mutilated" by the IRA are not sustainable. The wounds as described can be explained by the nature of the ammunition used. This information was not known to the medical or military personnel at the time. The types of injury inflicted and the location of those injuries on the ADRIC personnel would indicate that the ADRIC were shot at very close quarters and that at least four of the victims had their arms in the air when shot.

In relation to the type of rifles used by the volunteers at Kilmichael, we must consider the possible hand of Britain's Naval Intelligence Division in the equipping of Barry's column. Barry needed three vital items of equipment to wage war – arms, ammunition, and explosives – and it is obvious the lengths the IRA would go to procure them. The British were well aware of such shortages and also of the difficulties that the rebels had in sourcing sufficient stocks. Given the influence that Reginald 'Blinker' Hall had on the conduct of intelligence operations during the First World War and the interest he had in Irish affairs, most noticeably his role in the arrest of Roger

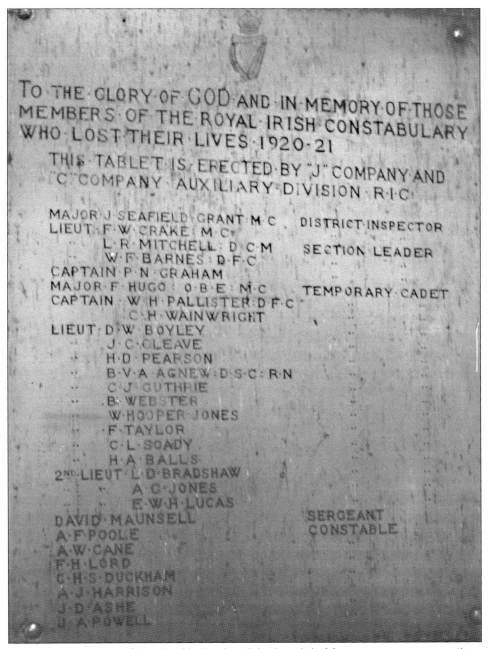

The plaque from the Church of Ireland parish church in Macroom commemorating the ADRIC members who died at Kilmichael. The plaque is currently located in Aherla, County Cork.

The graves of the IRA dead at Castletown-Kinneigh near Ballineen, County Cork

Casement, it is not unrealistic to expect that he and his successors would bring their experience and skills to bear against the republicans. The likelihood that Coastguard stations would be raided was obvious. The likelihood that the coastguards themselves would mount a robust defence was improbable. Here was an opportunity to equip the rebels with defective rifles by allowing them to fall into their hands. The Royal Navy sloop docking in Bantry against the advice of the RIC and the weapons being subsequently stolen, the re-equipping of Howe's Strand Coastguard station only days after a successful raid, and the lack of a military or police response when it was raided for a second time – these incidents, occurring over a short period of time, suggest a policy of allowing particular arms to be "acquired" by the rebels with a purpose that would soon become apparent. If such a policy existed, and there is evidence to suggest that it did, then it remains another aspect of the Kilmichael ambush which will contribute to maintaining it as the most intriguing engagement of the War of Independence.

How this knowledge impacts on the understanding of what transpired

There is little doubt or disagreement about the outcome. After what appears to have been a relatively brief encounter, the ADRIC patrol was annihilated. The outcome, from a military perspective, was a resounding success for the IRA.

We are left with considering a remarkable result. The volunteers suffered modest casualties, which was surprising because of the reportedly ultra-hostile nature of the engagement as characterised by the hand-to-hand nature of the combat and its intensity and reported duration.

For a military analyst, the difficulty lies in reconciling the disparities between the combat capabilities of the opposing forces with the eventual outcome. An analysis of this operation from a purely military perspective has sought to measure it against accepted concepts of warfare and its conduct. In that regard, consideration focussed on the use of ground, the deployment of the forces, the equipment available to both, the organisation of the forces, and what training they had received. The analysis then moved to a closer examination of individual actions and the fire-power that each combatant was capable of bringing to bear on the enemy. When all of those factors were considered the analysis moved to the more abstract exercise of assessing the combat power that each of these units possessed. Combat power has been defined as an "evaluation of a unit's capabilities considering numbers, weaponry and training, as well as the human factors of espirit de corps, leadership, and discipline."[2]

This examination has considered the action measured within these parameters. The analysis does not support a view that an untrained, inexperienced, inadequately equipped, and irregular grouping of IRA guerillas were militarily capable of defeating a regular, professional, well-armed, well trained and more experienced ADRIC patrol purely through conventional tactical means.

What then are the alternatives? A more plausible explanation lies in focussing on the single-minded attitude of Barry towards the desired outcome. Barry was intent on destroying the ADRIC patrol, and once the IRA gained the upper hand the result was inevitable. How and when this upper hand was achieved remains debatable. This might well be the real mystery of Kilmichael; any theory can only be speculative, but in this instance the speculation is on an informed basis.

The IRA achieved total surprise in the initial conduct of the operation, both lorries being allowed to proceed into the ambush area before being engaged. Barry's description, however, of appearing on the side of the road in a military tunic in order to slow or halt the convoy would certainly have been novel but, in this writer's opinion, unlikely. It would have taken from the element of surprise, an element so crucial to the ambush's success. Barry's description of throwing a grenade to the limit of its range so accurately that it landed in the lorry's cab needs to be treated with caution. It may have been theoretically possible but it is not realistic. Such an achievement is far too dependent on chance to be given serious consideration, particularly since there did not appear to have been an alternative plan to fall back on if the ruse did not work. The first lorry was more likely stopped by a volley of gunfire. As the lorry drove directly towards the IRA command post it would have presented a much easier target for those positioned behind the walls. With fire being delivered from the higher ground by No.1 Section, the first lorry was caught in a very effective cross-fire, straight on and from the side (enfilade). Once the lorry was immobilised, Barry and the other occupants from the command post would then have appeared on the road in order to take the ADRIC members captive, disarm them, and move them up the lane directly in front of the command post and under the watch of No.1 Section on the high ground. Barry's team was unlikely to have been opposed at this juncture. We make this presumption because, as shown from the experiment conducted with the Webley revolver, it is highly unlikely that the ADRIC, having opened fire with their Webleys at point-blank range, would have all missed their IRA targets. Barry's team in intimate contact with the enemy would have taken some casualties.

A more plausible view would suggest that the ADRIC were stunned by the opening fusillade, were confused about where the fire was coming from and the numbers that they were being engaged by, and put up little or no resistance. They would have been aware through their own operational briefings that only a month previously, on 22 October at Toureen on the road between Cork and Bandon, a patrol of the Essex Regiment had found themselves in a similar position. On that occasion the patrol surrendered, had their weapons and ammunition confiscated, and were sent on their way, unmolested.

The situation may have been slightly different at the scene of the second attack. No.2 Section failed to have any substantial impact on the second lorry and its occupants. The ADRIC members were far from incapacitated and were returning fire. Jim O'Sullivan was killed once he fired his first round. His colleagues mistakenly attributed his death to fire from the ADRIC. Accepting that O'Sullivan was killed by the action of his own rifle is to reject Barry's description of O'Sullivan being killed by ADRIC fire, and thereby calls into question the circumstances pertaining to the false surrender, if not the false surrender itself.

It is not at all certain, given McCarthy's location, that his injury and subsequent death can be attributed to the ADRIC fire alone. We have discussed the possibility of fire from No.3 Section posing a substantial threat to those deployed on the higher ground where No.2 Section was located. Once engaged, the ADRIC managed to deploy, and the lorry succeeded in extracting itself by reversing from its original position. There may have been a very quick exchange of revolver gunfire, which was over in minutes. Had there been a prolonged gun battle involving rifles, then either Lordon or Hennessy, given their close proximity to ADRIC members Pallester and Taylor, would have been killed, as both Pallester and Taylor had effectively outflanked No.2 Section while Pearson and Forde would have "fixed" Lordon and Hennessy's position.

A more credible account would be that the ADRIC members at the second lorry also surrendered following an initial exchange of revolver fire. O'Sullivan's death, Deasy and McCarthy's serious injuries, and the wounding of Hennessy and possibly Lordon added to the absolute confusion – the "fog of war" that permeated the engagement. The fact that this was the first time the majority of the volunteers had been engaged in such activity meant emotions were running high, and it is possible that those emotions were vented on the enemy. The ADRIC personnel whose bodies were found close to No.2 Section displayed extensive injuries, thus supporting this contention. Barnes and Jones had ten bullet wounds between them and displayed gunshot wounds to the axilla. Both were most likely shot first while their arms were in the air, and the additional shots administered subsequently. Taylor and Pallester exhibited similar injuries (inflicted at extremely close range with shot guns) to the region of the heart, while Pallester also appears to have been hit by a blunt instrument, probably the butt of a rifle. Those killed in the lane displayed an assortment of injuries inflicted to the front, side, and back, and many inflicted at close range. The specifics of the injuries and the subsequent location of the bodies would support a theory that they were surrounded when shot.

If it was the case that prisoners were shot, then such shootings would not have been a spontaneous event. It could only have been ordered by the column commander. The desire or willingness on the part of the IRA to shoot prisoners was not uncommon, and in a similar engagement only the personal intervention of General Seán MacEoin, in the aftermath of an ambush at Clonfin in Longford on 1 February 1921, prevented the Auxiliary prisoners there being executed by their IRA captors.

Barry may have been faced with a dilemma. He and his column perceived the ADRIC to be a "super force." The IRA had expected the fight to have been a far more difficult event and had not counted on taking so many prisoners. The outcome was unexpected. The engagement was over in minutes, and they were now faced with two large groups of captives. The column itself had taken physical casualties but the psychological effect was even deeper. At any moment an unexpected patrol could arrive, and it was questionable if the column would be in a position to defend itself. The safety of the column would have been foremost in the commander's decision making. Critical decisions had to be taken, and taken quickly in an atmosphere of euphoria, fear, and exhaustion. There was no possibility of moving such a large group of prisoners through West Cork, as the follow-up searches for the missing would be intense and relentless. The option of releasing the ADRIC was not feasible either, as Barry and his men may have feared the consequences for themselves and for the local population of being identified.

Ultimately, the historical narratives have left conflicting views and recollections as to what transpired. While this might appear to a casual reader be a more recent development, the disparity was recognised many years ago by John McCann. McCann, a politician, author and journalist writing in 1946, was one of the first writers to give two versions of what may have happened. He details the "false surrender" version but also another much different account of events attributed to Brigadier General Crozier, a former commander of the Auxiliary Division. McCann provides a direct quotation from Brigadier General Crozier's memoirs, which interestingly he describes as "worth noting":

> Some eighteen policemen of the [ADRIC] Division were killed. It was stated by the Government that the bodies were mutilated by the Sinn Feiners. When I returned to Ireland, as a civilian, at the request of Sir Hamar Greenwood to give evidence, I took particular care to enquire into this story of mutilation, as it appeared to me to be quite unlike the normal or abnormal act of Irishmen. The correct story I found to be as follows: - The lorries were held up by land mines and the leading lorry was partly destroyed. The men were called upon to surrender and did so, throwing up their hands and grounding their rifles. Each policeman carried a revolver in addition to a rifle. One policeman shot a Sinn Feiner at close quarters with his revolver, after he had grounded his rifle and put his hands up. A hand to hand combat of the fiercest kind ensued, the butts of rifles, revolvers, crow-bars and hammers being used, hence the battered condition of the police. When it is intended to kill a man with the butt-end there is no hitting him in the legs.
>
> The commander of the company to which these policemen belonged committed suicide on Wandsworth Common in 1920, having been let down by the Government and having become destitute. He was a colonel. [Author's insert]

Crozier's description is coincidentally supported by the captured ammunition figures in Barry's narrative. Crozier describes the patrol laying down their rifles, thus not firing them. Barry describes a haul of 1,800 rounds of ammunition, supporting a contention that no rifle shots were fired. It is not beyond the bounds of possibility that Pat Deasy was killed in the manner as described by Crozier.

In order to arrive at a reconciliation or a different understanding of what happened, the action requires examination in much closer detail than that achieved to date by the existing historical studies. The facts from a battlefield analysis perspective speak for themselves. They do not lend strong support to Barry's account of what transpired.

Did the Kilmichael ambush achieve its purpose? If the purpose was to confront the ADRIC and inflict a resounding victory, the answer is undoubtedly yes. Barry achieved the total destruction of the patrol with few casualties. The IRA also secured a considerable quantity of arms and ammunition for future operations. They had laid down a marker. There may, however, have been an unintended consequence. Michael Hopkinson believes that the Kilmichael ambush, in addition to the "Bloody Sunday" assassinations of twelve British agents by Michael Collins's squad a week earlier, may have delayed peace efforts:

> *Very probably, Bloody Sunday and Kilmichael had a profoundly negative effect on the peace moves in progress at that time. Any public readiness to compromise with Sinn Fein and the IRA would have appeared totally objectionable to military and public alike.*[3]

The Kilmichael ambush, as a military engagement, has been described by historians to me as "*the* ambush" and "*the* action of the War of Independence", but when pressed to explain such an elevated status commentators struggle for something beyond the body count. As to its importance as a military action, I have not uncovered any evidence to show that the ambush was being studied in any significant detail outside Ireland. Its interest to military professionals is purely historic and then only at the tactical level. For historians, its significance rests in the signal it sent to the British authorities that they needed to revise their assessments; the IRA was now packing a heavier punch and capable of using it. Intensity levels on both sides were raised, with the British, shortly afterwards, imposing martial law in the south of the country.

Kilmichael now

Kilmichael, a battlefield that hosted a bloody, vicious, and chaotic event has

The members of the executive of the Kilmichael and Crossbarry Memorial Committee after carrying out an inspection at the ambush site before finalising plans for the erection of the memorial in 1965. Front, from left – Rev C O'Brien, PP, chairman; P O'Brien, vice-president; Tom Barry, president; Tom Hales, vice-chairman; Major Maurice Donegan, vice-president. Back – Daniel O'Leary, treasurer, Jim Barry, Cork sub-committee; Willie Hales; Flor Crowley, NT, secretary.

undergone its latest transformation. What was once an unadulterated conflict site has morphed into a heroic theatre, resplendent with a grandiose war memorial and, more recently, a guide to a movie, *The Wind that Shakes the Barley*. With the passing of time, the horror and sheer brutality of the engagement is fading to be replaced by a pleasing, misty–eyed romanticism – a romanticism that has been further safeguarded by the latest inclusion of concrete footpaths and meandering walkways, thus taking the harsh and serrated edge off this tiny battlefield.

A picnic area with family benches now protects the flank of No.1 Section, with a small ornamental wooden bridge providing a direct path to where the bodies of ADRIC members Pallester and Taylor lay in the aftermath of the engagement. The centre of the engagement is now marked with a large stone circle and decorative bench. The dead ground between No. 1 and No.2 Section positions has been landscaped and extensively planted with ground cover. The natural undulations and cover that the ADRIC would have used to counter the actions of No.2 Section are gone. In order to accommodate a viewing and seating area, the position once occupied by No.2 Section has been mechanically sculpted to allow more seating and an elevated view of the destruction.

Kilmichael, intentionally or otherwise, has become a "softer" battlefield, which tells one side of a violent action. In the one instance where the Auxiliaries are afforded a semblance of remembrance, a memorial stone declares incorrectly that ". . . on this road too died seventeen terrorist officers of the British forces." Sixteen had been killed in the battlefield, of which only a few died on the road, while one, Cadet Cecil Gutherie, who escaped the carnage, was executed after being taken prisoner by IRA men a number of miles from Macroom.

Observers with a passing interest will have no difficulty in ascertaining where the IRA sections were deployed, and in the case of one volunteer, Jim O'Sullivan, a cross has been erected to mark the spot where he met his death. No such guidance exists to detail the ADRIC positions or to mark where, in an instant, their lives were taken from them.

The Kilmichael battle site has changed utterly. Wrapped in nostalgia, its "fictive kin" have ensured its continuing relevance as an altar to those who marched away victorious that evening, with victors' spoils not confined to war booty but the also the spoils of historical remembrance. It is a justifiably famous republican triumph, where "the victors' story of what happened there has been written, sung, told and commemorated many times."[4] The zealous efforts to sustain the levels of commemoration and remembrance continue, but it is a particular "truth" that is remembered, a truth that has been appropriated by those wishing to sustain a heroic vision which will forever edify the justness of the action, a vision of heroic volunteers and the "terrorist officers" of the Auxiliary Division of the Royal Irish Constabulary.

The debate continues

There is unlikely to be a final word on Kilmichael, and this examination does not pretend to provide all the answers. It seeks to simply add to the debate in an informed and relevant way and hopefully provide material that is of interest to those either immersed in Kilmichael or engaging with the subject for the first time. So much is uncertain but so much is yet to be uncovered. It will take others with different skill sets to advance our knowledge even further.

In this analysis we have focussed on the military aspects of the engagement, in which the false surrender understandably occupies a central position. Its centrality has been created by Barry who justified the annihilation of the patrol as a consequence of the false surrender. Were the volunteers deceived by the ADRIC calling a false surrender, or has history been deceived by the subsequent accounts of the engagement? Ultimately it is for the reader to decide.

Kilmichael was never going to be a fair fight. It was a guerrilla action and a youthful one at that. The volunteers were stepping into the unknown, placing all their trust in a young, ruthless and determined commander who had told them it would be a fight to the finish. The rank and file volunteers probably never understood the enormity of what they were about to engage in, but they participated nevertheless. Fear and anxiety would have been the prevailing emotions, but a powerful group bond, close deployments, side by side with neighbours, and Barry's influence would have held these in check. Once the destruction unfolded before them, it is obvious that some found the pressure too much and were incapacitated both physically and psychologically. Given the state of his troops, as evidenced by the immediacy requirement to drill them in the aftermath of the action, and the subsequent ineffectiveness of the Dunmanway participants, Barry was left with few options. Under enormous physical and psychological pressure he made decisions that were informed by the need to protect his troops and the local population on whose behalf he no doubt felt he was fighting. Barry, at 22 years of age, was a young man and such decisions are generally left to, or guided by, older counsel.

Professor John A. Murphy writing in the *Irish Independent* in 2000, proposed the following:

> *What seems certain is that Barry meant Kilmichael to be a fight to the finish. Not only would it be a major challenge to British military might but his own commitment to the cause would be clearly demonstrated, thus resolving all doubts arising from his Great War service and his loyalist family background.*[5]

Maybe there was a personal motivation to the commander's actions, but I am not convinced that the outcome would have been anymore different if there had not been. This was a guerrilla war, a case of big boys' games being played by big boys' rules. Every engagement posed its own challenges, requiring improvisation and on-the-spot decisions. It was also an action of its time with little knowledge of The Hague Convention or the general rules of war. It was an action undertaken in the immediate aftermath of the Great War where accounts of merciless trench warfare, serrated bayonets, dum-dum bullets, and blinding gas had received widespread coverage in the only media outlet available to the young volunteers, the newspapers. How would they have known about the rules of warfare? The volunteers, along with the West Cork people generally, were in fear, rightly or wrongly, of the Auxiliaries. It shouldn't come as a surprise that they sought to kill them all. The only question remains: how was it done?

The monument at Kilmichael.

The Court of Inquiry

Proceedings of a Court of Inquiry held at Macroom on the 30th November, 1920, to enquire into the circumstances under which 15 cadets of the ADRIC police and one temp constable R.I.C. were killed on the 28th November, 1920.

> Major A. Stapledon,   ) President.
> 1st Bn. Manchester Regt.   )
>
> Lt. C.F. Luffman,   ) Member.
> 1st Bn. Manchester Regt.   )

R.M. Taylor, Capt. D.I. 3. ADRIC Div. R.I.C. being duly sworn states:-
Iidentified the 16 bodies and was present when the superficial examination was carried out by Dr. Kelleher.
(Sgd) R. Taylor, Capt. 3. D.I.

The Court having assembled proceed (sic) to take evidence.

Doctor Jeremiah Kelleher being duly srown (sic) states :-

At Macroom on the 29th of November, 1920. I was called into Macroom Castle at about 4 p.m. and made a superficial examination of the bodies which I found there total 16.

In the case of Temp. Cadet late Major F.Hugo. I was informed that his age was 38 years, he had a compound fracture of the skull, a compound fracture of the femur, and extensive lacerated wounds of the lower extremities. In my opinion bomb wounds. His death was due to shock and haemorrhage resulting from these wounds.

In the case of Temp. Cadet late Lieutenant E.W.H. Lucas whose age was stated to be 31 years. Gun shot wound on the head and several wounds of neck and body which had fractured the femur (or thigh bone). Death due to shock and haemorrhage resulting from the wounds.

In the case of Temp. Cadet late Lieutenant Hooper Jones whose age was stated to be 27 years. Wound of groin and axilla his death was due to haemorrhage.

Temp Cadet F.W. Crake, D.I.3. late Captain, whose age is stated to be 26 years. He had a gunshot wound through the head. Death was due to shock.

Temp. Cadet P.N. Graham, late captain, whose age was stated to be 32. Explosive bullet wound through the neck, extensive lacerated wounds of the extremities and body, and fracture of the thigh bone (femur) cause of death shock and haemorrhage.

Temp. Cadet H.D. Pearson, late Lieutenant, whose age was stated to be 34 years. He had a wound of the head lacerated wound of the forearm and bullet wound of the leg. The wound of the forearm was caused by an explosive bullet or portion of a bomb. His death was caused by shock and haemorrhage.

Temp. Cadet B. Webster, late Lieutenant, whose age was stated to be 32 years. He had a gaping wound of the shoulder, fracture of the humerus, 3 rifle bullets through the back, death due to shock and haemorrhage resulting from the wounds.

Temp. Cadet A.G. Jones late 2/Lieutenant, whose age was stated to be 35 years. He had bullet wound of axilla, six other bullet wounds on limbs, and body, which fractured the femur (thigh bone). Death was due to shock and haemorrhage.

Temp. Cadet W.T. Barnes late Lieutenant, stated to have been 27 years of age. Gaping wound of axilla, four other bullet wounds and large gun-shot wound scorched over the heart inflicted after death. Death result of shock and haemorrhage.

Temp. Cadet L.D. Bradshaw, late Lieutenant, whose age was stated to be 22 years, wound of right shoulder with fracture of the lumerous(sic), wound of left axilla, big poforating(sic) wound over the liver which must have been fired at close range with an ordinary shot gun. Three other wounds in various parts of the body. Death due to shock and haemorrhage.

<u>Temp. Cadet Cristopher(sic) Wainwright, late Captain</u> whose age was stated to be 36 years. He had two wounds on the back of the right chest, one on the left side of the chest and one wound of abdomen. Death due to shock and haemorrhage.

<u>Temp. Cadet W. Pallister, late Captain</u> whose age was said to be 25 years. He had a large wound over the right side of heart caused by a explosive bullet a wound of the right hand had a large compound fracture of the skull through which the brains rotruded(sic), this wound was inflicted after death by an axe or some similar heavy weapon. Death due to shock and haemorrhage.

<u>Temp. Cadet F. Taylor late Lieutenant</u> whose age was stated to be 23 years. One pofarating(sic) wound upper right chest, one large shot gun wound over the heart fired at close range. A large gaping wound of the left shoulder caused by a explosive bullet or bomb, three other gun shot wounds. Cause of death shock and haemorrhage.

<u>Temp. Cadet C.S.W. Bayley late Lieutenant</u>, whose age was stated to be 22. He had a bullet wound behind the right ear one through the back of his chest and one slight wound of the right hand. Death was due to shock.

<u>Temp Cadet J.C. Cleave, late Lieutenant</u>, whose age was stated to be 21 years. He had a gun-shot wound over the heart one upper chest and a large lacerated wound left side of pelvis by an explosive bullet. He had one large gaping wound on his chest fired at point blank range by a shot-gun. Death due to shock and haemorrhage.

<u>Temp. Constable A.F. Poole, R.I.C.</u> whose age was stated to be 19 years. He had four bullet wounds of the neck and shoulder. Extensive depressed fractures of the bones of the face and head caused by some heavy blunt instrument and inflected after death. Death due to shock and haemorrhage from the wounds in the neck and shoulder.

(Sgd)   J. Kelleher.

Lieut. H.G. Hampshire D.I.3 ADRIC Div. R.I.C. being duly sworn states:-

On the 29th November, 1920 I went out to the road 1$^{1/2}$ miles past Kilpatrick Post Office and found 16 bodies of No.2 platoon , C, Company. All bodies were badly mutilated. From my experience as a soldier I should imagine that about four had been killed instaneously (sic) and the others butchered.
(Sgd) H.G. Hampshire,
T/C. D.I. 3.

OPINION

The Court are of the opinion that Temp. Cadet F. Hugo.
Temp. Cadet H.W.H. Lucas,
  ''   ''   Hooper Jones,
  ''   ''   F.W. Crake D.I.3
  ''   ''   P.N. Graham,
  ''   ''   H.D. Pearson,
  ''   ''   B. Webster,
  ''   ''   A.G. Jones,
  ''   ''   W.T. Barnes,
  ''   ''   L.D. Bradshaw,
  ''   ''   Christopher Wainwright,
  ''   ''   W. Pallister,
  ''   ''   F. Taylor,
  ''   ''   C.S.W. Bagley,
  ''   ''   G.C. Cleave,
Temp. Constable A.F. Poole, R.I.C.,
were ambushed near Kilpatrick on the 29th November, 1920 and wilfully murdered and mutilated by some persons unknown. In most cases they were murdered after being wounded.
Signed at Macroom this 30th day of November, 1920.

(Sgd) A. Stapledon, Major,
1st Bn. Manchester Regt.
President.

(Sgd) C.F. Luffman, Lt.
1st Bn. Manchester Regt.
Member.

The Ross Rifle and its defects

THE ROSS RIFLE was the brainchild of a wealthy Scottish industrialist, Sir Charles Ross, who arrived in Canada in 1897 and began to invest in a number of business opportunities such as public transport in Vancouver and hydro-electricity in British Columbia. Even though these were successful ventures in their own right, it was rifle design that most occupied his interests. Sir Charles was fortunate in that an opportunity to indulge his passion for firearms was presented in 1901 as a consequence of Canada's participation in the Boer War in South Africa. Up until 1900 the Canadian armed forces were equipped with obsolete British equipment and the Canadians quickly realised that their Martini–Henry rifles were no match for the longer range and much more accurate Mauser and Mannlicher rifles that the Boers used. The Canadians requested 15,000 Lee-Enfields from British manufacturers, but none could fulfil the request as they were fully occupied trying to meet British needs. The Canadians had no alternative but to turn to their own industrialists for a solution. Sir Charles seized the opportunity and won the contract in 1902 to supply 12,000 rifles in 1903. The rifles were two years in production and finally in 1905 the first batch of 1,000 Ross Mark I rifles were delivered to the Royal Canadian Mounted Police. They were beset with problems and subsequently withdrawn from service following an incident during a firing practice when part of a bolt was blown back into the face of a police officer, blinding him in one eye. Another incident involving the Mark I and the subsequent perception of the rifle's safety is described by Roger Philips as follows:

> By this time the Conservative [party] critics of the Ross had received word of Ross failures across the country, most having occurred during annual range qualifying practices of the militia held during the summer and fall of 1906. The bursting of a Mark I Ross breech, which mortally wounded a militiaman, moved one critic of the rifle in Parliament to charge that the Ross, "kills as much behind as in front."[1]

Sir Charles attempted to address these issues, and soon the Ross Mark II appeared, but it also required on-going modifications and finally, after it had reached the less than illustrious status of Ross Mark II★[5] (each ★ representing a new series of modifications), it was designated the "Rifle, Ross, Mark III." The Mark III was the rifle that the Canadian forces in France and Belgium were equipped with and which subsequently emerged in the hands of the IRA in West Cork.

Difficulties with the Mark III manifested themselves as soon as it was used in action. Michael Sheehan, a Canadian soldier, described his experience with the Ross rifle:

> I'll never forget our first sight of the Germans. We had those beautiful Ross rifles. They were absolutely the slickest rifles you could find anywhere, but no good for war. The Germans were coming, we could see them coming across down there. So we opened up with these Ross rifles, and I bet we didn't fire more than a dozen shots before it seized. It got hot. (It was made so beautifully.) They had absolutely seized, everything just as tight as could be. We stood on the bolt to try to open the breech, nothing doing! The rifles were absolutely useless.[2]

The Mark III's performance was so poor that it was effectively abandoned by Canadian troops during the First World War, who had resorted to equipping themselves with Lee-Enfield rifles recovered from dead British soldiers. The history of the Canadian Expeditionary force describes the fact that almost a third of the 5,000 troops who had survived the ordeal at Ypres "…had given an unmistakable verdict by throwing away the Ross and picking up the Lee-Enfield."[3]

The Mark III's inadequate performance "became an issue in empire politics – one that was to strain to a considerable extent the ties between the two countries during World War I."[4]

The weapon's suitability, or lack thereof, gave rise to some remarkable actions and correspondence on the part of British Army commanders. In a letter to the Houses of Parliament dated 19 June 1915, Field Marshal French, Commander-in-Chief, British Army in the Field, pulled no punches and laid the matter before the politicians in the following terms:

> I heard rumours that there was a growing want of confidence in this rifle, as evidenced by the fact that the infantry of the Canadian Division were taking every opportunity of exchanging their rifles with those of the Lee-Enfield pattern from casualties on the battlefield.
>
> To satisfy myself whether there was any real justification for this state of affairs…I gave instruction for the assembly of a small Committee at my General Headquarters to test the rifle with the various natures of ammunition in use, including ammunition of Canadian manufacture, of which a small supply was obtained from England for the purpose, none having been

sent out to this country for use with the rifle.

The proceedings of this Committee were laid before me on the eve of a serious offensive operation in which the Canadian Division was to take part, and I was at the same time informed that over 3,000, or more than one third, of the infantry of this Division had already succeeded in re-arming themselves with the Lee-Enfield rifle without any authority having been given for them to do so.

Looking –

- *to the unanimous opinion of my Committee that the Ross rifle could not be relied upon to work smoothly and efficiently in rapid fire with any ammunition other than that of Canadian manufacture;*
- *to the fact that no ammunition of this nature was available in this country, and that sufficient supplies could not be obtained from England; and*
- *to the want of confidence in the rifle which a large number of the infantry evidently felt, as evidenced by the fact that over 3,000 had, without authority, exchanged their rifles for those used by their British comrades, and taken from casualties on the battlefield;*

I did not feel justified in sending this Division into battle with the Ross rifle, and ordered the re-arming of the infantry of the Division with the Lee-Enfield rifle, which was carried out before they went into action on the 15th instant.[5]

The Division that Field Marshal French was referring to in this instance was the 1st Canadian Division, and the re-arming that he ordered occurred on 12 June 1915. It is remarkable that almost a year later other Canadian units were still armed with the Ross Mk III and requested to be re-armed with the Lee-Enfield, as an extract from a letter dated 28 May 1916 from General Douglas Haig, Commander-in-Chief, British Armies in France, testifies:

I have satisfied myself, after extensive inquires carried out throughout the Canadian Corps, that, as a Service rifle, the Ross is less trustworthy than the Lee-Enfield, and that the majority of the men armed with the Ross rifle have not the confidence in it that it is so essential they should possess. The inquiry on which these conclusions are based was the outcome of an urgent application from a battalion of the 3rd Canadian Division for re-armament with the short Lee-Enfield rifle, in consequence of a high percentage of jams experienced with their Ross rifles during a hostile attack on the 1st May 1916.[6]

At a political level the Canadians were not taking this matter lightly, and in a follow-up response from the Governor-General of Canada to the Secretary of State for the Colonies the Canadians requested that the tests be re-run, saying that they were willing to abide by General Haig's judgement, but only after ". . . thorough investigation and adequate tests."[7] Haig curtly replied, "I have the honour to inform you that the efficiency of the Ross rifle has been thoroughly tested *by actual fighting in the field* [emphasis added]."[8]

The controversy over the difficulties with the Ross rifle was a raging political issue in Canada and was a significant contributor to the dismissal of the Canadian Minister of Defence, General Sam Smyth, in 1916.

The official correspondence was obviously pitched at a certain level and for many reasons it is short on technical detail other than referring to jamming and that fact that soldiers had, "lost confidence in the weapon."

For our purposes there was, however, yet another serious defect with the weapon and that related to the bolt:

> *The Canadian army carried it proudly into World War 1 and when one Canadian armorer-sergeant first announced it was unsafe, his camp commandant bawled him out unmercifully. But within half an hour, the sergeant had demonstrated the rifle's dangerous action before the officer's astonished eyes and soon after that the Ross was withdrawn from army use and its manufacture ceased.*[9]

The sergeant being referred to was Sergeant Lindsay Elliot who became aware of an issue with the rifle's mechanism. The Canadian Ross Rifle Mk III had a serious and extremely dangerous design defect: after the weapon was stripped down and the bolt removed, it was possible to reassemble the bolt mechanism by repositioning the bolt-head incorrectly, replace it in the rifle's mechanism, and still fire a round from the weapon even though the bolt was unlocked. If it was assembled incorrectly and the bolt failed to lock prior to firing the cartridge then the bolt could be driven back, causing a serious or fatal injury to the firer depending on how close the firer's face was to the rear of the mechanism and whether the firer was firing right or left-handed. Sergeant Lindsay saw a comrade dead in the trenches,

> *. . . with the firing-pin, mainspring and cocking piece of his Ross embedded in his face; another dead with the bolt out of his rifle and the lugs badly torn. He saw a group of buddies set up a "trench mousetrap" with a Ross; the cocked and loaded rifle aimed at a piece of cheese with a string from cheese to*

198

trigger and the bolt blew out of the rifle when the trap went off.[10]

Further details relating to very similar injuries as that suffered by Jim O'Sullivan at Kilmichael are provided by Roger Phillips as follows:

Instances of Ross bolts blowing back and maiming or killing the shooters have been recorded. One occurred near Brant, Alberta, when a H.A. McNeil had half his face blown away. He lived. Less fortunate was Louis Lavalley, of Keith, Alberta, who died eleven hours after an M-10 bolt tore away part of his head. When the bolt of Lavalley's rifle was recovered it was found to be assembled in the wrong position.[11]

H.V. Stent provides some additional information relating to Lavalley's death and another instance of a Ross blow-back:

A man named A.L. Thompson, in California, had a Ross bolt let go on him in 1922. Thompson was lucky he shot right handed and escaped with serious wounds. An Alberta man named Louis Lavalley had a .280 Ross bolt blow when he fired from his left shoulder. Instead of hitting the side of his face it struck full centre and Lavalley died eleven hours later.[12]

The latent defect associated with the Ross rifle was the subject of litigation before the Canadian Supreme Court in 1921 which provided an authoritative determination as to the likely consequences of the rifle being used by those lacking in experience with firearms.

The facts were that the respondents in the case, Charles O. Dunstall and Sloan M. Emery, had separately purchased the civilian equivalent of the military rifle. To prevent rust, the guns were heavily oiled by the manufacturer, and purchasers were warned to wipe them out before using. In order to do this the bolt had to be taken apart, but no instructions were given by the manufacturer as to the manner of reassembling the parts.

Both Dunstall and Emery were both injured by the bolt of the rifle being driven back from the breach when it was used for the first time after purchase. Even though the bolt had appeared to be in the locked position it had fired a round but in doing so propelled the bolt to the rear. Each of the men lost the use of his right eye besides suffering other injuries to the head and face. The court felt it necessary to state that both Dunstall and Emery were experienced in the use of firearms but, when injured, were using the Ross rifle for the first time. The court found as a matter of fact that the rifle could be fired when the bolt wasn't locked and, equally important for the purposes of this analysis, that this could not happen with a Lee-Enfield:

> *If then it be fired, and it can be thus fired, the bolt is thrown back in the face of the user. In other rifles with a bolt action, such as the Mauser,* Lee-Enfield, *Lebel, Mannlicker, Nagant, United States Springfield, the rifle cannot be fired until the bolt is locked [emphasis added].*[13]

A government expert's opinion was admitted as part of the proceedings. A series of questions were put to this expert, Major Blair:

> **Question**: *What have you to say regarding a rifle that could have its bolt assembled in the wrong way and yet fire?*
> **Answer**: *Well, in the hands of one unacquainted with its mechanism, in the hands of the everyday individual, I would have to say that there was danger.*
> **Question**: *Would you call that a faulty design?*
> **Answer**: *In my opinion, it would be a fault in design.*
> **Question**: *Would you consider it a dangerous defect?*
> **Answer**: *I would in the hands of a person who did not know whether it was rightly or wrongly assembled; there would be a danger of his getting it into action in a wrong manner which would, if he did so, of course, be dangerous to the firer.*
> **Question**: *I am asking you whether there is anything from the external point of view in the rifle to show that the rifle is assembled in the wrong way?*
> **Answer**: *To one who knows it, yes; to one who does not know it, there is not; in my opinion there is not.*[14]

There is no way that the IRA of mid–1920 could have been aware of the danger that an improperly assembled bolt posed to the firer. It appears that even after the war had ended and participants were writing their memoirs, they were still unaware of the issues that it presented. A visual inspection carried out by those inexperienced in weapons handling would not have disclosed the difficulties. To an inexperienced eye it was simply an attractive rifle, a fact not lost on the Bantry IRA, as described by Flor Crowley:

> *There neatly arranged on their racks, like pins in a paper, were ten carefully oiled, perfectly preserved rifles. It was a sight that some of those Bantry youths will never forget. Ten excellent Ross-Canadian rifles, the first of their kind they had seen – they looked to those young IRA men what the Manna in the desert must have looked to Moses.*[15]

Liam Deasy was aware of the significant contribution that such rifles would make to the IRA efforts and he makes it clear that they were used in subsequent important engagements:

> *This capture considerably improved the volunteers' position in the Bantry Battalion and indeed in the West Cork Brigade generally. Not merely did the success of the raid greatly boost the morale of the men, but the arms were a welcome addition to the Brigade armament. Good use was made of them in many important engagements later in the war.* [16]

While the Ross was an excellent hunting or target rifle, it was not suited to combat firing, primarily due to the fine tolerances associated with the weapon, as the breech was easily fouled by even small quantities of dirt. Its large size made it unsuitable for the narrow confines of trench warfare as it was awkward to handle and consequently became dirty quite easily. Rather than possessing the chief characteristic of any good general issue combat rifle – reliability under harsh conditions – the Ross was a finely tuned instrument requiring a level of knowledge, attention, and care that was simply beyond the limited abilities of the West Cork IRA.

Storing the weapons and ammunition presented other difficulties. The consequences of arms and ammunition being found on someone's property were very serious, so most munitions were stored "off-site" in dumps, which invariably meant being buried underground or hidden in walls. Ernie O'Malley recognised the difficulties that this presented: "It was hard to keep our weapons in repair, harder still to keep arms and stuff dry and clean." [17] Therefore even when the rifles were not being used, they were exposed to those conditions that would most impede their performance.

Notes

Chapter 1

1   Hart, P. (1999) *The IRA & Its Enemies, Violence and Community in Cork 1916-1923*, Oxford: Clarendon Press, p. 21.

2   Meda Ryan, a historian and journalist with West Cork roots, has authored a number of books, including *Tom Barry: IRA Freedom Fighter*. She is described by Martin Mansergh in a review as having crossed swords convincingly with Peter Hart.

3   Peter Hart was a Canadian historian whose book, *The IRA & Its Enemies: Violence & Community in Cork, 1916-1923*, has been described as controversial and provocative and has had a considerable impact on how the events at Kilmichael can be understood.

4   Not all the Crown forces ambushed at Kilmichael were Auxiliaries. There was also a temporary constable (a Black and Tan), Arthur Poole, killed. Poole was part of a drivers' section that had been created purely for transport duties.

5   Barry, T. (1989) *Guerilla Days in Ireland*, Dublin: Anvil Books, hereafter referred to as *Guerilla Days*.

6   Jim's son Cathal reminded me that Jim, although an active column member, had not taken part in the Kilmichael action as he had injured his foot a number of weeks previously in an accident.

7   Barry, *Guerilla Days,* p. 89.

8   Hopkinson, M. (2002) *The Irish War of Independence*, Dublin: Gill & McMillan, p. 105.

9   Kingston, D. (2013) *Beleagured; A History of the RIC in West Cork during the War of Independence*, Skibbereen: Inspire Design and Print, p. 117.

10   Feehan, J.M. (1981) *The shooting of Michael Collins; Murder or Accident*, Cork: Royal Carbery Books, p. 27.

11   O'Hea O'Keefe, J. (2013) *Voices from the Great Houses of Cork and Kerry*, Cork: Mercier Press, p.113.

12   Murphy, G. (2011) *The Year of Disappearances; Political killings in Cork 1921-1922*, Dublin: Gill & Macmillan, p. 6.

13   FCA was the part-time reserve at that time. It is now known as the Reserve Defence Force (RDF).

14   There were a number of Defence Forces personnel who influenced, encouraged and nurtured my marksmanship skills thereby making the victory possible. However I would have to acknowledge the encouragement and assistance of particular members of my unit such as Colonel Brian Dowling, Lt Col Tim Donovan, Comdt Larry Devaney, Comdt Don

Crowley, C/S Martin Hamilton, C/S Murt Teehan, C/S Richard Walker, Sgt Billy Barry, Sgt William O'Donovan, Sgt Liam Stack, Sgt John Meere, Cpl Mossy Gould and Pte John Cashman. All were Ordnance specialists, marksmen, shooting enthusiasts and competitors of the highest order. Between 1988 and 2001 they amassed more shooting honours in the automatic pistol and rifle competitions than any other unit of comparable size in the Irish Defence Forces. A true 'band of brothers'.

Chapter 2

1 One member of the patrol, Cadet Forde although seriously wounded, survived the attack and another member Cadet Gutherie escaped only to be captured and shot by other IRA members not associated with the ambush.

2 McCann, J. (1946) *War by the Irish,* Tralee: Anvil Books, p. 128.

3 "Eyewitness" (1941) 'Kilmichael' *An Cosantóir*, Dublin: Defence Forces Printing Press, Vol. 1, No.22 p. 649. It is claimed that 'Eyewitness', who wrote the article, was in fact Tom Barry writing under a pseudonym.

4 Butler, E. (1971) *Barry's Flying Column*, London: Leo Cooper Ltd, p. 64.

5 Deasy, L. (1973) *Towards Ireland Free*, Cork: The Mercier Press, p. 172.

6 Barry, T. (1974) *The Reality of the Anglo Irish War 1920-21 in West Cork: Refutations, Corrections and Comments on Liam Deasy's 'Towards Ireland Free'*, Tralee & Dublin: Anvil Books, pp.13–14.

7 The publication of Hart's work created an unprecedented level of interest played out primarily in the pages of *The Irish Times* in the latter 6 months of 1998.

8 Hart, *The IRA & Its Enemies*, p. 36.

9 Ferriter, D. (2004) *The Transformation of Ireland*, England: Profile Books, p. 224.

10 Hart, *The IRA & Its Enemies*, pp. 25-26.

11 Ryan, M. (2003) *Tom Barry, IRA Freedom Fighter*, Cork: Mercier Press, p. 74.

12 Coogan, T.P. (1993) *The IRA*, London: Harper Collins, pp. 69-70.

13 *The Irish Times*, 05 April 2014.

14 McCall, E. (2013) *The Auxiliaries: Tudor's Toughs*, Newtownards: Red Coat Publishing, p.102.

15 Von Loringhoven, H. (1911) 'The Power of Personality in War', *Roots of Strategy,* Book 3, USA: Stackpole Books, p. 240.

16 Ruan O'Donnell writing in 2008 in the introduction to *Troubled History; A 10th anniversary critique of Peter Hart's The IRA and its Enemies* by the Aubane Historical Society.

17   Ryan, M. (2007) "The Kilmichael Ambush, 1920: Exploring the Provocative Chapters", *History Ireland* 92(306), p. 236.

Chapter 3

1   Ewell, J. J. and Hunt, I. (1995) *Sharpening the Combat Edge: The Use of Analysis to Reinforce Military Judgement*, Washington DC: Department of the Army, p. 235.

2   Bassford, C. (1994) *Clausewitz in English: The Reception of Clausewitz in Britain and America, 1815-1945*, New York: Oxford University Press. Available at; http://www.clausewitz.com/readings/Bassford/CIE/Chapter19.htm,[Accessed on: 11 June 2012]

3   Artéus, G. *Military History, A historiography*, p.2. Available at; https://www.fhs.se/Documents/Externwebben/forskning/Milit%C3%A4rhistorisk%20Tidskrift/gunnar-arteus-military-history-a-historiography.pdf, [Accessed on: 12 June 2012].

4   Duffy, C. (1998) *The Military Experience in the Age of Reason,* Hertfordshire: Wordsworth Editions Limited, p. 189.

5   Von Clausewitz, C. (1982) *On War*, London: Penguin Books, p. 330.

6   Naveh, S. (1997) *In pursuit of Military Excellence: The evolution of operational theory*, Oxford: Frank Cass publishers, p. 1.

7   Morillo, S. (2013) *What is Military History?* Cambridge: Polity Books, p. 106.

Chapter 4

1   Ainsworth, J. (2001) *The Black and Tans and Auxiliaries in Ireland, 1920-1921: Their Origins, Roles and Legacy,* A paper presented to the Annual Conference of the Queensland History Teachers' Association, 12 May 2001.

2   Murphy G. (2011) *The Year of Disappearances: Political Killings in Cork 1921-1922*, Dublin: Gill & McMillan, p. 13.

3   Beaumont, R.A. (1979) 'Military Elite Forces: Surrogate War, Terrorism, and the New Battlefield', *Parameters*, Vol (IX), No.1 p. 20.

4   Hart, P. (Ed.). (2002) *British Intelligence in Ireland 1920-1921: The Final Reports*, Cork: Cork University Press, p.19.

5   Black, J. (1999) 'War and the World 1450-2000', *The Journal of Military History*, Vol.(63), No.3 p. 671.

6   Bishop, P. & Mallie, E. (1988) *The Provisional IRA*, Great Britain: Corgi, p. 30.

7   Interview with General Sir Rupert Smith on 07 January 2007 in London by Toni

Pfanner (Editor-in-Chief of the International Review of the Red Cross), available in International Review of the Red Cross: Humanitarian debate: Law, policy, action: Methods of Warfare, Volume 88 Number 864 December 2006 at p. 721.

8   Reydams, L. (2006) 'A la guerre comme a la guerre: patterns of armed conflict, humanitarian law responses and new challenges', *International Review of the Red Cross,* Volume 88 Number 864, p. 732.

9   Barry, *Guerilla Days*, p. 23.

10   *An t-Óglach* (1920) "Guerilla Warfare", Vol II, No.5, January 15th p.2.

11   Hughes, D.J. (Ed.). (1993) *Moltke on the Art of War: Selected Writings*, New York: Ballantine Books, p. 45.

12   Barry, *Guerilla Days*, p. 36.

13   Edmonds, S. (1971) *The Gun, the law and the Irish people*, Tralee: Anvil Books, pp. 85-86.

14   Figgis, D. (1927) *Recollections of the Irish War*, London: Billing & Sons, p. 308.

15   Browne, C. (2007) *The Story of the 7th*, Cork: Schull Books, p. 39.

16   O'Casey, S.(1980) "Inisfallen, Fare Thee Well" in *Autobiographies* Vols 2, London, p. 40.

17   Brady, A.J.S. (2010) *The Briar of Life*, Dublin: Original Writing Limited, p. 170.

18   Ainsworth, J. 'British security policy in Ireland, a desperate attempt by the Crown to maintain Anglo-Irish unity by force'. Queensland University of Technology. Available at: http://eprints.qut.edu.au/6/1/British_Security_Policy_in_Ireland.pdf   [Accessed on: 11 June 2011]

19   Laqueur, W. (1977) *Guerilla*, London: Weidenfield and Nicholson, p. 180.

20   Briollay, S. (1922) *Ireland in Rebellion*, Dublin: The Talbot Press Limited, p. 99.

21   Brady, *The Briar of Life*, p. 173.

22   McCall, *The Auxiliaries: Tudor's Toughs*, p. 288.

23   Gleeson, J. (1962) *Bloody Sunday*, London: Peter Davies Ltd, p. 62.

24   Cohen, E.(1978) *Commandos and Politicians*, Cambridge, Massachusetts: Harvard University Press, p. 17.

25   Beaumont, R.A. (1979) 'Military Elite Forces: Surrogate War, Terrorism, and the New Battlefield', *Parameters*, Vol (IX), No.1, p. 20.

26   Black, J. (1999) 'War and the World 1450-2000', *The Journal of Military History*, Vol. (63), No.3, p. 671.

27   I am greatly indebted to Mr. Andrew Nelson of Northumbria University for allowing me to make extensive use of his research contained in his article 'The other boys of

Kilmichael': No.2 Section, 'C' Company, Auxiliary Division Royal Irish Constabulary, 28 November 1929 published in *Historical Research* DOI;10.1111/1468-2281.12057.

28   MacKenzie, S.P. (1992) *Politics and Military Morale: Current Affairs and Citizenship Education in the British Army 1914-1950*, Oxford: Clarendon Press, p.3.

29   Sheehan, W.(2009) *Hearts and Mines: The British 5th Division, Ireland, 1920-1922*, Cork: The Collins Press, p. 60.

30   Gleeson, J. (1962) *Bloody Sunday*, London: Peter Davies Ltd, pp. 57-58.

31   McRaven, W.H. (1996) *Spec Ops; Case Studies in Special Operations Warfare, Theory and Practice*, USA: Ballantine Books, p. 391.

32   Bennett, R. (1970) *The Black and Tans*, Great Britain: New English Library, p. 111.

33   Gleeson, J. (1962) *Bloody Sunday*, London: Peter Davies Ltd, pp. 57-58.

34   Kitson, F. (1971) *Low intensity operations: Subversion, Insurgency and Peacekeeping*, London: Faber and Faber, p. 95.

35   There exists a possibility, as reported in *The Times* of 02 December 1920, that they were specifically searching for an informant from the Dunmanway area who had gone missing.

36   Augusteijn, J. (2003) *From Public Defiance to Guerilla Warfare; The Experience of Ordinary Volunteers in the Irish War of Independence 1916-1921*, Dublin: Irish Academic Press, p. 212.

37   Van Crevald, M. (1982) *Fighting Power; German and U.S. Army Performance 1939-1945*, USA: Greenwood Press, p. 4.

38   I have not counted scouts as being part of the actual combat but I do recognise the important role that they provided.

39   Laqueur, W. (1977) *Guerilla*, London: Weidenfield and Nicholson, p. 181.

40   Graber, G.S. (1978) *History of the SS*, London: Robert Hale, p. 26.

41   Acknowledgements to local historian, Mary O'Leary for making the plans of Courtmacsherry Coast Guard Station available for this publication.

42   John Roche, pension application, WMSP34REF1950 JOHNROCHE at p. 11. Available at: mspsearch.militaryarchives.ie [Accessed on: 5 May 2014].

43   BMH.WS1603 of Michael J.Crowley at p. 6. Michael J. Crowley (1957) Bureau of Military History 1913-1921, Document No. W. S. 1603, p. 6.

44   Report made available to author by local historian Ms Mary O'Leary

45   BMH WS1530 of Christopher O'Connell at p.13 states that the station was garrisoned by 12 marines and that they recovered 12 Ross rifles. I have established in correspondence with the Weapons and Ordnance section at the National Museum of the Royal Navy that

the short magazine Lee Enfields(SMLE) was issued to those Royal Marines deployed ashore on operations. By way of information and in a similar role, Lee Enfield's were issued to Royal Marines who were engaged in coastal defence duties in the Orkney Islands.

46   BMH WS1527 of Liam O'Dwyer at p.15 or BMH WS1567 of James McCarthy at p. 16.

47   Acknowledgements are extended to the staff at Naval Historical Branch, HM Naval Base, Portsmouth for assistance. Keith Jeffrey's *MI6: The History of the Secret Intelligence Services 1909-1949* is recommended for more in-depth study on this area.

48   James McCarthy (1954), Bureau of Military History 1913-1921, Document No. WS1567, p. 11.

49   Ibid., p.16.

50   Sheila O'Neill, pension application, WMSP34 REF49981, available at: mspsearch.militaryarchives.ie [Accessed on: 5 May 2014].

51   Denis O' Callaghan interview tape.

52   Hammond, B. (1977) *Soldier of the Rearguard; The story of Matt Flood and the Active Service Column,* Fermoy: Eigse na Mainistreach Publications, p. 9.

53   O' Callaghan tape.

54   Hughes, D.J. (Ed.). (1993) *Moltke on the Art of War: Selected Writings*, New York: Ballantine Books, p. 34.

55   Alonso, R. (2007) *The IRA and Armed Struggle*, Oxon: Routledge, p. 154.

56   Keegan, J. (1983) *The Face of Battle*, London: Penguin, p. 13.

57   Available at http://theauxiliaries.com/INCIDENTS/Kilmichael-ambush/Kilmichael. html [Accessed on: 21 July 2013].

58   *An t-Óglach* (1920) "Bogs as Military Obstacles", Vol II, No.5, January 15th, p. 4.

59   *An t-Óglach* (1921) "Lorry Fighting 1", Vol II, No.22, February 1st, p. 4.

60   Deasy, *Towards Ireland Free*, p. 170.

61   Barry, *Guerilla Days*, p. 42.

62   Deasy, *Towards Ireland Free*, p. 171.

63   *The Times*. (1920) Kilmichael ambush press report, December 02

64   Costelloe, F. (2003) *The Irish Revolution and Its Aftermath; 1916-1923 Years of Revolt*, Dublin: Irish Academic Press, p. 98.

Chapter 5

1   Ryan, M. (2005) "Peter Hart and Tom Barry", *History Ireland,* May/June 2005, p.13.

2   Laqueur, W. (1977) *Guerilla,* London: Weidenfield and Nicolson:, p. 178.

3   Bishop, P. & Mallie, E. (1988) *The Provisional IRA*, Great Britain: Corgi, p. 30.

4   Barry, T. (1974) *The Reality of the Anglo Irish War*, p. 8.

5   I have come across a reference which suggests that the move from Clogher to Ahilina occurred on the previous Wed (24 November) and that the column were holding two British soldiers as prisoners. I haven't come across another reference which supports this, see Kilmichael Historical Society (2010) *Kilmichael through the Ages*, Skibbereen: Inspire Design and Print, p. 107.

6   Buckley, D. (2008) *The Battle of Tourmakeady, Fact or Fiction; A study of the IRA Ambush and its Aftermath*, Dublin: Nonsuch Publishing, p. 38.

7   Barry, T. (1974) *The Reality of the Anglo-Irish War*, p.14.

8   Corrigan, G. (2003) *Mud, Blood and Poppycock*, London: Cassell Military Paperbacks, p. 108.

9   Barry, *Guerilla Days*, p. 42.

10   Von Clausewitz, C. (1982) *On War*, London: Penguin Books Ltd, p. 164.

11   Naveh, S. (1997) *In pursuit of Military Excellence: The evolution of operational theory*, Oxford: Frank Cass publishers, p. 74.

12   Hughes, D.J. (Ed.). (1993) *Moltke on the Art of War: Selected Writings*, New York: Ballantine Books, p. 52.

13   Barry, *Guerilla Days*, p. 43.

14   James ("Spud") Murphy (1957) Bureau of Military History 1913-1921, Document No. W.S. 1684, p. 6.

15   Deasy, *Towards Ireland Free*, p.171. The account given in this publication which was published in 1973 does not give a reference as to when Paddy O'Brien supplied this detailed description of what transpired nor does it give an origin or explanation as to how Deasy secured this version of events.

16   Paddy O'Brien (1953) Bureau of Military History 1913-1921, Document No. W.S. 812, p. 15.

17   Edward Young (1956) Bureau of Military History 1913-1921, Document No. W.S. 1404, pp. 15-16.

18   Michael O'Driscoll (1955) Bureau of Military History 1913-1921, Document No. W.S. 1297, pp 4-5. In Michael O'Driscoll's statement a section of the sentence, "A bomb

was thrown into the front of the lorry and" has a line through it as if to signify that this was later withdrawn or redacted or struck out of the statement.

19   Jack Hennessy (1955) Bureau of Military History 1913-1921, Document No. W.S. 1234, p. 5.

20   Timothy Keohane (1955) Bureau of Military History 1913-1921, Document No. W.S. 1295, p. 6.

21   Barry, *Guerilla Days*, p. 39.

22   Ibid., p. 41.

23   Support for the assumption of nine Auxiliaries being in the front lorry is provided by the Kilmichael Historical Society (2010) *Kilmichael through the Ages*, Skibbereen:Inspire Design and Print, p.108.

24   Corrigan, G. (2003) *Mud, Blood and Poppycock*, London:Cassell Military paperbacks, p. 136.

25   'Eyewitness' describes the grenade being thrown a distance of fifty yards. This can be rejected as wholly implausible.

26   War Office. (1938) *Infantry Section Leading*, London: HMSO, p. 12.

27   Barry, *The Reality of the Anglo Irish War*, pp. 15–16.

28   Stephenson, M. (2013) *The last full measure; How soldiers die in battle*, London: Duckworth Overlook, p. 229.

29   James ("Spud") Murphy (1957) Bureau of Military History 1913-1921, Document No. W.S. 1684, p. 6.

30   Doubler, M.D.(1994) *Closing with the Enemy: How G.I.s fought the War in Europe*, 1944-1945, USA: University Press of Kansas, p. 37.

31   Barry, *Guerilla Days*, p. 44.

32   Stephenson, M. (2013) *The last full measure; How soldiers die in battle*, London: Duckworth Overlook, p. 192.

33   Barry, *Guerilla Days in Ireland*, p. 44.

34   Keegan, J. (1983) *The Face of Battle*, London: Penguin Books Ltd, p. 47.

35   Rinker, R. (1998) *Understanding Ballistics; Basic to Advanced Ballistics Simplified, Illustrated & Explained*, USA: Mulberry House Publishing, p. 105.

36   Kilmichael Historical Society (2010) *Kilmichael through the Ages*, Skibbereen: Inspire Design and Print, p. 108.

37   Chivers, C.J. (2010) *The Gun; The AK-47 and the Evolution of War*, Great Britain: Allen Lane, p. 267.

38   Spiers, E.M.(Ed.). (2006) *Between the South African War and the First World War in Big Wars and Small Wars: The British Army and the lessons of War in the 20th Century* , Oxford: Routledge, p. 30.

39   "Eyewitness" (1941), 'Kilmichael', *An Cosantóir*, Dublin, Defence Forces Printing Press, p. 649.

40   Barry refers to the engagement at the first truck lasting nearly 5 minutes, *Guerilla Days*, p. 44.

41   Edward Young (1956) Bureau of Military History 1913-1921, Document No. W.S. 1404, p. 16.

42   Barry, *Guerilla Days,* pp. 44-45.

43   Timothy Keohane (1955) Bureau of Military History 1913-1921, Document No. W.S. 1295, pp. 6-7.

44   Jack Hennessy (1955) Bureau of Military History 1913-1921, Document No. W.S. 1234, pp. 5-6.

45   Michael O'Driscoll (1955) Bureau of Military History 1913-1921, Document No. W.S. 1297, p. 5.

46   Paddy O'Brien (1953) Bureau of Military History 1913-1921, Document No. W.S. 812, pp 15-16.

47   James ("Spud") Murphy (1957) Bureau of Military History 1913-1921, Document No. W.S. 1684, pp. 6-7.

48   Department of Health and Children, (1998) *Hearing Disability Assessment: Report of the Expert Hearing Group*, Dublin: Stationery Office, p. 9.

49   Bak, M. Fiszer, M. Kotylo, P. Sliwinska-Kowalska, M. (2004) 'Temporary changes in hearing after exposure to shooting noise in *International Journal of Occupational Medicine and Environmental Health,* 17(2): 285-293.

50   Barry, *Guerilla Days,* p. 44.

51   Ibid., p. 47.

52   Ryan, M. (2012) *Tom Barry: Freedom Fighter*, Cork: Mercier Press, p. 66.

53   Ibid., p. 70.

54   Hart, *The IRA & Its Enemies*, p. 34.

55   Ibid., p. 34, footnote 58.

56   WS 1297, available at the Defence Forces, Military Archives, Cathal Brugha Barracks. The "S" file is the investigating officer's assessment of the reliability of the witness. It was drafted separately and after the witness statement had been taken.

57   Lucy, J.F. (1992) *There's a Devil in the Drum*, England: The Naval and Military Press Ltd, p. 225.

58   Deasy, *Towards Ireland Free*, p. 172.

59   Acknowledgements to Dr Eve Morrison, School of History and Archives, University College Dublin for bringing this letter to my attention.

60   Barry, *Guerilla Days*, p. 65.

61   Francis Davis (1951), Bureau of Military History 1913-1921, Document No. WS496, p. 28.

62   McMahon, P. (2008) *British Spies and Irish Rebels; British Intelligence and Ireland 1916-1945*, Great Britain: CPI Anthony Rowe, p. 17.

63   Hall's successor as the Director of Naval Intelligence in 1919 and therefore in place at the time of the ambush was Commodore (later Admiral) Hugh Francis Paget Sinclair. He was equally as proficient and industrious as Hall creating the Government Code and Cypher School (GC&CS), later GCHQ. He went on to become the Director of SIS (MI6) from 1923. He argued for the creation of a unified intelligence service, which would have brought together SIS, GC&CS as well as MI5 and counter intelligence thus demonstrating his ability to see the bigger picture.

64   Ramsay, D. (2008) *'Blinker' Hall: Spymaster*, UK: Spellmount Ltd., Introduction.

65   Beesley, P. (1982) *Room 40; British Naval Intelligence 1914-18,* Oxford: Oxford University Press, p. 38.

66   Ramsay, *'Blinker' Hall: Spymaster,* p. 87.

67   Ibid., p. 132.

68   *Rebel Cork's Fighting Story* (1949) Tralee: *The Kerryman*, p. 54.

69   According to the Kilmichael Historical Society's account, Michael McCarthy didn't die during the engagement but was seriously injured and died later while being carried by horse and cart to Buttimer's house in Gortroe. Kilmichael Historical Society (2010) *Kilmichael through the Ages*, Skibbereen: Inspire Design and Print, p. 115.

70   Philips, R. (1969) *Sir Charles Ross and his rifle; Historical Arms Series No.11,* Canada: Ontario Museum Restoration Service, p. 22.

71   *Swindon Evening Advertiser*, 01 December 1920.

72   Edward Young (1956) Bureau of Military History 1913-1921, Document No. W.S. 1404, p. 15.

73   Ibid., p. 15.

74   Barry, T. (1989) Guerilla Days in Ireland, Dublin: Anvil Books, p. 45.

75   Paddy O'Brien mentions John Lordon being wounded but Barry said he "wasn't even scratched" as reported in *The Reality of the Anglo Irish War* at p. 17.

76   Barry, *Guerilla Days*, pp. 44-45.

77   See generally Small Arms Training, Vol I, Pamphlet No.II, Pistol (.455=inch).
78   Doubler, M.D.(1994) *Closing with the Enemy: How G.I.s fought the War in Europe, 1944-1945*, USA: University Press of Kansas, pp. 238-239.

Chapter 6

1   McRaven, W.H. (1995) *Spec Ops: case studies in Special Operations Warfare: Theory and Practice*, New York: Ballantine Books, p. 11.

2   Hackett, J. (1983) *The Profession of Arms*, New York: Macmillan, p. 146.

3   Van Creveld, M. (2006) *The Changing Face of War: Lessons of Combat from the Marne to Iraq*, New York: Ballantine Books, p. 14.

4   Townsend, C. (1983) *Political Violence in Ireland; Government resistance since 1848*, Oxford: Clarendon Press, p. 336.

5   Barry, *Guerilla Days*, p. 39.

6   Ibid., p.36.

7   Ibid., p.48.

8   McCall, *The Auxiliaries; Tudor's Toughs*, p. 288.

9   War Office (1936) *Text Book of Ammunition*, London: HMSO, p. 223.

10   Sheehan, W. (2009) *Hearts & Mines*, Cork: The Collins Press, p.94.

11   War Office (1914), *Field service pocket book 1914*, London: HMSO, p. 162.

Chapter 7

1   Edson, M. "Scope Sights on .22 and Value of Marksmanship", p.19. Available at: http://www.rifleman.org.uk/Historical_notes_and_extracts_Main.html [Accessed on: 18 July 2012]

2   Pegler, M. (2012) *The Lee-Enfield Rifle*, UK: Osprey publishing ltd, p. 22.

3   Hogg, I. & Gander, T. (2005) *Jane's: Guns Recognition Guide*, London: Harper Collins Publishers, p. 257.

4   Hughes, D.J. (Ed.). (1993) *Moltke on the Art of War: Selected Writings*, New York: Ballantine Books, p . 154.

5   Stevenson, R. (2013) *To Win the Battle: The 1st Australian Division in the Great War, 1914-1918*, Cambridge: Cambridge University Press.

6   Barry, *Guerilla Days*, p. 9.

7   Stephenson, M. (2013) *The Last Full Measure: How Soldiers Die in Battle*, London: Duckworth Overlook, p. 297.

8   Hogg, I. & Gander, T. (2005) *Jane's: Guns Recognition Guide*, London: Harper Collins Publishers, p. 267.

9   Johnson, M. and Haven, C. (1943) *Automatic Arms*, New York: William Morrow and Co, pp. 185-186.

10   Defence Forces (1932) *Rifle Marksmanship, Training Regulations No.3,* Dublin: The Stationary Office, p. 59.

11   Many thanks to the project team who are currently conducting an historical evaluation of the Battle of Mount Street for their cooperation in the conduct of the experment.

12   Barry, *Guerilla Days*, p. 47.

Chapter 8

1   Lindee, S. (2007) "Experimental Wounds: Science and Violence in Mid-Century America", *Dark Medicine: Rationalizing Unethical Medical Research*, Lafleur, W.R. and Bohme, G. and Shimazono, S. (2007) US: Indiana Universtiry Press, p. 123.

2   Farrar, C.L. & Leeming D.W. (1983) *Military Ballistics-A Basic Manual,* Oxford: Brassey's Publishers Ltd, p. 163.

3   Rinker, R.A. (1998) *Understanding Ballistics*, USA: Mulberry House Publishing, pp. 298-299.

4   Houghton Beck, H. (1900) *History of South Africa and the Boer-British War,* Philadelphia: Globe Bible Publishing Company, p. 404.

5   The origin of these expanding bullets is attributed to the work of a British officer, Capt. Bertie Clay at the arsenal at Dum Dum, India. He developed a bullet that would peel back on impact by opening the jacket at the nose of the round thus exposing the lead core causing the bullet to mushroom on impact and greatly increasing the lethality of the bullet's impact.

6   *"The Contracting Parties agree to abstain from the use of bullets which expand or flatten easily in the human body, such as bullets with a hard envelope which does not entirely cover the core, or is pierced with incisions."*

7   Pegler, M. (2012) *The Lee-Enfield Rifle, Chin*a: Osprey Publishing Ltd, pp. 24-25.

8   Junger, E. (2003) *Storm of Steel,* London: Allen Lane/The Penguin Press, p. 150.

9   Barnes, F.C. (2006) *Cartridges of the World*, USA: Gun Digest Books, p. 356.

10   Farrar, C.L. and   Leeming, D.W.(1983) *Military Ballistics-A Basic Manual*, Oxford: Brassey's Publishers Ltd, p. 166.

11   Junger, E. (2003) *Storm of Steel*, London: Allen Lane/The Penguin Press, p. 64.

12   Smith, J.C. "The scope is the proof" p.20 Available at http://www.rifleman.org.uk/Historical_notes _and_extracts_Main.html [Accessed on: 18 July 2012].

13   Kilmichael Historical Society (2010) *Kilmichael through the Ages*, Skibbereen: Inspire Print and Design, p. 111.

14   Von Clausewitz, C. (1982) *On War,* London: Penguin Books Ltd, p. 160.

15   *Rebel Cork's Fighting Story* (1947) Tralee: The Kerryman, p. 106.

16   Turner, W.A. (1915) Remarks on cases of nervous and mental shock. BMJ 1915;I: 833-5 in "Shell shock, Gordon Holmes and the Great War", *The Journal of the Royal Society of Medicine*, 2004 February: 97(2): 86–89 by AD Macleod , Available at http://www.ncbi.nlm.nih.gov/pmc/articles [Accessed on: 3 July 2012].

17   Belenky, G.L. Sodetz, F.J. and Tyner, F.C. (1983) *Israeli Battle Shock Casualties: 1973 and 1982*, Walter Reed Army Institute of Research, Washington, DC 20307, US Army Research and Development Command, p. 3.

18   Gabriel, R. (1986) *Soviet Military Psychiatry: the Theory and Practice of Coping with Battle Stress*, New York: Greenwood Press, p. 49.

19   Barry, *Guerilla Days*, p. 46.

20   Kearney, P. (1950) Bureau of Military History 1913-1921, Document No. W.S. 444, pp. 15-16.

21   Barry, *Guerilla Days*, p. 54.

22   John Roche, pension application, WMSP34REF1950 JOHNROCHE at p. 11. Available at: mspsearch.militaryarchives.ie [Accessed on: 5 May 2014].

23   Jerome O'Hea, pension application, WMSP34REF9787 at p. 15. Available at mspsearch.militaryarchives.ie [Accessed 5 May 2014].

24   Available at http://www.theauxiliaries.com/companies/c-coy/c-coy.html [Accessed on: 29 Dec 2013].

Chapter 9

1   *The Times*, 02 Dec 1920.

2   *Swindon Evening Advertiser*, 1 December 1920.

3   Scheipers, S. (2013) 'Fighting Irregular Fighters, Is the law of Armed Conflict Outdat-

ed?' *Parameters* 43(4) Winter 2013-14, p. 46.

4   *The Lieber Code,* p. 39, avalable at http://www.icrc.org/ihl.nsf [Accessed on: 15 May 2013].

5   Montgomery, B. (1958) *The Memoirs of Field Marshall Montgomery*, London: Collins Clear Type Press, pp. 39-40.

6   War Office (1914) *Manual of Military Law*, London: HMSO, p. 217.

7   Ibid., para 10, p. 218.

8   CO904/168, UK National Archives, London.

9   Geib, R. (2006) 'Asymmetric conflict structures', *International Review of The Red Cross* Vol 88, No.864, December.

10   Convention (IV) respecting the Laws and Customs of War on Land, The Hague, 18 October 1907, Art. 1.

11   See Art 43(1) of the 1977 Protocol 1 to The Geneva Conventions of 1949.

12   Regulations respecting the Laws and Customs of War on Land, The Hague, 18 October 1907, Section 1, Chapter 1, Art. 1.

13   War Office (1914) *Manual of Military Law*, London: HMSO, p. 239.

14   Kilcullen, D. (2009) *The Accidental Guerilla*, London: Hurst & Co, p. 30.

15   Article 14, *The Lieber Code* Available at http://www.icrc.org/ihl.nsf [Accessed on: 15 May 2013].

16   Ignatieff, M. (1999) T*he Warrior's Honor: Ethnic war and the Modern Conscience,* London: Vintage, p. 118.

Chapter 10

1   Rotte, R. and Schmidt, C. (2002), "On the production of victory: Empirical Determinants of Battlefield Success in Modern War" IZA Discussion Paper No.41, p.4.

2   Von Clausewitz, C. (1982) *On War,* London: Penguin Books, p. 86.

3   Johnson, R. (1989), *Lanchester's Square Law in Theory and Practice*, p. 3, available at www.dtic.mil [Accessed on: 3 June 2013].

4   Geldenhuys, G. and Botha, E. *A note on Dupuy's QJM and the New Square Law,* Orion, Vol.10, No.1/2, pp. 45-55.

5   Lindee, S. (2007) "Experimental Wounds: Science and Violence in Mid-Century America", *Dark Medicine: Rationalizing Unethical Medical Research*, Lafleur, W.R. and Bohme, G. and Shimazono, S. (2007) US: Indiana Universtiry Press, p. 125.

6   Choi, J (2009) *Combat evolved: Lanchester's Laws in Modern Warfare*, p.9, available at www.aladinrc.wrlc.org [Accessed on: 3 June 2013].

7   Engel, J.H. (1954) "A verification of Lanchester's Law" in *Journal of the Operations Research Society of America*, Vol. 2, No.2 (May, 1954), pp. 163–171.

8   "Eyewitness" (2009) *Our struggle for Independence: Eye-witness accounts from the pages of An Cosantoir*, edited by Terence O'Reilly, (Mercier Press), p. 103.

9   Rotte, R. and Schmidt, C. (2002), *On the production of victory: Empirical Determinants of Battlefield success in Modern War*, Discussion Paper No.491

10   Gray, C.S. (2010) *The Strategy Bridge*, Oxford: Oxford University Press, p. 215.

11   Gabriel, R.A. and Savage, P.L. *Crisis in Command: Mismanagement in the Army*, New York: Greewood Press, p. 51.

12   Begley, D. (1999), *The Road to Crossbarry: The Decisive Battle of Ireland's War of Independence 1991-1921*, Cork: Deso Publications, p. 101.

13   Keegan, J. (1987) *Mask of Command*, New York: Viking Penguin, p. 329.

14   Begley, D (1999), *The Road to Crossbarry: The Decisive Battle of Ireland's War of Independence 1991-1921*, Cork: Deso Publications, p. 101.

15   Ewell, J.J. and Hunt, I. (1995) *Sharpening the Combat Edge: The Use of Analysis to Reinforce Military Judgement*, Dept of the Army, Washington, DC, p. 78.

16   Marshall, S.L.A. (1947) *Men Against Fire, The Problem of Battle Command*, US: University of Oklahoma Press, p. 50.

17   Chambers, J.W. (2003) "S.L.A. Marshall's *Men Against Fire*: New Evidence Regarding Fire Ratios", *Parameters*, Autumn 2003.

18   See Dave Grossman (2009) "S.L.A. Marshall revisited…?" in *Canadian Military Journal*, Vol 9, No.4, 2009.

19   Lord, F.A. (1995) *Civil War Collector's Encyclopedia*, US: Blue and Grey Press.

20   Keegan, J. (1976) *The Face of Battle*, London: Penguin Books, p. 28.

21   James Murphy (1957), Bureau of Military History 1913-1921, Document No. WS1684, p. 4.

Chapter 11

1   Ignatieff, M. (1999) *The Warrior's Honor: Ethnic war and the Modern Conscience,* London: Vintage, p. 117.

2   Doubler, M.D. (1994) *Closing with the Enemy: How G.Is Fought The War in Europe, 1944-1945*, USA: University Press of Kansas, p. 8.

3   Hopkinson, M. (Ed.). (2002) *The Irish Revolution, 1913-1923*, UK: Palgrave MacMillan, p. 124.

4   Hart, P. (2003) *The IRA at War 1916-1923,* Oxford: Oxford University Press, p. 81.

5   Murphy, J.A. (2000) 'Bloody fable of Kilmichael's dead' *Irish Independent* (26 Nov) Available at http://www.independent.ie/opinion/analysis/bloody-fable-of-kilmichaels-dead-26257440.html [Accessed on: 13 June 2013].

Appendix II: the Ross Rifle

1   Philips, R. (1969) *Sir Charles Ross and his rifle; Historical Arms Series No.11,* Canada: Ontario Museum Restoration Service, p. 16.

2   Read, D. (ed.) (1978) The Great War and Canadian Society; An Oral History, Toronto: New Hogtown Press, p. 153.

3   Nicholson, G.W.L. (1962) *Canadian Expeditionary Force 1914-1919*, Ottawa: Queen's Printer, p. 156.

4   Philips, R. (1969) "Sir Charles Ross and his rifle", *Historical Arms Series,* No.11, Ontario: Museum Restoration Service, p. 16.

5   Letter from Field Marshall J.D.P French of 19th June 1915 contained in "Correspondence relating to the use of the Ross rifle by the Canadian troops in France", presented to both Houses of Parliament by Command of His Majesty (1916) London, HMSO, p. 1.

6   Letter from General Douglas Haig, Commanding-in-Chief, British Armies in France of 28th May 1916, contained in "Correspondence relating to the use of the Ross rifle by the Canadian troops in France", presented to both Houses of Parliament by Command of His Majesty (1916) London, HMSO, p. 3.

7   Paraphrase telegram from the Governor-General of Canada to the Secretary of State for the Colonies dated 6th Nune 1916, contained in "Correspondence relating to the use of the Ross rifle by the Canadian troops in France", presented to both Houses of Parliament by Command of His Majesty (1916) London, HMSO, p. 4.

8   Ibid., p. 4.

9   Stent, H.V. "The Ross Rifle Ruckus" in *Guns Digest*, May 1958, Vol IV, No.5-41, p. 40.

10   Ibid., p. 41.

11   Philips, R. (1969) *Sir Charles Ross and his rifle; Historical Arms Series No.11,* Canada: Ontario Museum Restoration Service, p. 30

12   Stent, H.V. "The Ross Rifle Ruckus" in *Guns Digest*, May 1958, Vol IV, No.5-41, p. 40.

13   Supreme Court of Canada, Vol. LXII, 1921, Ross V Dunstall, Ross V Emery, p. 416.

14 Ibid., pp. 411–412.

15 *Rebel Cork's Fighting Story*, Traleee, The Kerryman, p.53.

16 Deasy, *Towards Ireland Free*, p. 89.

17 O'Malley, E. (1979) *On Another Man's Wound*, Dublin: Anvil Books Ltd, p. 211.

Bibliography

Books

Augusteijn, J. (2003) *From Public Defiance to Guerilla Warfare; The Experience of Ordinary Volunteers in the   Irish War of Independence 1916-1921*, Dublin: Irish Academic Press.

Barnes, F.C. (2006) *Cartridges of the World*, USA: Gun Digest Books.

Barry, T. (1989) *Guerilla Days in Ireland*, Dublin: Anvil Books.

Beckett, F.W. (2010) *Modern Insurgencies and Counter Insurgencies: Guerillas and their opponents since 1750,* London: Routledge.

Beesley, P. (1982) *Room 40; British Naval Intelligence 1914-18,* Oxford: Oxford University Press.

Begley, D. (1999) *The Road to Crossbarry: The Decisive Battle of Ireland's War of Independence 1991-1921*, Cork: Deso publications.

Bennett, R. (1970) *The Black and Tans*, Great Britain: New English Library.

Bishop, P. & Mallie, E. (1988) *The Provisional IRA*, Great Britain: Corgi Books.

Borgonovo, J. (2007) *Spies, Informers and the 'Anti-Sinn Féin Society'*, Dublin: Irish Academic Press.

Brady, A.J.S. (2010) *The Briar of Life*, Dublin: Original Writing Limited.

Briollay, S. (1922) *Ireland in Rebellion*, Dublin: The Talbot Press Limited.

Browne, C. (2007) *The Story of the 7th*, Cork: Schull Books.

Browning, E. (2011) *Slaughtered like Animals*, Surrey: Grosvenor House Publishing Limited.

Buckley, D. (2008) *The Battle of Tourmakeady, Fact or Fiction; A study of the IRA Ambush and its Aftermath*, Dublin: Nonsuch publishing.

Butler, E. (1971) *Barry's Flying Column*, London: Leo Cooper Ltd.

Canadian Army (1914) *Rifle and Musketry Exercises for the Ross Rifle*, Ottawa: Government Printing Board.

Chivers, C.J. (2010) *The Gun; The AK-47 and the Evolution of War*, Great Britain: Allen Lane.

Clinton, E. (1993) *Small Arms of The World, A Basic Manual of Small Arms*, New York: Barns and Noble Books.

Cohen, E. (1978) *Commandos and Politicians*, Cambridge, Massachusetts: Harvard University Press.

Coogan, T.P. (1993) *The IRA*, London: Harper Collins.

Corrigan, G. (2003) *Mud, Blood and Poppycock*, London: Cassell Military Paperbacks.

Costelloe, F. (2003) *The Irish Revolution and Its Aftermath; 1916-1923 Years of Revolt*, Dublin: Irish Academic Press.

Craven, C. & Humphreys, G. (1997) *Military Law in Ireland*, Dublin: Round Hall Sweet & Maxwell.

Daly, E. (2007) *Skibbereen and District: Fact and Folklore*, Cork: Heron's Way Press.

Deasy, L. (1973) *Towards Ireland Free*, Cork: The Mercier Press.

Doubler, M.D. (1994) *Closing with the Enemy: How G.Is Fought The War in Europe, 1944-1945*, USA: University Press of Kansas.

Duffy, C. (1998) *The Military Experience in the Age of Reason,* Hertfordshire: Wordsworth Editions Limited.

Edmonds, S. (1971) *The Gun, the law and the Irish people*, Tralee: Anvil Books.

Farrar, C.L. & Leeming D.W. (1983) *Military Ballistics-A Basic Manual*, Oxford: Brassey's Publishers Ltd.

Ferriter, D. (2004) *The Transformation of Ireland*, England: Profile Books.

Figgis, D. (1927) *Recollections of the Irish War*, London: Billing & Sons.

Gabriel, R.A. & Savage, P.L. (1978) *Crisis in Command: Mismanagement in the Army,* New York: Hill & Wang.

Gabriel, R. (1986) *Soviet Military Psychiatry: the Theory and Practice of Coping with Battle Stress*, New York: Greenwood Press.

Gleeson, J. (1962) *Bloody Sunday*, London: Peter Davies Ltd.

Gray, C.S. (2010) *The Strategy Bridge*, Oxford: Oxford University Press.

Hackett, J. (1983) *The Profession of Arms*, New York: Macmillan.

Hammes, T.X. (2004) *The Sling and the Stone: On war in the 21st Century*, US: Zenith Press.

Hammond, B. (1977) *Soldier of the Rearguard; The story of Matt Flood and the Active Service Column,* Fermoy:,Eigse na Mainistreach Publications.

Hanley, B. (2010) *The IRA: A documentary history 1916-2005*, Dublin: Gill and Macmillan.

Hart, P. (1999) *The IRA & Its Enemies, Violence and Community in Cork 1916-1923*, Oxford: Clarendon Press.

Hart, P. (2003) *The IRA at War 1916-1923*, Oxford: Oxford University Press.

Hickey, P. (2002) *Famine in West Cork: The Mizen Peninsula Land and People 1800-1852,* Cork: Mercier Press.

Hogg, I. & Gander, T. (2005) *Jane's: Guns Recognition Guide*, London: Harper Collins Publishers.

Hopkinson, M. (Ed.). (2002) *The Irish Revolution, 1913-1923,* UK: Palgrave MacMillan.

Hopkinson, M. (2002) *The Irish War of Independence*, Dublin: Gill & McMillan.

Houghton Beck, H. (1900) *History of South Africa and the Boer British War*, Philadelphia: Globe Bible Publishing Company.

Hughes, D.J. (Ed.). (1993) *Moltke on the Art of War: Selected Writings*, New York: Ballantine Books.

ICRC. (2005) *Rules of International Humanitarian Law and Other Rules Relating to The Conduct of Hostilities*, Geneva: ICRC.

ICRC. (2006) *International Review of the Red Cross: Methods of Warfare*, Vol. 88, No. 864, Geneva: ICRC.

Ignatieff, M. (1999) *The Warrior's Honor: Ethnic war and the Modern Conscience*, London: Vintage.

Irish Permanent Defence Forces (1932) *Rifle Marksmanship, Training Regulations No.3*, Dublin: The Stationary Office.

Johnson, M. & Haven, C. (1943) *Automatic Arms*, New York: William Morrow and Co.

Junger, E. (2003) *Storm of Steel,* London: Allen Lane/The Penguin Press.

Kautt, W.H. (2010) *Ambushes and Armour: the Irish Rebellion 1919-1921*, Dublin: Irish Academic Press.

Kautt, W.H. (2014) *Ground Truths: British Army Operations in the Irish War of Independence*, Dublin: Irish Academic Press.

Keane, B. (2014) *Massacre in West Cork: The Dunmanway and Ballygorman killings*, Cork: The Mercier Press.

Keegan, J. (1983) *The Face of Battle*, London: Penguin Books.

Keegan, J. (1987) *Mask of Command*, New York: Viking Penguin.

Kilcullen, D. (2009) *The Accidental Guerilla*, London: Hurst & Co.

Kilmichael Historical Society. (2010) *Kilmichael through the Ages*, Skibbereen: Inspire Print and Design.

Kingston, D. (2013) *Beleagured; A History of the RIC in West Cork during the

War of Independence, Skibbereen: Inspire Print and Design.

Laqueur, W. (1977) *Guerilla*, London: Weidenfield and Nicholson.

Letourneau, G. (1995) *Commission of Inquiry into the Deployment of the Canadian Forces to Somalia*, Ottawa: Farr Spriggs Reporting Inc.

Lindee, S. (2008) 'Experimental Injury: Wound Ballistics and Aviation Medicine in Mid-century America' in *Dark Medicine: Rationalizing Unethical Medical Research,* La Fleur, W.R. (Ed.). US: Indiana University Press

Lord, F.A. (1995) *Civil War Collector's Encyclopaedia*, US: Blue and Grey Press.

Lucy, J.F. (1992) *There's a Devil in the Drum*, England: The Naval and Military Press Ltd.

Mackenzie, S.P. (1992) *Politics and Military Morale: Current Affairs and Citizenship Education in the British Army 1914-1950,* Oxford: Clarendon Press.

Marshall, S.L.A. (1947) *Men Against Fire, The Problem of Battle Command*, US: University of Oklahoma Press.

Mitchell, A. (2013) *16 Lives: Roger Casement*, Dublin: The O'Brien Press.

McCall, E. (2013) *The Auxiliaries; Tudor's Toughs*, Newtownards: Red Coat Publishing.

McCall, E. (2013) *The Auxies*, Newtownards: Red Coat Publishing.

McMahon, P. (2008) *British Spies and Irish Rebels; British Intelligence and Ireland 1916-1945*, Great Britain: CPI Anthony Rowe.

McRaven, W.H. (1995) *Spec Ops: case studies in Special Operations Warfare: Theory and Practice*, New York: Ballantine Books.

Montgomery, B. (1958) *The Memoirs of Field Marshall Montgomery*, London: Collins Clear Type Press.

Morillo, S. (2013) *What is Military History?*, Cambridge: Polity Books.

Murphy, B.P. (2006) *The Origins and Organisation of British Propaganda in Ireland 1920*, Cork: Aubane Historical Society.

Murphy, G. (2011) *The Year of Disappearances; Political Killings in Cork 1921-1922*, Dublin: Gill & McMillan.

Naveh, S. (1997) *In pursuit of Military Excellence: The evolution of operational theory*, Oxford: Frank Cass publishers.

O'Casey, S. (1980) 'Inisfallen, Fare thee well', *Autobiographies*, Vols 2, London.

O'Malley, E. (1979) *On another man's wound,* Dublin: Anvil Books Ltd.

O'Shea, B. & White, G. (2003) *Irish Volunteer Soldier 1913-1923*, Great Britain: Osprey Publishing Ltd.

Ó Súilleabháin, M. (2013) *Where Mountainy Men Have Sown: War and Peace in Rebel Cork in the turbulent years 1916-1921*, Cork: Mercier Press.

Pegler, M. (2012) *The Lee-Enfield Rifle*, China: Osprey Publishing Ltd.

Philips, R. (1969) *Sir Charles Ross and his rifle; Historical Arms Series No. 11*, Canada: Ontario Museum Restoration Service.

Ramsay, D. (2008) *'Blinker' Hall: Spymaster*, UK: Spellmount Ltd.

Read, D. (Ed.). (1978) *The Great War and Canadian Society: An Oral History*, Toronto: New Hogtown Press.

Regan, J.M. (2013) *Myth and The Irish State*, Dublin: Irish Academic Press.

Richards, F. (1983) *Old Soldiers Never Die*, London: Anthony Mott Ltd.

Rinker, R. (1998) *Understanding Ballistics; Basic to Advanced Ballistics Simplified, Illustrated & Explained*, USA: Mulberry House Publishing.

Ryan, A. (2007) *Comrades: Inside the War of Independence*, Dublin: Liberties Press.

Ryan, M. (2003) *Tom Barry, IRA Freedom Fighter*, Cork: Mercier Press.

Sheehan, W. (2005) *British Voices from the Irish War of Independence 1918-1921*, Cork: The Collins Press

Sheehan, W. (2009) *Hearts and Mines, The British 5th Division, Ireland, 1920-1922*, Cork: The Collins Press.

Sheehan, W. (2011) *A Hard Local War: The British Army and the Guerilla War in Cork 1919-1921*, England: The History Press.

Singer, P.W. (2003) *Corporate Warriors: The Rise of the Privatized Military Industry*, USA: Cornell University Press.

Smith, R. (2005) *The Utility of Force: The Art of War in the Modern World*, England: Penguin Books Ltd.

Spiers, E.M. (Ed.). (2006) *Between the South African War and the First World War in Big Wars and Small Wars: The British Army and the lessons of War in the 20th Century* , Oxford: Routedge.

Stephenson, M. (2013) *The last full measure; How soldiers die in battle*, London: Duckworth Overlook.

Stevenson, R. (2013) *To Win the Battle: The 1st Australian Division in the Great War, 1914-1918*, Cambridge: Cambridge University Press.

Tilly, C. (2003) *The Politics of Collective Violence*, Cambridge: Cambridge University Press.

The Kerryman (1949) *Rebel Cork's Fighting Story*, Tralee: The Kerryman Ltd.

Townshend, C. (1975) *The British Campaign in Ireland 1919-1921; The Development of Political and Military Policies*, London: Oxford University Press

Townshend, C. (1983) *Political Violence in Ireland; Government resistance since 1848*, Oxford: Clarendon Press.

Townshend, C. (2013) *The Republic: The Fight for Irish Independence*, London: Allen Lane.

Ungoed-Thomas, J. (2008) *Jasper Wolfe of Skibbereen*, Cork: The Collins Press.

Dupuy, T. (1987) *Understanding War: History and the Theory of Combat,* New York: Paragon House Publishers.

Van Crevald, M. (1982) *Fighting Power: German and U.S. Army Performance 1939-1945*, USA: Greenwood Press.

Van Creveld, M. (2006) *The Changing Face of War: Lessons of Combat from the Marne to Iraq*, New York: Ballantine Books.

Von Clausewitz, C. (1832) *On War*, London: Penguin Books.

Von Loringhoven, H. (1911) 'The Power of Personality in War', *Roots of Strategy,* Book 3, USA: Stackpole Books.

Walsh, M. (2008) *The News from Ireland: Foreign Correspondents and the Irish Revolution*, London: I.B. Tauris Ltd.

War Office (1914) *Field service pocket book 1914*, London: HMSO.

War Office (1914) *Manual of Military Law*, London: HMSO.

War Office (1936) *Text Book of Ammunition*, London: HMSO.

War Office (1938) *Infantry Section Leading*, London: HMSO.

War Office (1937) *Small Arms Training*, Vol. I, Pamphlet No.II, Pistol (.455=inch), London: HMSO.

Journal Articles

An T-Óglach (1921) *Lorry Fighting* 1, Vol II, No.22

An T-Óglach (1920) *Bogs as Military Obstacles*, Vol II, No.5

An T-Óglach (1920) *Guerilla Warfare*, Vol II, No.5

Badsey, S. (2007) 'The Boer War (1899-1902) and British Cavalry Doctrine: A Re-Evaluation', *The Journal of Military History*, Vol.71, No.1, pp.75-97.

Bak, M. Fiszer, M. Kotylo, P. Sliwinska-Kowalska, M. (2004) 'Temporary changes in hearing after exposure to shooting noise in International' *Journal of Occupational Medicine and Environmental Health*.

Beaumont, R.A. (1979) 'Military Elite Forces: Surrogate War, Terrorism, and the New Battlefield', *Parameters*, Vol (IX), No.1.

Belenky, G.L., Noy, S., Solomon, Z. (1985) 'Battle Stress: The Israeli Experieince', *Military Review*, 65(7). pp. 28–37.

Belenky, G.L. Sodetz, F.J. and Tyner, F.C. (1983) *Israeli Battle Shock Casualties: 1973 and 1982*, Walter Reed Army Institute of Research, Washington, DC 20307, US Army Research and Development Command.

Beyerchen, A. (1992) 'Clausewitz, Nonlineraity and the Unpredictability of War', *International Security*, pp. 59–90.

Black, J. (1999) 'War and the World 1450-2000', *The Journal of Military History*, Vol. (63), No.3.

Bolt, A. & Ó'Ceilleachair, S. (2005) 'Peter Hart and His Enemies', *History Ireland*, Vol.13, No.5 (Sep-Oct), pp. 12-14.

Chambers, J.W. (2003) 'S.L.A. Marshall's *Men Against Fire*: New Evidence Regarding Fire Ratios', *Parameters*,

Engel, J.H. (1954) 'A verification of Lanchester's Law', *Journal of the Operations Research Society of America*, Vol. 2, No.2.

Fox, S. (2005) 'Tom Barry and the Kilmichael Ambush', *History Ireland*, Vol. 13, No.6, pp. 14-15.

Geib, R. (2006) 'Asymmetric conflict structures', *International Review of The Red Cross,* Vol. 88, No.864.

Geldenhuys, G and Botha E, 'A note on Dupuy's QJM and the New Square Law', *Orion*, Vol.10, No.1/2.

Gilmore, R. (1976) 'The New Courage: Rifles and Soldier Individualism 1876-1918', *Military Affairs*, Vol. 40, No.3, pp. 97-102.

Grossman, D. (2009) 'S.L.A. Marshall revisited…?', *Canadian Military Journal*, Vol. 9, No.4.

Hardaway, R.M. (1978) 'Vietnam Wound Analysis', *Journal of Trauma*, 18(9), pp.635-643.

Hart, P. (2005) 'Peter Hart and His Enemies…', *History Ireland*, Vol. 13, No.4 (Jul-Aug), pp.16-19.

Jeffery, K. (1981) 'The British Army and Internal Security 1919-1939', *The Historical Journal*, Vol. 24, No.2, pp. 377-397.

Lindee, S. (2011) 'Experimental Wounds: Science and Violence in Mid-Century America', *Journal of Law, Medicine and Ethics*

Murphy, I. Lavell, L. Ní Mhurchú, E. McCarthy, R. Heffernan, E. (2014) 'Imaging of Gunshot Injuries in a

West Dublin Teaching Hospital: A Ten Year Review', *Irish Medical Journal*, September, Vol. 107, Number 8.

Nelson, A. 'The other boys of Kilmichael': No.2 Section, 'C' Company, Auxiliary Division Royal Irish

Constabulary, 28 November 1920', *Historical Research* DOI;10.1111/1468-2281.12057.

Reydams, L. (2006) 'A la guerre comme a la guerre: patterns of armed conflict, humanitarian law responses and new challenges', *International Review of the Red Cross,* Volume 88, Number 864.

Ryan, M. Meehan, N. O'Riordan, M. (2003) 'Peter Hart and Tom Barry', *History Ireland,* Vol. 13, No. 3 (May–Jun), pp.13–15.

Ryan, M. (2004) 'Tom Barry', *History Ireland,* Vol 12, No.3 (Autumn) pp.16–17.

Ryan, M. (2005) 'Tom Barry and the Kilmichael Ambush', *History Ireland*, Vol. 13, No.5, (Sep–Oct), pp. 15–18.

Ryan, M. (2006) 'Tom Barry and the Kilmichael Ambush', *History Ireland*, Vol. 14, No.1, (Jan–Feb), p.14.

Ryan, M. (2007) 'The Kilmichael Ambush, 1920: Exploring the 'Provocative Chapters', *History Ireland* 92(306).

Scheipers, S. (2013) 'Fighting Irregular Fighters, Is the law of Armed Conflict Outdated?' *Parameters* 43(4).

Stent, H.V. (1958) 'The Ross Rifle Ruckus', *Guns: Finest in the Firearms Field*, (May), Vol. IV, No.5–41.

Townshend, C. (1979) 'The Irish Republican Army and the Development of Guerilla Warfare 1916-1921', *The English Historical Review*, No.371 pp. 318–345.

Turner, W.A. (1915) Remarks on cases of nervous and mental shock. BMJ 1915;I: 833-5 in 'Shell shock,

Gordon Holmes and the Great War', *The Journal of the Royal Society of Medicine*, 2004 February: 97(2): 86–89 by AD Macleod , Available at http://www.ncbi.nlm.nih.gov/pmc/articles. [Accessed: 03 July 2012]

Walls, T. (2003) 'Merry Christmas from Ireland?', *History Ireland,* Vol.11, No. 4.

Williams, B.S. (2010) 'Heuristics and Biases in Military Decision Making', *Military Review*, (September/October), pp. 40–52.

Selected Reports

Anonymous (undated) The Short Magazine Lee-Enfield Rifle (S.M.L.E) Available at: http://www.rifleman.org.uk/The_Rifle_Short_Magazine_Lee-Enfield_main.htm [Accessed on: 18 July 2012]

Ainsworth, J. (2001) *The Black and Tans and Auxiliaries in Ireland, 1920-1921: Their Origins, Roles and Legacy,* A paper presented to the Annual Conference of the Queensland History Teachers' Association, 12 May 2001.

Ainsworth, J. 'British security policy in Ireland, a desperate attempt by the Crown to maintain Anglo-Irish unity by force'. *The Australian Journal of Irish Studies.* Available at: http://eprints.qut.edu.au/6/1/British_Security_Policy_in_Ireland.pdf [Accessed on: 11 June 2011]

Artéus, G, *Military History, A historiography,* Available at: https://www.fhs.se/Documents/Externwebben/forskning/Milit%C3%A4rhistorisk%20Tidskrift/gunnar-arteus-military-history-a-historiography.pdf [Accessed on: 12 June 2012]

Bassford, C. (1994) *Clausewitz in English: The Reception of Clausewitz in Britain and America, 1815-1945,* New York: Oxford University Press. Available at: http://www.clausewitz.com/readings/Bassford/CIE/Chapter19.htm, [Accessed on: 11 June 2012]

Choi, J. (2009) *Combat evolved: Lanchester's Laws in Modern Warfare*, College of Arts and Sciences, American University, Washington, D.C.

Department of Health and Children, (1998) *Hearing Disability Assessment: Report of the Expert Hearing Group*, Dublin: Stationary Office

Edson, M. 'Scope Sights on .22 and Value of Marksmanship', p.19. Available at: http://www.rifleman.org.uk/Historical_notes_and_extracts_Main.html [Accessed on: 18 July 2012]

Ewell, J. J. and Hunt, I. (1995) *Sharpening the Combat Edge: The Use of Analysis to Reinforce Military Judgement*, Washington DC: Department of the Army.

Ferriter, D. (2014) 'Picking a fight over the rights and wrongs of our history' Irish Times, 05 April. Available at: http://www.irishtimes.com/culture/books/picking-a-fight-over-the-rights-and-wrongs-of-our-history-1.1747128 [Accessed on: 24 April 2014]

Johnson, R. (1989) *Lanchester's Square Law in Theory and Practice*. School of Advanced Military Studies. United States Army Command and General Staff College. Fort Leavenworth, Kansas.

Lewis, F.A. (2002) 'Is there a place for Elite Forces in the Canadian Army?', Thesis, Command and General Staff College, Fort Leavenworth, Kansas.

Murphy, J.A. (2000) 'Bloody fable of Kilmichael's dead' *Irish Independent* (26 Nov) Available at: http://www.independent.ie/opinion/analysis/bloody-fable-of-kilmichaels-dead-26257440.html [Accessed on: 13 June 2013

Rotte and Schmidt (2002), 'On the production of victory: Empirical Determinants of Battlefield Success in Modern War' *IZA Discussion Paper* , No.491

Smith, J.C. *"The scope is the proof"* p.20 Available at: http://www.rifleman.org.uk/Historical_notes _and_extracts_Main.html [Accessed on: 18 July 2012]

Supreme Court of Canada, Vol. LXII, 1921, Ross V Dunstall, Ross V Emery

The Irish Times, 05 April 2014.

The Lieber Code Available at: http://www.icrc.org/ihl.nsf [Accessed on: 15 May 2013]

The Swindon Evening Advertiser, 01 December 1920

The Times, (1920) Kilmichael ambush press report, December 02.

War Office (1916) *Correspondence relating to the use of the Ross rifle by the Canadian Troops in France*, London: HMSO.

Watkins, T. (undated) Lanchester's Theory of Warfare. Available at: http://www.sjsu.edu/faculty/watkins/war.htm [Accessed on: 16 November 2013]

Index